Buddhism
and
Christianity

Buddhism
and
Christianity
Some Bridges of Understanding

by

WINSTON L. KING

THE WESTMINSTER PRESS

Philadelphia

LIBRARY OF CONGRESS CATALOG CARD NO. 62–11075

PRINTED IN THE UNITED STATES OF AMERICA

Contents

Preface

One humid Monday afternoon in October, 1958, I was sitting in a room in the dwelling of the Venerable U Thittila, Lecturer in Abhidhamma at the University of Rangoon, Burma, frustrated in mind and bathed in nervous perspiration. He also, though a native Burman and presumably used to Burmese weather, was looking uncomfortable in his yellow monk's robe. Now and then he discreetly fanned himself and wiped his face with a handkerchief.

Both of us were at a standstill in our efforts to communicate what we wanted to say to each other. I had submitted to him, three days or so before, a résumé of our conversation of the previous week, in which I had tried to set out as clearly as I knew how what I thought he had said about the Buddhist doctrine of the sheer momentariness of human personality and its relation to the karmic continuity of human existence. Apparently I had failed. And half an hour of conversation had done absolutely nothing to clear up our difficulty. He was politely and gently, but definitely, dissatisfied with what I had written and was saying; and I was acutely disappointed at failing to grasp what he had said. Then suddenly, with a light in his eyes, he asked, "Are you speaking here in terms of *one* or *many* lives?" "I'm speaking in terms of one life, of course," I said, with a firm Western assurance that one always takes this for granted. Said he with a relieved smile: "Well, that explains it. I was thinking in terms of many lives. If you are speaking of one life,

I have no objection to what you say here." So it had been that for a full half hour, using the same vocabulary—though it was in my language rather than in his—and trying our level best to communicate, we had yet failed because of our differing Eastern- and Western-style presuppositions.

During the rest of my twenty-month stay in Burma I came upon this same problem again and again: the inability of two faiths, in particular Christianity and Buddhism, to communicate at crucial points. It came out when I was teaching a class in which sat a young monk. I was trying to explain to him what an "inspired" Old Testament prophet was like. For a time I make no progress. Then his face lighted up and he told me that now he understood; the prophets were "possessed" just as some Burmese professional dancers become possessed by the nats (earth, tree, sky spirits) in the midst of their dance. I am not sure that I ever led him to understand the difference in the quality of an Amos' or Isaiah's "possession" from that of one possessed by a nat; to him this latter was the proper explanatory category. And he also told me on another occasion that whenever Christians used the term "love" it always meant to him possessive, or sexual and erotic, love—therefore, of a much lower order than Buddhist *mettā,* or loving-kindness.

Not even Burmese Christians themselves, I discovered, were always able to communicate with their Buddhist friends. One of the former told me that when he attempted to talk to Buddhists about the relation of the two faiths he felt as though they were traveling on "parallel but never-meeting tracks." And I had the impression, perhaps accurate only in part, that there was indeed little genuine intellectual or experiential intercommunication between Buddhist and Christian communities in Burma. Each thought of the other's faith and practice as something quite different, something that made any efforts but those of proselytization or polemic interchange futile or dangerous. Hence there seemed to have been no genuine religious dialogue between the two faiths for many years.

From these experiences came the basic idea for the present volume, which represents, in the words of the title, an effort toward building some bridges of understanding between the two religions. This is, of course, by no means the first attempt to relate them in some way or other. If one may criticize the generality of such efforts, however, either they tend to portray the eternal and absolute separation of the two faiths, or, particularly in the West, they tend to hasten joyfully and uncritically toward immediate syncretism or the discovery that they are at bottom identical.

The attempt here is hopefully to avoid these extremes in the interest of some sort of genuine dialogue. If it is held that the separation between faiths is absolute and that they can communicate only by what Professor Hocking calls the method of the "radical displacement" of the other, then the only "dialogue" that can ensue is largely epithetical and argumentative. If, on the contrary, Buddhism and Christianity are indeed one at bottom or may be easily syncretized with violence to the essense of neither, then also dialogue is impossible. There remains only the music of a hallelujah chorus celebrating the unifying love feast. But if a dialogue is to occur, there must be a proper sense of both difference and likeness. The sense of difference recognizes that traditions and views historically separate, and radically variant for centuries, cannot be immediately and readily joined together without remainder. But the sense of likeness makes possible some hopefulness for a quality of communication across the lines of difference that will yet escape a blurring of essential distinctions. The intention of this volume is to contribute to such a discussion some further stimulus, looking toward its still further and better continuance.

It should be said in all honesty, but with charity, that at present most interest in mutual understanding flows from the West eastward; for the East in its newly independent mood wishes now to reverse the missionary current and proclaim *its* faiths to the West, not caring to learn much more than it already knows about the West and its Christianity, which is little enough. This perhaps complicates still further the already difficult problem of understanding a quite different faith set in a different culture, resulting as it does in the Buddhist attempt to commend Buddhism to the West as the perfect solution to all its problems. Obviously, traditional Buddhism is somewhat changed in the process. But, then, this is a process that has also occurred in Christianity more than once during its varied career as it has sought to commend itself anew in changed circumstances and to strange peoples. For this is the manner in which all religions grow and change; and it is one of the most interesting aspects of the contemporary Buddhist situation that an age-old and long-static tradition is now adapting itself to new circumstances—even though it makes the task of one who would describe "Buddhism" more difficult.

One specific limitation of the scope of this volume should be pointed out. Its portrayal of "Buddhist" teaching and practice is largely confined to what is variously called Southern, Hinayana (Lesser Vehicle), or Theravada (doctrine of the elders), Buddhism, the scriptural and conservative Buddhism of Southeast Asia, as contrasted with the more "liberal" and speculative Northern, or Mahayana (Great Vehicle), Buddhism of China, Korea, and Japan. (Some occasional references are made to the specific differences of the latter from the portrayal given here.) It is true, of course, that there are basic Buddhist likenesses found in both varieties, especially when contrasted with Christianity. But the heavy emphasis upon karma and rebirth, taken in a literal sense, and upon the no-soul doctrine is especially characteristic of Southern Buddhism. Indeed, Northern Buddhism has so modified these and other Buddhist doctrines in a somewhat Christian direction that it makes an interesting subject in itself. But because the author's primary direct experience has been with Southern Buddhism, and because there are so many varieties within Buddhism as to make the single term "Buddhist" too general for accurate use, it is Southern Buddhism that is here compared with Christianity. Thus when "Buddhist" or "Buddhism" are used without qualification, "Southern Buddhism" is to be understood. However, the *Northern* Buddhist (Sanskrit) forms "Nirvana," "Karma," and "Dharma" are used because of their greater familiarity in the West.

Of course, something of the same difficulty also relates to the use of the word "Christian" as a descriptive adjective in view of a like variety within Christendom. And the author must plead guilty to using the term with regard to what *he* understands the central Christian tradition to be— though his background and perspective is that of liberal Protestant, which inevitably colors the interpretation here given to Christianity. But to make complete comparisons of all possible Christian and Buddhist versions of all matters at all points would be an encyclopedic task. The attempt here is more modest: to speak from within the Christian tradition and its basic perspective about the Buddhist perspective, particularly that of Southern Buddhism; and, without glossing over or magnifying likeness *or* difference, to try to achieve a greater understanding of Buddhism on the part of Christians, with perhaps, as a by-product, a deeper and more intelligent interest in their own faith.

W.L.K.

(I)

Concerning the
Christian Understanding of Buddhism

1. *The Historical Separation*

In the thought and experience of most Westerners, Buddhism and Christianity are a world, perhaps a universe, apart—geographically, historically, culturally, and religiously. All the connotations of the two terms "Buddhist" and "Christian" are those of separateness, difference, and incommunicability. Buddhism originated in India and has been concentrated in the Far East ever since; Christianity originated in the Middle East but early moved westward, and due to subsequent historical circumstances became almost concentrated in Europe and the New World—European civilizations.

To be sure, the mutual exclusiveness has not been absolute. It seems reasonably certain that Nestorian Christianity strongly influenced Chinese Buddhist ritual and that Greek culture powerfully affected northwest (Buddhist) India. And it is also true, though less definitely specifiable, that for centuries both before and after the beginning of the Christian Era, Eastern (Hindu-Buddhist) philosophical and religious influences flowed through the Middle Eastern screen of peoples and cultures into the Greek and Greco-Christian civilization. From these Eastern sources, that mysticism which flowered within the Christian tradition during its medieval European period undoubtedly drew its aboriginal nourishment—though by that time the mystical nourishment had been assimilated and re-formed several times over.

13

How directly it affected the beginnings of Christianity (Were late Judaism and Jesus affected by Buddhist teaching?) is a matter of unclear, imprecise conjecture whose flavor depends largely upon the religious bias of the conjecturer.

But whatever the extent or nature of those early mutual influences, other cultural forces and historical events subsequently pushed the two traditions farther and farther apart. There was, for instance, the intrusion of Islam between the two geographically. Rising in the seventh century of the Christian Era, Islam expanded with literally explosive force through all the Middle East. Westward it put Christianity on the defensive, penetrating as far west and north as southern-central France by the eighth century, and again threatening Christendom from the east in the Turkish invasion of the Balkans in the fifteenth and sixteenth centuries. Within four or five centuries it had conquered much of India, displacing Buddhism in the northwest and central areas and contributing to Buddhism's rapid decline and eventual disappearance from the land of its birth. The net result was the erection of an almost impenetrable cultural and religious barrier of three thousand miles or more in geographical width and a good thousand years in chronological length between Christian and Buddhist cultures.

It was, therefore, perhaps inevitable that the two religions should grow ever farther apart rather than along parallel lines. Not only were they diverse in their beginnings—one formed by the Semitic and the other by the Aryan-Hindu religious genius—but in their separated worlds social, cultural, and political events moved them along quite different lines. Of course, some of this divergent development was due to the influence of the religions themselves and hence can be seen as an extension of their original differences; but others represent a mingling of factors external to and independent of the religions. Before its decline and reabsorption by Hindu India, Buddhism had been carried to other cultures: to China, where it was a minor partner, religiously, with Confucianism and Taoism; to Japan, where it was an equal and sometimes dominant partner with Shinto; and to Southeast Asia, where it settled into gentle, contemplative, tradition-bound dominance of the predominantly agrarian societies found there. But wherever it went and whatever its local modifications and dilutions, Buddhism tended to remain detached and aloof from the political power struggles of the mighty, concentrating on the disciplines that would bring better rebirths in future lives or upon the hope of final deliverance in Nirvana, far beyond all space-time realities.

In Christian Europe things progressed far differently. Faithful to its Jewish heritage, Christendom within a few short centuries became inextricably involved with the social, historical, and political forces of its culture—even while the otherworldly mystical life was sedulously cultivated within the monasteries of the church. For the church had an outward face, a sense of historical destiny, as well as the hope of inward realization and of heavenly reward. When Islam pressed in upon it, Christendom fought back with physical force to preserve its institutional existence, and was successful, though not without profound interior changes. And then in breathless succession—in part, the result of Christendom's concern with the contemporary social and political realities—came those great events which moved it still farther away from the Buddhist course of development: the Renaissance, in which the concrete human and natural world grew to a new significance; the Reformation, which sought to bring the devout forth from their contemplative inaction within church walls into sociomoral action in the secular world; the massive force of the industrial revolution, the profoundly disturbing and exciting growth of the new science, and the subsequent conquest and colonization of the nonindustrial, nonscientific East by the industrialized, scientized West.

And so, ironically enough, after a thousand years of almost complete separation, Christianity encountered Bud-

dhism again, this time borne as the religion of the con-
queror on the ships of colonial imperialists. The differences
were profound; the contrast could scarcely have been more
complete: on the one hand, Western religion and culture
inextricably intermingled, materially advanced, dogmatically confident of superior worth, humanitarian, activist,
determined to convert the rest of the world without remainder to its ways, values, and beliefs; on the other hand, Eastern religion (Buddhism, in particular), politically indiffer-
ent for the most part, socially passive and stratified,
in economically primitive contexts, and religiously contemplative and mystical.

It seems small wonder, then, that the work of a few
scholars during the past hundred years or more, and some
sporadic missionary contacts through the same period of
time, have not sufficed to bridge the gulf created by ten or
fifteen centuries of development in almost "opposite" directions. Thus it is that whenever vital religious concerns of
belief, way of life, or practice come to be considered, it
seems that Buddhist and Christian perforce express themselves in radically contrasting ways. Attempts at communication seem to reveal that each is "wholly other" to the
other. The rapid expansion of Buddhist-Christian contacts
in our own time has led to a re-examination of these differences on a more intensive scale than ever before in both
Christian and Buddhist circles. And some have immediately come to the conclusion that there is no hope of genuine
intercommunication. The only method of approach is the
proclamation of one's own faith to persons of the other faith
in the hope of their conversion to it, and the eventual evan-
gelization of the other faith out of existence. Professor
Hocking has termed this the method of "radical displacement," by which one religion literally displaces the other,
completely and finally. We may note two expressions of
such views. First, from the Buddhist side, we read the following assertion in a publication of a modern Buddhist

missionary organization, the World Fellowship of Buddhists:

The world is doomed unless enmity, concord, and understanding can be brought about between the peoples and countries set against one another in mortal conflict. The Buddha Dhama points to the root cause of these evil forces and also provides a sure remedy. . . . Furthermore Buddhism is the only religion acceptable to the scientific mind, as has been said by Einstein. Buddhism is the religion for the present age of science and reason.[1]

But the Christian world too, or at least many Christians within it, equally stoutly maintains that there can be no real communication from, or cross-fertilization of its own faith by, a non-Christian one. We may allow Dr. Hendrik Kraemer, the eminent Dutch scholar, to speak for this view. With regard to the religions of India, China, and Japan ("naturalist religions"), he writes:

It is not to be marvelled at that the prophetic religion of Biblical realism does not show this syncretistic, pragmatist, relativist, and subjectivist trend of the naturalist religions. It contrasts entirely with the endless assimilative and adaptive elasticity of naturalistic monism. It is disturbing by its "exclusivist" attitude, that is not lessened in the least by the fact that the Bible radiates with the lustre of love and freedom of the spirit. . . . This enigmatic "Exclusivism" brought it about that amidst the tolerant and conforming mystery-cults Christianity stood alone "intolerant" and non-conformist.[2]

Nor is this exclusivism something to be repented of, but rather it is to be accepted as an intrinsic and essential part of the Christian faith, according to Dr. Kraemer. And though in subsequent books he has somewhat softened the rigor of his earlier pronouncements at least in details, he still conceives the relation of Christian to non-Christian religions as one primarily of noncommunicative contrast. Thus:

> Above all, in regard to the Biblical thesaurus, the primary reason [for the special place of this treasure of Biblical and theological language] is that the cardinal Biblical concepts and expression about God, man, and the world, in their cohesive unity, are unique in this sense that *they are discontinuous with all other expressions and attitudes.*[3]

Since the central thesis of this work is that it is both possible and desirable to attempt to throw bridges of understanding across the centuries-old chasm between Buddhism and Christianity—and not just for the instrumental purpose of gaining converts from the other side—I cannot fully accept either of the above statements (Buddhist or Christian) as the final word on the matter. (Nor does Dr. Kraemer, for that matter; for he keeps making further attempts to express his understanding of the non-Christian faiths to his fellow Christians as a matter of intrinsic importance.) There is, however, enough of truth in these statements to put us on our guard against the casual ecumenicity of our generation that, in the interests of universal human brotherhood, of course, would lightheartedly wash out all religious distinctions and values by such simple (and fallacious) statements as, "After all, religions are all the same at bottom" and "All religions are equally true and good." This has not been historically true in the past; nor does it seem an evaluation that does justice to the deepest insights and experiences of the sincere devotees of the faiths in question.

The approach hopefully espoused here is that of sympathetic interpenetration. This does not mean a cessation of mutual Buddhist-Christian missionary activity. Quite the contrary; for when one genuinely seeks to explain his faith to one of another faith, he must learn something of the other's faith, as well as more of his own, to do so. And if he does his work well, he must penetrate to some better than usual understanding of the nature and locus of the basic similarities of structure and experience, as well as differences, between the two religions. To make such exploration of the interfaith terrain meaningful, there must be a genuine attempt to understand the strange faith "in depth," avoiding the merely superficial similarities and differences, trying to relate religious deep to religious deep in accordance with actual function and essence in each respective faith. And it is perhaps most meaningful, or at least encouragingly concrete, when this is done in terms of certain specifics in each faith rather than in generalized terms. With this in mind we turn first to a preliminary statement of some of the basic Christian-Buddhist oppositions of doctrine, attitude, and practice with whose facets we shall deal more in detail in the following chapters.

2. *The Oppositions*

a. *Conceptions of Ultimate Reality*

The Christian term for ultimate reality is, of course, God. Now, there have been many variations on the significance of the word "God" in the Christian tradition, far too many to deal with here. But certain basic features seem to inhere in the Christian idea of God, whatever its variability in certain specifics. By "God," Christianity means that force which created and sustains the physical and personal world; the power that determines its destiny in the large; that this creative power is in some sense "personal," i.e., characterized by consciousness, activity, and sensibility; that in "him" are found moral and spiritual excellence in their supremely possible form, i.e., that God is "holy."

For the Buddhist there is no God in the Christian sense, though there may exist beings temporarily greater in power and length of existence than human beings.[4] And these beings may have a certain subordinate control over, or influence upon, the course of natural and historical events. Yet subsuming all other categories of existence under its form is that of *impersonal process*. It is impersonal because it is governed by the law of causality, including mental causes as well as physical, but all of them nonpersonal. Each being, "thing," or event, including "persons," is only a cluster of rapidly changing elements that are mutually dependent upon each other. According to Buddhism, there was no creation in the sense of "something from nothing" but only an eternal process that never began, or of whose beginnings we can never know. There is no supreme Guide or Guardian of the way the world takes, nor any goal toward which all "creation" moves, only the formation and dissolution of many successive universes whose elements have been always in existence.

b. *The Meaning of World History*

The opposition here can be put in the form of a nearly absolute contradiction. For Christianity the world has a purpose foreseen and moved toward by the providence of God; for Buddhism the world has no inherent or all-over purpose, only regularities of a causal order, as noted above. In keeping with its concept of the nature of God, Christianity has viewed the world as the "handiwork" of God, in part gone astray from the divine purpose, yet in essence good. Its essential worth or goodness is manifest in its order and beauty and in its capacity for redemption. Though the world order is derivative from God, and hence of less than absolute worth, God moves purposefully within its nature and historical events for its final redemption in holiness and goodness. The name given by Christianity to the redeemed order, social and natural, is the Kingdom of God or the Kingdom of Heaven, in which the human and divine wills shall achieve complete harmony. Hence man is called upon to share creatively by means of dedicated historical (social, political, economic, personal) action in God's purpose, which has been revealed in Jesus Christ and the Christian community.

Contrastingly, according to one class of Buddhist statements at least, world process, as such, has neither meaning nor purpose. It is going nowhere in particular, save through another cycle of dissolution-renovation-stability-degradation-dissolution and so on ad infinitum. Nothing that man can do, either individually or collectively, can permanently change the character of world process; it is only a succession of birth-death linkages, both of individuals and world orders, whose basic characteristics are three: impermanence, suffering, and emptiness. The properly ultimate goal for man, no matter how much he may line his way through birth-death by flower beds of temporary betterment or pleasure, is to escape world process completely in timeless, spaceless, distinctionless Nirvana.

c. *The Nature of Man*

As we might well expect, Christianity and Buddhism vary radically in their conceptions of human nature. Though Christian philosophy here is often a somewhat confused combination of Jewish body-soul unity and Greek dualism of immaterial soul imprisoned in a material body till death, in general we can say that Christianity has emphasized the personal, that is, the unique, unitary self-conscious, individuality of man, as being his essence. This is essentially what it means by "soul": the continuing unity and identity of self-awareness through many changes and hopefully on into life after death. Hence, Christianity finds in the service and worship of a personal God the enhancement and guarantee of the integrality of the individual self and its future glorification.

Buddhism, however, is a religion of *anātman,* or no-soul. Southern, or Theravada, Buddhism in particular stresses this as one of its most essential and distinctive doctrines. By "no-soul" it means precisely that. There is no real enduring and identical self that passes through life's many diverse experiences and persists on after death. On the contrary, what we call "self" is only a temporary, momentarily changing compound of five psychophysical factors that arise in mutual dependence upon each other and upon external stimuli, coagulating around a center of karmic force. Such an individual can only be thought of as a minuscule part of the total world process of cause and effect, one of its cause-effect sequences. Upon death the fivefold compound called sentient being simply disintegrates into the world process, like a momentary swirl in a stream of water dissolving into the main current again. Actually what happens in death has been happening every split second through life—the "death" of each momentary body-mind self and its "birth" in a new body-mind self, governed by cause and effect.

There are two corollary beliefs about man in Buddhism that contrast strongly and importantly with Christian beliefs. The first seems quite surprising in view of the no-soul doctrine: it is that, after all, *something* of the sentient individual does pass on from moment to moment, or life to life. It is not a soul or self, says Buddhism, but karmic energy. Around this thrust of karmic energy from the dying life, a new individuality is formed, a new sentient being is born, in whatever shape and nature the quality of his past deeds has entitled him to—in hells of suffering, heavens of pleasure, as a miserable animal, or in the mixed status of a human being. This process, governed by Karma (morally directed causality), in which the new being reaps what the old one sowed, has been going on for all eternity and will continue to go on for another eternity unless and until the individual achieves final escape into Nirvana from the endless rounds of birth and death. This is clearly an adaptation of the Hindu doctrine of transmigration of souls. Its contrast to the Christian one-life view of man is obvious and the effects on Buddhist religious life important, but we cannot enter into the wide range of differences between them here.

d. *Salvation*

The processes of salvation in Buddhism and Christianity are functions of their respective doctrines of ultimate reality and the nature of man. In a phrase we might sum up Buddhism's view: salvation is *from* the self *by* the self. To start with the last: Buddhism insists that it believes and practices *self*-salvation. The Buddha was not saved by any revelation or grace from any god. He was the self-enlightened one; by the power of his own past lives of virtue, which finally produced piercing insight-wisdom, he came to the knowledge or the saving insight into things "as they are." He literally made himself into a Buddha and subsequently entered into Nirvana. Though few men will become Buddhas—those beings who have the power of enlightening others—the way to Nirvana trod by the Buddha is that which every man himself must take; that is, for *everyman* it is also a way of self-salvation. Only by his own efforts, under the guidance of the teaching of the Buddha and inspired by his example, can a man attain release. Nothing but his own deed (karma) will save him. Thus literally a man is his own savior and creator: by his present deeds he may make himself, somewhat in this life and completely in future lives, into what he wills to be. As to salvation *from* self, Buddhism conceives belief in the integrality and reality of the self to be the major obstacle to man's salvation.[5] Selfhood is man's major illusion; it is the essence of that primordial and all-pervasive ignorance which binds man to ever new births. Because he believes that he is a self, he is greedy (attached to self and its pleasure) and full of hatred (fear of other competitive selves). Destroy the illusion of the self, realize that it is in fact not real, and the bond of "attachment" that makes man a prisoner of the wheel of life is cut; rebirth and redeath are at an end. Two implications are of course obvious. One is that Buddhism considers individualized existence as the primary evil which is to be escaped; salvation is its destruction in Nirvana, not in its continuation in heaven. The other is that the way of salvation is primarily through enlightenment or knowledge rather than through repentance for sin. Man is ignorant rather than depraved.

The contrasting Christian view has been implied throughout the above description of the Buddhist view. According to Christianity, man cannot save himself. Though he knows the good, at least enough of it to feel himself guilty, he is not able to perform it. "For I do not do the good I want, but the evil I do not want is what I do." (Rom. 7:19.)

Only by the freely given grace of God, a power not man's own, can man be saved. His response is that of repentance from past sin, denial of present intention to sin, and response by an act of accepting in faith God's saving and renewing grace. By Christianity man is accounted a sinner, one who has deliberately set his will against the Divine Will, though he is aware of the nature of that Will. Ignorance may compound man's sin, but basically man is a deliberate rebel and in need of a transformed will. The saved man will be a renewed individual, capable of communion with God—not an individual "gone out" from individuality into nonindividuality.

e. *Spiritual Technique* (*Worship*)

Worship is a word, strictly speaking, that can be used only in Christianity. As the origin of the word suggests, it is an acknowledgment of that which one reveres; primarily it is absolute reverence for absolute or divine worth. For the Christian, prayer is the most characteristic and distinctive form of worship. Prayer, of course, is many faceted: adoration of God, as that Being of supreme worth, i.e., holiness; thanksgiving for benefits experienced in the created order; confession of sin and petition for forgiveness; petition for one's own and others' physical and spiritual needs. The basic image, however, is that of two-way communication, call and response of some sort, or, as we might term it, genuine personal fellowship in the mode of the "Our Father" prayer.

For the Buddhist, there is no supernal worth to be worshiped in the sense of adoration. The Buddha was a wayshower, not a god; Buddhas in Nirvana do not answer prayers. Karma is a law of cause-effect, inexorable justice, not a power to be placated. And Nirvana, though of supernal worth, is not a Being, but a dimension beyond time and space in which there is no personal existence or need. The basic Buddhist spiritual technique is therefore that of individual meditation. It is a depersonalized contemplation on self-chosen or teacher-suggested subjects that may range from one's own bodily processes, through various types of external physical objects, up to themes such as the Buddha's virtues, peace, or the infinity of consciousness. One of its main methods is to sit detachedly apart in the attitude of "Bare Attention," i.e., as unemotional self-spectator, analyzing every act of "self" into its component parts and thereby destroying the illusion of separate or integral self. Or, to state it more positively, its purpose is to replace the narrow awareness of self-consciousness with a superindividual, universal consciousness that looks upon all beings with equal love and charity.

f. *Ethical Attitudes*

Again, as one might expect from the divergent Buddhist and Christian conceptions of the meaning of history and the nature of man, there is a radical division with regard to ethical language. Viewing historical events and occurrences in the natural world as the arena of divine purposive activity, and men as real individuals, Christianity is concretely and actively ethical. Its genius is one of prophetic concern for, and involvement in, practical human life. Some of its great words are truth, justice, and mercy. It reaches its apex in the quality of love supremely manifested in that love which enters into the lives and concerns of others and gives of itself freely, even unto death. By love Christianity seeks to redeem not only human individuals but the created historical and social order.

It is rather of *detachment* and *equanimity* that Buddhism speaks when defining its ethical ideas. Detachment may have to do with objects: one must be emotionally detached from material possessions, earthly goals, bad or good, and from other individuals as individuals. It also has to do with attitude: equanimity, a cool balanced benevolence toward all sentient beings, including oneself, and an unemotional acceptance of the world order as one finds it—for it is beyond his power of improvement, just as other individuals are essentially beyond one's help. To be sure, there are modern tendencies in Southern Buddhism to pick up the compassionate theme of Northern Buddhism by strongly emphasizing the self-giving deeds of that being who became the Buddha in his last life, and to underline the practical nature of his teaching (as the Buddha) to the laymen who came to hear him. But the classic pattern of Buddhist saint-liness is that of the holy man meditating within his cell and radiating therefrom positive benevolence to all creatures in all worlds rather than of a Master healing disease or a Savior upon a cross.

g. *Positive and Negative Attitudes*

Finally, and importantly for the next section, it may be pointed out that Buddhism and Christianity characteristi-cally approach fundamentals in quite different styles. Simply, and somewhat inaccurately, it may be put thus: Christianity affirms and Buddhism denies. Some of this has already been apparent: Christianity affirms a Creator-God, a continuing human self or soul, a meaningful world order in which man co-operates with God by active ethical and social involvement. But Buddhism denies God, the reality of the human soul, the meaning of the historical and natu-ral order, and seeks a noninvolved detachment as its highest good.

But we may extend this a little further and in doing so lay the groundwork for a statement of the fundamental difficulty to be found in attempting intercommunication between Buddhism and Christianity. It is this: Christianity seeks to affirm positively what it believes about its ultimate realities and experiences by stating what it means in clear theological propositions and philosophical concepts. For example, it calls God "the Father Almighty," "Creator," "good," "loving," "just"; it states that he has revealed himself in creation, in his written Word, and in the life of Jesus Christ; it prophetically identifies his action now in this event and now in that circumstance. Upon these, and other related themes, endless volumes of theological discourse have been written. Christianity is known by its massive theological structure.

On the other hand, Buddhism approaches *its* ultimates in terms of negatives. The profoundest truths, it affirms, cannot be arrived at by reasoning but by intuitive perceptions. The highest wisdom cannot be communicated by word; it is more often realized in silence. Ultimate realities —such as Nirvana—are absolutely indescribable. Qualifying phrases, descriptions, conceptualization may even distort or hide its true nature, and their mouthing become a substitute for the fullness of the reality itself. Truth in the ultimate sense is *realized,* not *known.*

3. *Negative and Positive Transcendence*

Thus far we have noted the fact of the wide historical separation of Buddhism and Christianity, a certain degree of intransigent denial on both sides that there can be any dialogue between them, and some specific areas of opposition or contrast that we find between them. With the last-noted and general quality of the two religions, the affirmativeness of Christianity and the negativeness of Buddhism, we come to the core of our problem of intercommunication between the two: How can the living structure of the opposing faith be truly understood? How can its centers of significance be truly related to the corresponding centers in one's own faith? To put it succinctly for the Christian: *How can he, theologically affirmative, find the locus of the true Buddhist affirmation under cover of Buddhist negativity?*

Such is the nature of the essential problem that I shall introduce in the remainder of this chapter and deal with in some half dozen specific forms in the following chapters. But before we face the problem head on, either generally or specifically, one or two preliminary comments must be made. The first of these is the very simple affirmation that Buddhism is a religion. This may seem to be a trivial truism. Yet it is important to indicate that this is my assumption for two reasons. First, some Buddhists as well as some non-Buddhists have denied that Buddhism *is* a religion. It may be a philosophy or a moralism, say they, but not a religion. And from our brief résumé of its differences from Christianity, which is admitted on all hands to be a religion, the reasons for this are obvious. Buddhism appears to deny the stock-in-trade, the distinguishing, characteristics of what we usually signify by the word "religion." How can we call a view of life that denies the existence of God, of the human soul, of any world purpose, of existence after death, and has no place for prayer or worship within it, a religion? It would certainly fail of fulfilling the role of religion according to most definitions.

I have no disposition to quarrel over a matter of definitions and will not here propose one that fits Buddhism for the role of a religion. Of course, in actuality one can observe that, practically and realistically speaking in terms of historical form, the Buddhist "philosophy and morality" have become as religious as any other religion, in whatever way one chooses to define religion. But even if we discard these actual forms as superstitious, non-Buddhistic accretions picked up through the centuries, what must we say of the core of Buddhism itself? This: It is a view of life that originates in a serious, even pessimistic, appraisal of the truly desperate condition of man—caught, world without end, in a succession of lives whose main characteristics are suffering, impermanence, and unreality; that proclaims that it has an infallible technique for freeing him from his bondage, made plain and available by the teaching of Gotama Buddha, and that there is a refuge for man, unfailing, immutable, absolute—called Nirvana—how can this be anything *but* religion in the ultimate analysis, whatever terms it may use to describe its ultimate? Obviously, it is a religion of the most emphatic sort; and the fact that millions have given to it a devoted reverence as the supremely good way of life through the centuries bears out this evaluation.

A second reason for reiterating that Buddhism is a religion lies in the author's assumption with regard to religion as such, Buddhist or Christian. It is this: All religion basically embodies a thrust toward some ultimate, transcendent factor or reality in human experience or hopefully accessible to it. It is in terms of the right relationship to this factor or reality that religions conceive their salvations. And if Buddhism *is* a religion and if as a religion it *does* promise salvation—as indeed it does—then even under its negative terminology there must be some sense of an ultimately transcendent reality by which men are saved. One of its terms for this reality, perhaps the supreme one, is, of course, Nirvana. And though it is usually defined (when it *is* defined) negatively, the following scriptural assertion leaves no doubt that it does in truth represent a substantive reality, a transcendent ultimate for the Buddhist:

There is, O disciples, an unborn, not become, not compounded, not constructed. If there were not this unborn, not become, not compounded, not constructed, no escape could be seen here from that which is born, become, compounded, constructed. *But* since there is an unborn, not become, not compounded, not constructed, so an escape is possible from what is born, become, compounded, constructed.[6]

What do we then have in the case of a religion like Buddhism? A positive emotion-filled awareness of a genuinely transcendent reality that yet hides beneath negative terminology and conceptual emptiness. This situation is well stated by Rudolf Otto with specific regard to Buddhism:

And this is also entirely true of the nature of Nirvana, which is only in appearance a cold negative state. *It is only concep-*

*tually that "Nirvana" is a negation; it is felt in consciousness as
in the strongest degree positive;* it exercises a "fascination" by
which its votaries are as much carried away as are the Hindu
or the Christian by the corresponding objects of their worship.

I recall vividly a conversation I had with a Buddhist monk.
He had been putting before me methodically and pertinaciously
the arguments for the Buddhist "theology of negation," the
doctrine of Anātman and "entire emptiness." When he had
made an end, I asked him what then Nirvana itself is; and
after a long pause came at last the single answer, low and
restrained: "Bliss unspeakable." And the hushed restraint of
that answer, the solemnity of his voice, demeanour, and ges-
ture, made more clear what was meant than the words themselves.[7]

What we have here—except for the name Nirvana—is
of course not absolutely unique with Buddhism, or totally
foreign to Christianity, for that matter. Buddhist attitudes
toward, and language about, Nirvana are those of the
mystic.[8] For mysticism, in whatever tradition, has characteristically maintained: (1) that ultimate realities are completely beyond description; that what one can describe in
words is both less and other than the ultimate reality of
mystic experience; that words may become false substitutes
(idols) for the living reality they seek to describe; (2) that
the kind of religious experience that is capable of reaching
ultimate reality (and hence, by definition, achieving salvation) is of an ineffable sort; that is, just as ultimate reality
itself cannot be described by words or concepts, so the experience of it is inward and direct, independent even of
the mediation of thoughts, let alone description in words.

Now Christians need to be reminded that the mystical
tradition is not unknown in their own faith, though it is
obscure and almost meaningless to most contemporary Christians. Even in the New Testament Paul wrote, obviously of
himself:

I know a man in Christ who fourteen years ago was caught
up to the third heaven—whether in the body or out of the

body I do not know, God knows. And I know that this man was caught up into Paradise . . . and he heard things that cannot be told, which man may not utter (II Cor. 12:2–4).

That this experience "that cannot be told" is mystical in character needs no urging. Of course, such experiences may not have been typical of Paul's daily life and were probably not characteristic of the rank and file of the early church membership. Yet the tendency was there. And under later influences, Neoplatonism in particular, which in turn may have been fed from Buddhist-Indian sources, Christianity in its medieval period became strongly mystical. Again one must say that the average medieval priest and layman were largely untouched by mysticism. Yet the saint who had forsaken the world for the monastic life and who therein received visions and direct revelations did indeed become the classic pattern of the true and highest Christian piety. What he thus experienced, certified and inspired the faith of those on the lower levels of faith. And to this we may add that an elaborate mystical technique, again borrowed in part from the East, became an integral part of the central Christian tradition of this period. Here indeed was full-fledged mysticism whose saints have produced some of the most precious writings in the Christian collection of spiritual treasures.

But many things have happened since then to break the hold of mysticism upon Western Christianity. We have already spoken of the humanistic Renaissance and the secularizing influences of the industrial revolution, scientific advance, and the global expansion of European political and economic control. Even more importantly, though stimulated by the above forces and at the same time strengthening them, the Jewish prophetic-practical root within Christian tradition reasserted itself, particularly in Protestantism. The contemplative life was demoted in favor of the active, practical, moralistic life; would-be saints who earlier might have entered the monastery turned to convert the burgeoning world of new cities and the newly conquered foreign do-

mains into the Kingdom of God. And even though the Roman Catholic Church maintained, and still does, its system
of monastic orders and glorifies the contemplative life in its
teaching, its accepted type of mysticism became practical
and churchly: a Francis of Assisi building chapels and
caring for the social outcasts of his day; a Teresa of Ávila
going on from visions to build monasteries and counter fast-
growing Lutheran influences in Spain; an Ignatius Loyola
constructing a set of semimystical Spiritual Exercises for
the encouragement and stimulation of his monkish soldiers
of the Counter Reformation. We might sum it up by saying that though mysticism made a long-continued assault
upon Christianity, even apparently capturing it for a time,
the inner citadel of the Christian heart was never captured;
and that Christianity remained essentially—though in a
modified form—the religion of the Jewish prophets with
their emphasis upon historical and moral action as the true
expression of religion.

At any rate, mystical awareness is so deeply buried in
the collective religious unconscious of the Western Christian that it is nonexistent for all practical purposes—save
that *all* vital religious experience has something of the mystical sense of direct personal relation to ultimate realities
within it. Hence, the contemporary Christian finds any type
of mysticism or mystical language far beyond his ken—
whether that of "unorthodox" Meister Eckhart or "orthodox"
Catherine of Siena, Julian of Norwich, the mild visionary
kind of George Fox, or the philosophical variety of Paul
Tillich's God of "Unconditioned Being." Take him, then,
into a totally foreign culture where *all* the landmarks are
strange, and to a mystical religious tradition that far out-
mystics the Christian mystics—who did at least keep the
name of God in their language—in its complete negativity
of rejoicing in "emptiness," the "Void," or a "going out" in
Nirvana, and he is at a total loss. To him, Buddhism seems
as strange as the other side of the moon.

This is not, of course, to say that all or most actual Buddhists are "practicing" mystics, or know what it is all about. Many of them have neither hope nor immediate stomach for the emptiness of nirvanic peace; they comfortably put off its serious quest for another thousand lives or so, meantime devoting themselves to the more colorful anxieties of the realms of rebirth. Probably the vast majority even of the monks, though sworn by monkish vow to Nirvana-questing, have no hope (or desire?) for it at *this* life's end. Yet even the Buddhist layman, analogously to the medieval Christian layman, reverences those who seek Nirvana by a monk's life or by meditation,[9] and is dimly and guiltily aware that his present life is not the *truly* Buddhist life. For from the beginning, both by the example and explicit teaching of the Buddha and by the continuing tradition of the homeless (monkish) seeker for Nirvana, the life of negative attainment has been enthroned at the center of Buddhism in a way that mysticism never was even in medieval Christendom. The Nirvana Road of no-God, no-soul, no-prayer, no-attachment, no-heaven, no-theology, and of final individual cessation in Nirvana *is* Buddhism.

Our problem, then, to restate it, is to orient the Christian, to whom even his own mystical tradition is foreign, to a totally strange "nonreligious" mysticism that is yet religious in some sense; to enable him to locate its centers of significance, its transcendent realities under the form of its seeming denial of all significance and transcendence, and thus make some meaningful connection with his own tradition which is of a different and more affirmative sort. It may be, strange as it may sound, that some of the negations of Buddhism are as affirmative as Christian affirmations, differently stated and focused, yet not hopelessly incomprehensible or *totally* other. To some of these negative affirmations we now turn our attention.

(II)

God in Four Parts

1. *The Buddhist Denial of God*

Nowhere is it so easy to misunderstand the nature of Buddhism as with regard to its denial of God. This is particularly true in Southern Buddhism with which we shall deal mainly in these chapters. For, contrary to the semi-deification of the historical Buddha by Northern Buddhism into a kind of metaphysical essence manifesting itself in a threefold manner[1] strongly suggestive of the Christian Trinity, Southern Buddhism insists that the Buddha is essentially Ideal Man and flatly denies the existence of a Supreme God in any form whatsoever. To the traditional Christian mind, however, the question of God's existence is often a matter of all or nothing: either there is a living personal God, personal in some sort of humanistic sense, or there is only sheer mechanical process in the world, which leaves man, as a living person of infinite hopes and aspirations, high, dry, and alone upon a cosmic beachhead into nowhere. For the Christian, godlessness signifies the flight of all meaning and purpose from life, both cosmic and individual. Human existence is a pointless accident if God is denied. Spiritual life and ethical discipline seem worthless and fraudulent.

Yet in Buddhism there is the curious phenomenon of a way of life ostensibly without God, but not without hope or purpose in the world. It is, furthermore, a way that is often characterized by a considerable degree of spiritual discipline

34

and an ethic that parallels the Judeo-Christian ethic in several important respects. To this we may add, as before maintained, that it is essentially a religious way of life, containing within it sufficient resources for a life of deep devotion and inner spirituality, the capacity for the achievement of true saintliness, and some sense of a luminous experience of the Transcendent.

We must, of course, acknowledge in all historical honesty that there have been compensatory "religious" modifications in the course of Buddhism's development, additions of a concrete sort that have made it more humanly easy to live with than its austere skeletal orthodoxy might suggest. Northern Buddhism "deified" the Buddha. To reverence for the Buddha as a teacher, Southern Buddhism added reverence for his relics, for the scriptural record of his words, for his disciples' relics, for his monks, and for rituals honoring his image. He has been elevated to the level of an omniscient viewer and teacher of the truth, unapproachable by other men in his power and glory. And surrounding the central cult of reverence for the Buddha, almost approaching adoration at times, has grown up a bastard cult of reverence for second-grade deities and spirits (devas) from whom may be gained practical benefits and who may to some extent help their worshipers on the Buddha's way to Nirvana.

Despite such changes in Buddhist practice, and the addition of non-Buddhist perversions, the central core of Buddhism both in theory and practice tends to remain non-theistic in the strict sense. Nor should we seek to evade or deny the strength of the Buddhist nontheistic conviction despite practical flaws in its purity. To repeat in part what was said in the previous chapter, we may observe that Buddhism does indeed deny that there is a Supreme and Almighty God in all the forms with which that doctrine has been clothed: First Cause, Unmoved Mover, Creator, Almighty Father, Supreme Being, Spiritual Presence, All-Knower, etc., etc. Even limited-God theories would be rejected, unless the limitation be such that God be reduced to deva (godling) level, i.e., that of the spirit of a just man made more powerful and blessed for a time in one of the heavens but incapable of even his own salvation. A characteristic statement from Southern Buddhism follows:

Question 5: (a) If Buddhism does not believe in God, why not? (b) Does not this make the universe without any purpose or meaning?
Answer: (a) Buddhism, like Louis Pasteur, confines its attention to prevention and cure. It does not bother its head about any copyright author or inventor of plague and a thousand million worldly woes. . . . Buddhism points to the law of righteousness to be conformed to, leaving alone favour-seeking as an industry. (b) If the purpose and meaning of plague is not investigated by Louis Pasteur or by any other scientist, why should we waste time to trace its sole author![2]

Nor can we call that luminous experience of the Buddhist saint (*arahat*) the experience of a Divine Presence—at least he would not agree if we did so. It has, rather, the quality of sheer aloneness; nor is it that Aloneness to which Christian mystics saw the aloneness in man responding in saintly ecstasies. The quality of saintly awareness in Buddhism is that of complete lucidity and emptiness of consciousness—so that even the self that is aware is not so much a *self* that is aware, but merely an act of awareness. And Nirvana, into which the saint will enter directly upon death, is the cessation of all interpersonal as well as intrapersonal consciousness—"the graveyard of the mind" as one Buddhist friend called it.

We may note again that the universe is not a universe of soul-making, as Christian philosophers have been wont to name it. It is, rather, a vale of the *un*making of that illusory entity which calls itself a self or soul. That is, personal, psychophysical beings are simply processes, integrally a part of the world process that is neither more nor less than an orderly causal flux, changing at every moment of its existence in every part of its existence (including "souls") into something else. If, in accordance with these facts, the self knows that it is not a self, and achieves a detached acceptance of this truth, it is on the way to liberation from the birth-death process that we call life.

What, then, remains? A sheer materialistic atheism of mere fluxing forces and whirling atoms, certain small collections of which somehow and somewhat crazily imagine themselves to be selves? It is true that Buddhists are fond of quoting the antitheistic arguments of Western freethinkers, agnostics, rationalists, and atheists in support of their own position. It is also true that they tend to regard adherence to belief in individual soul and personal God (the two are almost inseparable) as an injurious addiction.[3] It is further true that sometimes Buddhists are willing to be called atheists and now and then have shown a superficial sympathy for the "scientific atheism" of communism, though again they sometimes publicly appeal to all religious men to join them in fighting the philosophy of "godless communism."

However, one might properly use the term "divine atheism" with regard to Buddhism, not so much in the sense of approving the high purity of its atheism, but rather in the sense of a "spiritual" or "religious" atheism. For this is precisely what even the most purely atheistic Buddhism is —a deeply religious atheism. Though the cosmos may not be ruled by, or contained in the being of, a supreme deity, nor created by his act, it is nonetheless not a materialistic universe. For the Southern Buddhist it is filled with a multitude of sentient beings, both superhuman and subhuman, constantly being born in new forms on different levels and never ceasing to exist in some sentient form or other. Further, the Buddhist rejects the dialectical materialism of the communist just because it *is* materialistic in its assertion that different arrangements or states of material particles produce mind-states. Citing the opening verses of the Dhammapada (a scripture), "Mind foreruns (all evil, all good) conditions, mind is chief, mind-made are they,"[4] he asserts the Buddhist position to be that it is body-states and bodily forms that arise from mind-states, rather than the reverse. So also, as we shall see, he finds the universe in which he lives profoundly responsive to his spiritual, extra-sensory perceptions and projections of will-force. There is here obviously a striking similarity to pantheistic Hinduism, or to Christian Science in its affirmation of God as "Mind" or spiritual "Principle" rather than as person.

Much might be said along this line, but the above may suffice to suggest that there is more in Buddhist "atheism" than the mere word itself suggests. And this calls for further examination. We shall therefore turn our attention to four factors that form what I shall call a *reality-complex* or *reality-structure,* namely, Dharma, Karma, Nirvana, and the Buddha. These four elements embrace the highest order of realities that we can find in Buddhist theory and practice. And our interest here will be to note if, and in what way, they work together to provide a God-substitute or fulfill a God-function in Buddhism.

2. *The Fourfold Reality-Complex*

a. *The Orderly Universe of Dharma*

Dharma is a word that Buddhism inherited from India. It comes from a root meaning the "foundation" or "basic constitution" of whatever is spoken of, and in the course of centuries it has acquired both social and cosmic meanings. In Hinduism it is primarily, though not exclusively, used to indicate the caste order constitutive of Indian society. Thus used, dharma suggests a comprehensive and meaningful social order by which every individual and every racial group has its own proper place and function; and the implication, often voiced, is that this order mirrors, expresses, or is in accord with, a divine cosmic order.

In Buddhism, where caste was rejected, dharma came to have both narrower and wider meanings. Most narrowly interpreted, it means simply the teaching (law, norm, truth) of the Buddha. And there is something herein of the sheerly dogmatic Southern Buddhist assurance of the absolute truth of that teaching, that it is the account of all things, "as they are," which has been infallibly transmitted in the scriptures. But at its widest it also reaches out to include cosmic order. The following quotation will illustrate the contemporary Buddhist usage of dharma:

All the teachings of the Buddha can be summed up in one word: dhamma [the Pali form of dharma]. . . . It means truth, that which really is. It also means law, the law which exists in a man's own heart and mind. It is the principle of righteousness. . . .

Dhamma, this law of righteousness, exists not only in a man's heart and mind; it exists in the universe also. All the universe is an embodiment and revelation of dhamma. When the moon rises and sets, the rains come, the crops grow, the seasons change, it is because of dhamma, for dhamma is the law residing in the universe which makes matter act in the ways revealed by the studies of modern science in physics, chemistry, zoology, botany, and astronomy. Dhamma is the true nature of every existing thing, animate and inanimate.[5]

It is illuminating to observe the wide range of elements that dharma comprises. It includes the natural uniformities of the physical world at all levels, and it includes the inner human world of moral values. Human righteousness and the lawful organization of matter are all essentially dharma, says our author. Does this then signify the reduction of moral values and inner experiences to "epiphenomena," mere feelings that unaccountably and unmeaningfully arise alongside chemical and physical processes? No! Then does this mean the mechanization of the inmost states of the human soul? To some extent, the answer must be in the affirmative, for man is not to be conceived as a self or soul that floats along above mechanical world processes, airily and freely disregarding all the lawful order of those processes because he is, as a soul, made of completely other stuff. Buddhism expressly intends to include man in world process; each man himself is a small process, an integral part of the whole. Such is the essence of the no-soul doctrine.

But observe, then, what happens to that order (dharma) in which man's inmost spirit is integrally included. The order itself, however mechanically conceived, becomes spiritualized. Nowhere more so than in Buddhism. Thus, though the Buddhist says that man is *only* a set of factors, *four* of the five factors that comprise him are mentalistic in nature. These factors are sometimes called bodily form, or corporeality; feeling, or the power of sensation; the power of perceiving sense objects; "mental formations" of fifty types including tendencies, or what an older psychology called "faculties"; and consciousness, "which is the fundamental factor of all the other three."[6]

As the writer of this passage said to the author, "Man is indeed only a set of factors, but he is a very *unusual* set." To this may be added the consideration that Buddhism considers consciousness or mind-power, in another context than this, to be a sixth sense that is not dependent upon the ordinary five senses for its dynamism or for all its raw materials. (Hence the deep Buddhist interest in and sympathy for parapsychological research and extrasensory perception.) Man is thus no merely mechanical set of factors or neurochemical reaction pattern in the sense of behaviorist psychology.

There is yet more to be said about the nature of that set of factors called "man," that dharma in microcosm. He can exert actual effective influence upon other beings and physical realities by the sheer power of good-will force. Buddhist scriptures are full of tales of how the saints and the Buddha, in his lives both before and after becoming a Buddha, turned back the power of ravenous or enraged beasts, venomous snakes, and hostile men by the exercise of harmless benevolence, without lifting a finger physically. So likewise in many passages it is held that the saint—not necessarily a Buddha, though Buddhas in particular possess such powers in abundance—can develop such psychic powers that the molecules of his bodily form become obedient to his will. He may give himself multiple bodies, appear in different places simultaneously, and fly through air, water, or earth with the greatest of ease. While many modern Buddhists—like many contemporary Christians—would believe that such miracles belong almost exclusively to past and holier times and men, it is still a central conviction that such deeds are *possible* even now to the very holy; and that for all men in some perceptibly effective measure the "radiation" or transmission of good influence at a distance is a spiritual duty and reality. The scriptural statement here is as follows:

Herein is wealth, that a brother abides, letting his mind fraught with love pervade one quarter of the world, and so too the second quarter, and so the third quarter, and so the fourth quarter. And thus the whole wide world, above, below, around, and everywhere and altogether does he continue to pervade with love-burdened thought, abounding, sublime, beyond measure, free from hatred and ill will.[7]

It may be observed that though we have been speaking only of *man's* powers, the success with which such powers can be exercised clearly implies much about the nature of a universe in which such powers can be exercised. It must "co-operate" in remarkable fashion, or at least be of such a nature that spiritual-moral force can be exerted by means of it. Such a type of cosmos is surely no mere mechanical causal order that behaves only according to the laws of scientific physics. To the *spiritual* physics of dharma we shall next turn in our consideration of karma.

b. *Karma: The Moral Order Within the Universe*

Karma is perhaps the best-known Hindu-Buddhist word in all the world. It has often been capitalized as though it were some sort of God—which it is not, according to Buddhist thinking at least; therefore, we shall not ordinarily capitalize it here. Karma as the rule has also carried the connotation of fatefulness, an irrevocable, unhappy destiny riveted upon a man by his likewise irrevocable deeds in past lives. To such a deserved fate one can only passively yield. There is a considerable measure of truth in this conception, judged by the historical influence of the belief in karma, though contemporary Buddhist leaders are trying hard to change this fatalistic connotation by an emphasis upon the individual's power to change his present, and consequently future, karma through resolute deeds in the here and now.

In any case, karma (literally "deed") stands for the power of the deliberately willed action to produce future mental and physical results in keeping with its original quality. We may call karma the ethical subdivision of the dharmic causal order; it is the *ethical* life of man structured according to the cause-effect uniformity of the *natural* order of the outer world. Thus we can see the meaning of the Venerable U Thittila's statement that both inward and outward realities are all dharmic in nature. That is, a man's actions do not spring causeless into existence, nor his decisions that produce the actions. They are rooted in surrounding circumstances, and most importantly in a series of thoughts, decisions, and actions, stretching, chainwise with absolutely no breaks, into the infinite past of infinite previous lives. Nor is it only his states of mind, his emotions, his moral character, that are thus affected; the apparent accidents of birth, or different circumstances, appearance, and ability—in fact, all that "I" now am—are thus determined. This, obviously, is the Buddhist explanation of human inequalities of capacity and fortune, the Buddhist way of dealing with the problem of evil.

By the same token by which the dharmic order of the outer world is induced into the ethical and religious worlds in the hope of making the latter systematic and orderly— "scientific" in modern terminology—immense effort has been exerted to conform the operation of karma to the sheerly simple patterns of natural or physical causation. One must avoid all attempts to think of karma as Karma, i.e., a semipersonalized punishing and rewarding agency. Thus, to quote again the Venerable U Thittila:

We have seen in the discussion of dependent origination how the origination of existent things is a continuous process in which every existent being is an effect of previous causes. Every action produces an effect—it is cause first and effect afterward. We therefore speak of kamma [Pali form of karma] as "the law of cause and effect." Throwing a stone, for example, is an action. If the stone strikes a glass window and breaks it, the break is the effect of the action of throwing, but it is not the end, for the broken window will be the cause of further trouble. . . .

Kamma knows nothing about us. It does not know us any more than fire knows us when it burns us. It is the nature of fire to burn, to give out heat; and if we use it properly, it gives us light, cooks our food, burns up things we want to destroy— but if we use it improperly, it burns us and our property.[8]

Still further, we may think of the results of karma as the addition of mathematical sums in which a plus b equals c, no more, no less. Given all our past actions, what we now are or experience is but the correct, inevitable, or "right" result. In this sense, "right" seems to be another name for what exists; what now is, is "right" because it is the "right" sum of all past actions:

Everything that comes to us is right. Whenever anything pleasant comes to us and makes us happy, we may be sure that what we have done is right. When anything hurts us or makes us unhappy, our kamma is showing us our mistake. We must never forget that kamma is always just—it neither loves nor hates, it does not reward or punish, it is never angry, never pleased. It is simply the law of cause and effect.[9]

Thus is stated the rigid mathematical formula that presumably governs the inner moral life of man and makes it one indissoluble unity with outward dharmic chemical and physical uniformities. Yet a little further observation here will show how thoroughly the conception of karma (and through karma, of dharma) has actually been moralized in fact, if not in word. For example, in the above quotation those preponderantly ethical terms "right" and "just" are given a purely quantitative, mathematical formulation by Buddhism. Yet this formulation is faulty, for in the same passage, happiness—which has nothing mathematical about it—is linked to "right" and "just" as their *results*. We are happy, have good, i.e., pleasant, things happen to us— health, wealth, fame, friends, easy dying, birth in the pleasant heavenly worlds—because we have been *ethically* good. And the reverse effects for morally evil deeds likewise result. This is surely beyond the nature of the sheer mathematics of cause-effect observations. It is a faith that there is a moral order (karma) in the universe that "punishes" and "rewards"—no other words seem to fit, even though the deeds that produced these results were "mine" in previous life—the evil and good action. There is here a close analogue to the Christian conception of a judging providential order.

One other moralistic, and not mechanical-mathematical, feature of karma is yet to be mentioned. Or perhaps it is better termed a moralistic—but quite essential—loophole in the apparent mechanical determinism of karma. For if the present thought-word-deed pattern was inexorably caused by a previous thought-word-deed pattern, and so on back through infinite lives, where is there any hope for improvement? Especially does this seem to be the irresistible conclusion of the Buddhist denial of any substantial or independent soul which might act freely in its own right. But by what seems an illogical turn to the outsider, nearly all modern Buddhists strongly affirm the free will of man. The Venerable U Thittila may be our spokesman again:

Man has, therefore, a certain amount of free will and there is every possibility to mold his life or to modify his actions.

Even the most vicious person can by his own free will and effort become the most virtuous person. One may at any moment change for the better or for the worse.[10]

Thus does karma represent a thoroughly moralistic aspect of the rigid world order in which man lives. Of the inwardness of its relation to dharma we shall speak again at the end of the chapter. Here we must turn to a third factor in the reality-complex which, in every way, is the most important of them all. That is, of course, Nirvana.

c. Nirvana: Supreme Goal and Haven

How shall that greatest of all Buddhist ultimate entities be explained to a Christian? Buddhists would uniformly say that the task of explaining Nirvana is completely hopeless, not only to Christians but to Buddhists—except that for Christians it is *more* completely hopeless. For, as we have noted, the essence of Nirvana is that it is beyond all description or explanation of any sort. But there is not much more actual consistency here, whatever the theory, among Buddhists than among mystics in general, for whom the theoretically inexpressible experience and reality become fountainheads of endless and colorful attempts to express them. Therefore, by direction and indirection, Nirvana is found very often described in the Buddhist scriptures and tradition as deathless; the ambrosial; peace; calmness and coolness; release; bliss, the going out of greed, hatred, and delusion; a haven; an unborn, uncompounded (and therefore eternal) essence; and so forth. To some of these we shall return later, but for our purpose now we may take Buddhism more or less at its official word and refuse to characterize Nirvana directly by ascribing qualities to it. We shall, rather, characterize it with regard to its place and function in the Buddhist religious structure, which is both more in line with Buddhist procedure and may at the same time be more meaningful to the outsider. This is necessary if at all possible; for with Nirvana we come to that Buddhist term and experience most difficult to grasp, the apex of the problem of Buddhist-Christian incommunicability.

(1) *Nirvana is utterly transcendent*

It is perhaps impossible to overexpress Nirvana's complete transcendence of everything else to the Buddhist's satisfaction. We are unavoidably reminded of a similar Hindu refusal to characterize that ultimate reality called Brahman; to all attempted attributions or descriptions he responds, No, No; or Not that, Not that. Where shall we then begin with our denials of what Nirvana is? Almost anywhere will do, so to speak. Nirvana has neither beginning nor ending; we might call it eternal, save that eternity carries the flavor of a kind of countertime, whereas Nirvana is utterly atemporal. In keeping with this, those flashes of nirvanic awareness of which the saints become capable a few times in their last mortal lives are utterly timeless in their quality as experience. Nor is Nirvana in any sense spatial; it is not here, there, or yonder. This makes it difficult to relate it to anything else. Does it include *everything*, as "Being" may be held to comprise everything from atoms and stars, to men, angels, and God? Or is Nirvana *ex*clusive of everything else? There is no real answer. Presumably it is *not* the stuff of reality, as is the Dharmakaya of Northern Buddhism; yet nothing else is real compared to it. (See next subsection.) Perhaps we could call it absolutely infinite Infinitude with absolutely no limitations—yet again words like infinite do not seem to apply either. They are as meaningless, say Buddhist scriptures, when applied to Nirvana, as to ask in what direction a fire "goes" when it "goes out." All that we can say is that Nirvana is utterly different from anything we know about, or perceive in ordinary experience.

There are still other ways of indicating Nirvana's utter difference from all other known things. It is completely nonindividual. That is, there are no parts to it, no distinctions within it, no place for difference or change "inside" it. To use an analogy—one perhaps not acceptable to the Buddhist—Nirvana is like a world in which nothing exists

save a completely transparent atmosphere, yet with nothing
at all to see in its transparency, and no sense of being one
who is beholding this transparency, but of somehow being
the transparency itself. Now and then a Buddhist will suggest that Nirvana is more mental than it is physical; but he
almost immediately withdraws from active circulation any
suggestion that it *is* actually some sort of "mind-stuff." For
in Nirvana there is no consciousness in the ordinary
sense; and the reason for this is apparent: "consciousness"
always indicates division between the mind that is aware
and that of which it is aware, or between mind and matter,
or inner feelings and outward objects. And all such distinctions are held to belong to a lower level of reality than
Nirvana, which latter is utterly distinctionless.

Thus one might say: Name it, name *anything,* and Nirvana is different. It is neither temporal nor spatial; nor
mental nor physical; nor this nor that. We cannot even use
the terms "existent" or "nonexistent" with regard to Nirvana
or of one who has entered it. One who has "gone out" into
Nirvana has entered on a "trackless" way that cannot be
found or measured by any possible process. Nirvana is
"wholly other" in the fullest possible meaning of these
words.

(2) *Nirvana is utterly real*
This may seem to be contradictory to what has just been
said, and so it is, in the usual sense. Not that this would
bother the Buddhist logician who revels in logical contra-
dictions and finds in the *really* Real the confusion of all
logic. But if we use the word "real" with regard to Nirvana,
what do we then mean since it is presumably utterly transcendent of even terms like reality? Nirvana is not real in
any directly assignable sense, to be sure. It is not physically
real as the mountains, or implicitly real as the human self,
or inferredly real as God. Even to call it "unconditioned
being" or "ultimate reality" is not quite enough or exactly
right. In one sense, these terms do describe it as a functioning reality, one that is beyond every limitation and every

other reality. But "being" and "reality" have connotations of some kind of substance or life or position or quality about them. And by definition Nirvana has none of these.

We can perhaps speak of the *utter* reality of Nirvana— its special brand of reality—as the convergence of two lines of thought that reach their ideal limit in Nirvana. By an ideal limit I mean that point to which a certain development or kind of experience or thought process would come if carried on to its logical conclusion or its theoretical perfection, but which we never actually reach either in thought or experience. Thus one divides and subdivides a particle into half, ad infinitum, but never comes to an absolute Zero. So in another sense we may think of Nirvana as representing the joint ideal limit of two converging developments, both of which seek a maximum of "reality" in regard to categories of *time* and *substance*.

With regard to *substance* Nirvana is conceived as that which is absolutely unchanging. For change diminishes reality, according to Buddhism. Whatever changes, dies in part; change means that something has to disappear or be displaced by something else; otherwise, there would be no change. This indeed is the situation with regard to *all* perceptible realities (save Nirvana): they do change, that is, decay and die. The Buddhist writer agrees perfectly with the sentiments of the hymn writer, "Change and decay in all around [and in myself] I see." And for the Buddhist the essence of human suffering lies precisely in this: there is no true permanence. What is loved cannot be kept; and even the lover himself may change so that what he once loved he now hates. Even "God," if he is conceived as personal, must change, for change is the essence of "personality." And as changing He would be dying and diminishing. Therefore, Nirvana conceived as Absolute Permanence must also be conceived as Absolute Unchangeability.

The other line of development, or the other side of the coin, to change the figure for a moment, is that change occurs in *time*. Time and change are the twin assassins of

Reality. However "real" an experience of a moment may be, it is gone with the passing of the moment. Hence, it is not real in the full sense. And looking at the items of experience, wherein can we find any true lasting permanence? Be it the flash of a thought, the flight of a bird, a passing mood, a happy holiday, the length of a long human life, the enduringness of a mountain, the many-millioned years of existence in a deva world—all of these at last come to an end and when ended are as though they had never been. (Indeed, they do not truly even *endure,* for not even the mountain really lasts all this time, but is itself a process of continually passing away into something else, into subsequent states.) All of them are characterized by *anicca* (impermanence) and *anattā* (emptiness or unreality).

Therefore, the maximum case of Reality is that which does not change in any part or slightest degree and that which lasts unchanged for such an endless length of "time" that it is beyond time itself. Nirvana alone represents the meeting point of unchangeability and everlastingness in maximum degree; and hence Nirvana alone is real. And this is also the reason that Nirvana cannot be described. What can be described must have parts, or change from moment to moment or year to year, or be observed by some changing mind. Thus it is that we can describe dewdrops, mountains, stars, and persons, because either subject or object changes, and hence all are less than fully real. But the truly Real cannot be described save by silence.

(3) *Nirvana is utterly desirable*

How can the utterly different be desired? And how can we know enough about the utterly different to have any feelings about it at all? Difficult as it may seem, we must not make the mistake of equating the utterly different (in an intellectual sense) with utter Zero, particularly in the emotional sense. The quoted passage from Otto in Chapter I should remind us of this. We may say in a phrase that Nirvana is desirable by its sheer contrast with that changeable and empty reality that we know under the name of self-conscious human existence in the world of time and space. Whatever is to be fully desired must be totally different from the elements of that changeful level of being. And this is in some sense what the Buddhist does say. For it is taken as granted that wherever there are anicca (impermanence) and anatta (changing emptiness) there is also dukkha (suffering). We suffer because of change, as noted above. Hence, only the infinitely unchanging and infinitely enduring are infinitely desirable. And what achieves this condition but some such reality as Nirvana?

But there is a deeper and perhaps primary root of nirvanic desirability, and that is the nirvanic *experience*. As suggested in passing, at an earlier point, Nirvana may be experienced to some extent in this life. It is held that the Buddha daily refreshed himself in the early morning hours by achieving nirvanic awareness. Also there is the pure essence of Nirvana experienced momentarily by the higher orders of saints. An old tradition suggests that there are four such flashes, and then out into the real thing for the highest level saint, or arahat. And it is recognized that the *totality* of the saint's life is, in a somewhat lesser sense, nirvanic; and further, that even the ordinarily devout person may have a nirvanalike experience of peace and detachment that grows progressively deeper as such a one advances in the spiritual discipline of meditation. This partial but growing experience of Nirvana-in-this-life is undoubtedly the core of the Buddhist conviction of the absolute reality of ultimate Nirvana; and its time-transcendent quality produces an ever-growing desire for the fullness of Nirvana itself.

d. *Buddha: The Supreme Revelator and Example*

Even though the term "Buddhism" is one attached by outsiders—and not too welcome to Buddhists—it would be impossible to think of this way of life without the figure of the Buddha somewhere among its major realities and it was inevitable that the term "Buddhism" should result. For popular Buddhism, in Southeast Asia, the "presence" of the

Buddha, i.e., his pagoda and his image, is multitudinously present. Yet even here, or should we say especially here, the charge that these symbols are idols is resented and denied. Despite appearances—incense, candles, flower offerings, "prayers" before the images at the pagodas—it is denied the Buddha is a god or that he is worshiped in the Christian sense. Thus it is evident that the relation of the Buddhist to the Buddha is not entirely analogous to the usual Christian's relation to Christ.

Into the full relation of Buddha to Buddhists we cannot go here. But we must consider something of what this fourth element of the reality-complex contributes to the totality. *Roughly* speaking, the role of the Buddha is comparable to that of Jesus, the Christ, in Christianity. Gotama, the man, became a Buddha, or Enlightened One, as the result of spiritual power accumulated through millions of his successive lives and by virtue of one supreme final effort of concentrated meditation. After his enlightenment he became a supreme Teacher whose teachings are to be found in the scriptures. (Northern and Southern Buddhism have two somewhat variant scriptural canons.) Just before his death he told his disciples that he would continue to be present with them in these teachings, which fully portray the way to Nirvana.

Not only is the Buddha the supreme Teacher of the Truth, the only Truth that can bring men release from birth-death, but he is the supreme example of Perfect Manhood. Buddhists use the word "supernormal" rather than "supernatural" with regard to the Buddha. What he has done can in theory be done by any or every man. His godlike powers of omniscience—*not* of creativity—and his perfection of virtues represent only the sum of long lives of *human* endeavor. Thus, while no one exactly expects to become a Buddha thereby, and even the term "Buddhalike" is avoided, yet the virtues of the Buddha should be meditated upon in the hope of at least a weak imitation of them. Such is presumably what occurs when the worshiper kneels before the Buddha image.

Yet precisely at this point there enters in another decisive —and confusing—factor. As just implied, no one dreams of calling himself a Buddha in Southern Buddhism, or speaks, as in Northern Buddhism, of his own Buddha nature. Though the Buddha theoretically is only a man, he is a man of such proportions that he is truly Godlike, an incalculable distance beyond the average man in every way. The conviction that it takes millions of lives to produce a Buddha and that Buddhas appear only rarely after agelong intervals in our human universes is one way of making this point; another is that of emphasizing the fullness and richness of the knowledge and virtues of a Buddha. And though there have been many Buddhas—if we go back through uncounted universes—it is usually only the Gotama Buddha of whom we think when we today say "the Buddha."

What then *is* the essential religious value of the Buddha for Buddhism? The very least that can be said of him, and this is considerable, is that without his teaching—Christians would call it a revelation—no man can be saved. For the Noble Eightfold Path to Nirvana is not something that the ordinary man can discover for himself; it must be taught by a Buddha. The omniscience of the Buddha that discovered saving truth is rock-bottom reality for Buddhist faith. Further, there is no doubt that the stories of the Buddha's earthly life and the presence of his image give to "Buddha" the quality of a personalized center for religious devotion, even almost adoration. In the Buddha the higher life, and the power and hope of Nirvana, become tangible and personal. Therefore, in the end the Buddha becomes *functionally* and *actually* a savior God for many rank-and-file Buddhists.

3. *The Synthetic Unity of the Fourfold Complex*

Such, then, are the four components of that complex of basic realities which may be said to fulfill a God-function in Buddhism. The questions to which we turn in conclusion are those having to do with the degree and nature of this God-function. Do these four elements really add up to a "hidden" God in Buddhism? Do they function as an integral unity in the Buddhist scheme of things, as God does in the Christian? For the purposes of giving an answer we must note the genuinely God-quality of the elements and then the sort of unity they achieve or imply.

The dharma-karma combination of forces governing the world in which we live has many of the attributes of the Christian God. There is in it that kind of order necessary to achieve a cosmos or universe rather than a chaos. Most Christian scriptures and hymns speak of this order as a personally established and maintained one—an order achieved by God's "changeless decree," according to the hymn, and maintained by God's "faithfulness," according to the Bible. Recent Christian thought, however, has often spoken of the uniformity of nature, as observed in its physical laws, in less personalistic terms. Yet whichever approach is used, the universe is seen as an internally related organism held together by a principle (or being) of order, each part marvelously adapted to every other.

More important for our purposes is the karmic quality of this universe, for it suggests that despite mechanistic appearances the universe has a moral "heart." To be sure, the Buddhist would not speak of it thus, but insist that its "morality" is only that of impersonal causal order which applies to the moral realm as well as to the physical. Nevertheless, we have seen how karmic morality "gets out of hand" and ends up by pervading the whole structure. Karma represents a synthesis of the neutral, nonpersonal, physical order with the human spiritual-moral order in organic fashion, in which synthesis the moralistic quality becomes the dominating element. This is still further demonstrated in that spiritual quality of the dharma-karma order by which one may radiate benevolence throughout the length and breadth of the universe in an effective way; and by the manner in which developed mind-power can totally control and transform—at least in one's own person and his relation to the universe—the physical aspects of the universe in a near-magical way.

There is a further dimension of the karmic (moralistic) nature of the cosmic order only implied thus far, but quite important. It is this: the moral or immoral quality of the inhabitants of a universe determines its rise and fall as a universe. In several Buddhist scriptures there appears the theme of the gradual decline of the universe from a state of initial blessedness, of life up to 84,000 years in length, and of universal peace and common possessions, down to one in which men are divided in strife and competition and by mutual hatreds, ravaged by disease, and live only ten years at the maximum. (We are now in a period of decline, say contemporary Buddhists.) But when the nadir of misery is reached, men repent, and the cycle moves upward again toward the heights of splendor. One recent writer carries the process of dissolution due to moral decay to the ultimate degree—that of a completely disembodied universe that consists only of "suffering" heat units. When these have been purified by heatful suffering, they will gradually coagulate round about them a newly formed physical universe.

Thus with the two exceptions of an initial creation and a final climactic Kingdom of God, dharma-karma seems almost to equal God in its governance of the universe. For the dharma-karma order is as tightly controlled, and in essentially moralistic terms, as the Calvinistic world is by the sovereign God. Not one particle, one thought, or one stray breeze is out of context. To be sure, there are mysteries of inequality about the present situation. But just as the Calvinist can rely on man's sin or the inscrutable decree of God for explanation, so the Buddhist has faith in the invisible order of karmic justice for *his* explanation.

Turning to the *Buddha*-producing process—if it may be so termed—we may note that it is part of the dharma-karma order in some aspects. We may put it this way: This is such a universe that periodically the merits of certain rare individuals build up to Buddha height and a deliverer appears. For though Southern Buddhists primarily worship Gotama Buddha (who lived in the sixth century B.C. in India), they find in him only one of many, many Buddhas who have appeared, and presumably will appear, in the course of an infinite procession of universes. Gotama was the fourth Buddha in *this* world age, and one more, Maitreya, is scheduled to appear and temporarily "save" the world. But back beyond these, some twenty-three or twenty-four others are named; and some prayers speak of still other thousands, even millions, of Buddhas before these last-named.

In any case, this is a universe in which occurs the "incarnation" of Buddhas for men and for their salvation. How, then, is this to be regarded? Is there an overarching Mercy that brings forth or incarnates itself in Buddhahood periodically? Is there some ineluctable necessity in the nature of things that produces such individuals in "the fullness of time"? This is what Northern Buddhism seems almost to say: Dharmakaya (ultimate cause) produces Nirmankaya (historical Buddhas). Or, in more personalistic terms, all-seeing Bodhisattvas who have vowed never to enter Nirvana until all men are saved deliberately take on human forms as and when the world needs them. But with Southern Buddhism the case is not so clear. Revivalist preachers emphasize the long intervals between Buddha appearances and warn of the *rarity* of the privilege of living in epochs of Buddhist teaching. And there seems to be no regular schedule of appearances, though some may look for Maitreya's appearance in the near future. Rather, it seems that there are only sporadic individuals who take the Buddha vow and finally bring their vow to its fruition. Who knows when the next such a one shall come with any actual assurance?

Thus in Southern Buddhism it is doubtful whether we can speak of any genuine metaphysical synthesis of Buddha substance with dharma-karma order. It is true that the necessary foundation for Buddhahood is one built through the agency of karma—an infinitely large accumulation of karmic merit through long ages until it adds up to a Buddha. Yet the driving force in all of this is not so much karma force as the individual will of the Buddha-to-be who *uses* the karmic mechanism to achieve his goal. And besides this, when such a one actually becomes a Buddha, he enters another order whose relationships to dharma-karma are most ambiguous. I speak of the order of Nirvana.

We have been at pains to emphasize the "utterness" of Nirvana, which quite removes it from all earthly temporal orders. Do these qualities of "otherness" then constitute Nirvana the real "God" in Buddhism? To be sure, Nirvana is apparently a most unlikely candidate. It is often equated with distinctionless Suchness or Voidness or Nothingness in Northern Buddhism; it is the inexpressible reality into which the Buddha entered upon death. It is certainly not the creator of the universe or its sustaining order. It is indeed the antithesis of that universe both in general and particular, and seems to have no dynamism of any sort. One enters Nirvana instead of Nirvana entering him. And that entrance is the remedy for that pervasive evil in the universe called individualized life.

Yet there are Godlike qualities in Nirvana also, and very important ones. And paradoxically they turn out to be those very qualities which in the above context seemed to deny its "divinity." Thus Nirvana approximates the hiddenness, the inscrutability, the otherness of God, the essence of Divine Selfhood and majesty, the ultimate mystery of Divine Being. We in the Christian tradition should not need reminding that such ultimate mystery is a constituent element of even the Christian conception of God—though it is much lost sight of today. "For my thoughts are not your thoughts, neither are your ways my ways," says Jehovah (through Isaiah) to the chosen people. And we may also remember Paul's sense of the ultimate mystery of God's being and purposes, Augustine's and Calvin's sense of God's inscrutable will, Eckhart's unfathomable Godhead which is "beyond" God, Luther's *"Deus absconditus"* beyond the *"Deus revelatus,"* Barth's emphasis upon the Wholly Otherness of God —to mention only a few Christian statements. Hence, in its quality of that Reality beyond all words about it, the Utterly Real and Transcendent Nirvana is completely Godlike.

It is further true that Nirvana is the object of the Buddhist's fundamental passion as a devout Buddhist. It is the "long home" to which he desires to go; the other-side port of safety across the tides and storms of birth-death existence; it is the deathless for which he longs, in which conscious-ness may be swallowed up, yet which may be the beginning of perfect knowledge.[11] It can be described as "unutterable bliss." Here again is something analogous to a deep-lying Christian theme that man is made for God and that God's purpose and nature are, according to the Westminster Con-fession, that man should "enjoy God forever."

In the light of these considerations we might say that in Nirvana is to be found the *essence* of the God-function of the fourfold reality-complex in Buddhism. For here is that synthesis of ultimate reality and value with which religions have always sought to deal in their theologies, rituals, and experiences, and which in many is called Deity. To the ex-tent that Nirvana represents this synthesis of metaphysical reality and desirability, it would seem to represent more nearly than any other of the four elements in the complex the locus of theistic functions and values. And to the extent that the hope of Nirvana and the experience of nirvanic-quality peace and detachment, come to be the central and appropriable value in the higher reaches of the Buddhist religious life, it may be said that Nirvana is, functionally speaking, the God-equivalent in Buddhism.

Yet we cannot simply say, "For the Buddhist, Nirvana is God," no matter how illuminating its consideration in terms of God-function may be. Or, at the very least, we must be aware that the God-value of Nirvana is only partial so far as the Christian would be concerned, having *only* those God-values which the Christian *mystic* emphasized —"God" as the source of an experience of the inexpressibly real and desirable. Indeed, Nirvana is perhaps essentially and only that: the inexpressible mystic experience which, because of its inexpressibility, is also assumed to be the ulti-mate metaphysical reality. Nirvana is the Buddhist God-of-religious-experience, not of history, theological descrip-tion, or of morality. These latter functions of Deity, which the Christian mystic took for granted as the ordinary context of his mystical experience, the Buddhist refers to the areas of Dharma, Karma, and Buddha, but does *not* include in the Nirvana context.

We must therefore ask, Of what sort is the essential unity of the Dharma-Karma-Nirvana-Buddha complex? And we must reply—a point that the Christian must always keep in mind when thinking of Buddhism—that the result is a kind of loose-jointed deity complex rather than any entity that can be called God in the Christian sense. The complex does *not* have the tight integrality that Christianity has sought to achieve in its concept of God and in its distinctive religious experience. This Buddhist "God-complex" in its four parts works differently, and perhaps even antagonistically within itself, for different purposes at different levels and under different conditions.

To illustrate this, we may note two or three aspects of the relationship of these four elements to each other, implied but not specified in the foregoing description. Consider, for example, the relation of Buddhas to the other three elements. Can one say of the Buddhas that they are incarnations of ultimate reality in time and space, as the Christian doctrine of the Trinity says with regard to Christ? There are impressive parallels: the heavenly preparations for the birth of the Buddha-to-be; the heavenly choice and divine purity of the mother; marvels occurring at the time of that birth; the more than ordinary human quality of the life of the Buddha; his assumption of the chosen life role of teacher-revealer after his enlightenment (comparable to Christ at his baptism); and the Buddha's exemplification of nirvanic qualities in his life (comparable to the interpretation of Christ as God's son in the flesh or the incarnation of the Eternal Logos). Yet one cannot exactly say that the Buddha was Nirvana-become-flesh, for Nirvana is scarcely a divine principle or Person actively searching for the lost and the sinful with redemptive love. And as before remarked, the Buddhist insists upon the fact that Buddhas are not saviors sent redemptively into the world by a su-

perworld grace, but once-upon-a-time men who have per-
sisted in the way of wisdom or charity until they have
become Buddhas. The end result is somewhat the same,
a Being beyond all contemporary humankind who remains
in the world after his enlightenment out of redemptive
compassion for his fellows who are still caught in the bonds
of ignorance and rebirth; but it is not identical with the
Christian conception of a redemptive God, incarnating himself in a Savior.

But there is another and deeper factor in the situation,
suggested by the relation of Buddha to Nirvana, but best
apprehended in the innate duality, or even multiplicity, of
realities found in the Dharma-Karma-Nirvana interrelationship. For they are not integrally one order but are even
antithetically opposed to each other at times. There is the
tension between dharma and karma, for example. Dharma
is the impersonal, nonmoral causality found in the order of
nature. But karma is an absolutely just and impartial *moral*
order. The two obviously clash at many points, since the
natural order brings calamity, disease, death, pain, and the
like upon seemingly undeserving individuals. Yet Buddhist
faith makes them one by insisting that even the natural
order serves ethical ends, i.e., that whatever comes to a
man, either pleasant *or* unpleasant, is *morally* deserved
because of his past lives. Yet in order to avoid the theistic
problem of evil (God both good and almighty) the Buddhist
turns again and insists that the moral order that punishes
evil and rewards good is essentially only impersonal, scientifically perceived causality such as is found also in the
natural order. He is never willing to say that the dharma-
karma order "works together for good" for the good man,
but insists to the end that it impartially yields *both* good
and evil result for good and evil deed.

But there is further an even more serious tension between dharma-karma and Nirvana. The first has to do with
the order of mundane life whose main goal is the achievement of more pleasant rebirths of individual beings in space-
time worlds, and whose only means of advancement is

through ethical good deeds. Here is the way of the devout
Buddhist layman. But the Way of Nirvana is one of meditation, detachment from individual persons and worldly
goals and values whether good or evil. The goodness that
it seeks is above, or different from, ordinary ethical goodness
and its goal is far beyond history and the improvement of
society. This is the way of the monk. Thus the Buddhist
cosmos is split between the nonnatural, nontemporal, nonethical, nonhistorical order of Nirvana (and the way to it)
and the natural, temporal, ethical, and historical order of
dharma-karma (and the way to better rebirths). One pays
his currency of ethical-historical action or of meditative
detachment and takes his choice. And that element of the
God-complex which rules the way he has taken serves him
accordingly.

This multiplicity of level of operation and diversity of
form in the complex which fulfills the God-function for
Buddhism is perhaps lessened in two respects. First, the
saints and the Buddhas represent in their lives a joining of
this diversity into one kind of unity. For they do indeed
live in the space-time world (dharma-karma realm), and
have in the past followed *its* ways of virtue, progressing
even as others from birth to birth. Yet, building on this basis
of dharma-karma, causal-moral order, they have also
achieved nirvanic stature, or have escaped the former order
of life for the latter; and for one last lifetime they live as
Nirvana-experiencers in the world of dharma-karma. Thus
they are in the world of dharma-karma and rebirth, but not
of it.

And secondly, there is a current tendency in Buddhism
to join the two ways of life (dharmic and nirvanic) in one,
in the form of the life of worldly (layman's) activity *and*
simultaneous periodic meditation periods by that same layman. As part of this same bringing of Nirvana down to
earth, there is also present sometimes a tendency to think
of Nirvana as an active force in men's lives.

But despite these unitive tendencies, no full integral
synthesis of a divine world order is ever wholly or explicitly

achieved. The usual Buddhist synthesis of "God in Four Parts" may be typified by an experiment that the author tried with the Venerable U Thittila during a series of conversations. We took the Christian hymn, "Immortal, Invisible, God Only Wise" and deleted the personal names, and pronouns relating to God, with the following result:

Immortal, invisible _____ only wise,
In light inaccessible hid from our eyes,
Most blessed, most glorious, the Ancient of Days,
Almighty, victorious, _____ great Name we praise.

Unresting, unhasting, and silent as light,
Nor wanting, nor wasting, _____ rulest in might;
_____ justice like mountains high soaring above
_____ clouds which are fountains of goodness and love.

To all, life _____ givest, to both great and small;
In all life _____ livest, the true life of all;
_____ wisdom so boundless, _____ mercy so free,
Eternal _____ goodness, for naught changes _____.

Great fountain of glory, pure source of all light;
The (devas) adore _____, all veiling their sight;
All laud we would render; O help us to see
'Tis only the splendor of light hideth _____!

The project then was to see whether a Buddhist could fill in these blanks with any of *his* terms. And we actually made it, after a sort, by stretching some of the connotations a little! Into all these blanks one or more of the terms dharma, karma, Nirvana, or Buddha could be filled. Thus, for example, Nirvana and dharma might be termed immortal and invisible, and "only wise" applied to the Buddha. U Thittila objected to "inaccessible"—perhaps missing the innate mysticism of his own faith. But he cautiously agreed that most men did *not* understand the clear pure truth of the Buddha, and that Nirvana was hard to come by. "Almighty" was acceptable only when interpreted or paraphrased to mean "irresistible"—as applied to dharma-karma.

"Ancient of Days" was stretched to include the long ages of preparation that lie behind Buddhahood. Angels could be called "devas" or godlings (for which suggestion I was rewarded by a permissive chuckle), karma is just, and Nirvana the "fountain of glory, pure source of all light."

Needless to say, this analysis, however interesting, did not persuade the Venerable U Thittila that he was a theist unbeknownst to himself or convert him on the spot to an avowed theism. For, as he rightly insisted, Buddhism maintains that not *all* the four terms could rightly be used in *each* of the blanks. That is, the Buddhist "God" remains divided in function, and the Buddhist *cherishes* this very diversity and loose-jointedness as the peculiar hallmark of his faith. The union of these aspects in an integral personal Being is explicitly rejected. And notably absent from all the combined functions and qualities of all four elements of the Buddhist God-complex, however generously interpreted, is the world-creative function.

This leads to the last consideration. How shall we define the essential difference between Christian God and Buddhist reality or God-complex? It is to be found, I think, primarily and essentially in this last-mentioned distinction, creativity and noncreativity, and the implications flowing therefrom. The Christian doctrine of creativity puts God squarely in the middle of the world process. This joins ultimate reality, *both* creatively and redemptively, to the natural and historical orders of the world. The world as we know it, and live in it, is thereby considered essentially good and worthy of redemption; and the Christian faith in God, as seen in Christ, is that there is an active work of redemption going on in the midst of this world and its life. Thus is an integral unity of world concept and practical action achieved in Christian faith—at the cost of creating the intellectual and emotional problem of evil.

In Buddhism the solution of the world mystery and the problems attendant on this solution are different. The loose-jointedness of the Buddhist's God-complex enables him to deal more flexibly with the tensions between natural and

moral order, the disparities between individual circumstance and individual virtue. In a word he does not have to
justify the ways of God to man or solve the problem of
evil. Each man reaps what he has accumulated by way of
past good and evil actions. Yet the cost of this way of avoiding the problem of evil is the problem of an ultimate plural-
ity of worlds and values that in itself becomes a distressing
evil. There is in Buddhism no sense of world purpose; no
viable long-term sociohistorical goals, because history and
nature as such are meaningless and goalless. For into what
pattern of meaning, save that of his own individual salvation in Nirvana, shall man fit his life? The world as conceived and as experienced falls apart into diverse entities
not integrally related to each other. The nature of man's
present life is to be explained only by a series of past lives,
the knowledge of which is totally inaccessible to the ordinary
man, but which must be taken by faith on the word of
others. There is the world of ordinary moral virtue and
social action, but it is separated from the world of ultimate
spiritual worth (Nirvana) as by a chasm; the lesser and
the higher goods have no integral relation to each other.
Thus in the end the lack of an integral God-concept atom-
izes the Buddhist world and makes significant life-unity—
save on a purely individualistic level—most difficult. Those
positively creative and helpful aspects of the world process,
which the Christian calls God, can be acknowledged only
indirectly under cover of one's "own" karmic merit, if at all.

Which set of difficulties is the preferable one—the Christian God concept, whose internal tensions of power versus
goodness, and of impersonal natural order created by personal being, tend to explode it; or the Buddhist reality-
complex, which achieves no integral unity of inner and
outer lives and can scarcely frame a unifying philosophy
of historical action—is perhaps a question that requires
considerable study and further experience. And in the end
its answer for the individual may depend upon his personal
choice of religious values.

(III)

Love: Christian and Buddhist

Of course, as the whole world is aware, Christianity is the religion of love—at least in theory if not always in practice. Its two great commandments are both commandments to love. The primary commandment is that man should love God with his whole heart, soul, mind, and strength. The second and derivative commandment is that one should love his neighbor, elsewhere defined by Jesus as any human being with whom one has to do in any direct way, as one loves himself. And at numerous other places in the New Testament love is described as the highest and most comprehensive of all Christian virtues. Indeed, in his first epistle, John affirms that God himself is love.

Now in Buddhism there is no such overwhelming addiction to the language of love. This is not because the Buddhist has no words for love, nor, presumably, because he is unaware of the depth and strength of personal love. But he finds Christian love, or Christian love as he conceives it to be at least, wrongly oriented for expressing what he considers to be the highest religious quality of life. He prefers to use the word *mettā,* usually translated as "lovingkindness," to express the proper Buddhist attitude toward other beings; and his attitude toward his "God in four parts" varies with whatever part is in mind at the moment. But toward none of them, save perhaps the Buddha, would he extend what the Christian calls love.

What, then, is the nature of the essential difference be-

64

tween Buddhism and Christianity on the score of love? What does Christianity mean by love? And why does Christianity so warmly espouse it, while Buddhism criticizes it when it is considered to be the supreme religious virtue? What is the quality of that loving-kindness which Buddhism would put in the place of love? To these and related questions we give our attention in this chapter, first briefly characterizing the more familiar concept of love in Christianity and then proceeding at some length to try to understand what the Buddhist means by loving-kindness.

1. *Christian Love*

Many volumes have been written on the subject of Christian love. It has been variously and endlessly interpreted and reinterpreted, each Christian generation seeking to find in it a new and significant meaning for its own peculiar situation. We cannot hope here even to epitomize the width and breadth of this endeavor but will try to present only a few central and distinctive features of it, sufficient to enable some comparison with Buddhist metta and its related qualities. To begin with, we shall consider Christian love under three aspects: as a unitary quality of life; as personal; as mutual.

a. *The Unity of All Love*

It is often complained that Christian "love" represents, not one distinguishable essence or attitude, but a vast, imprecise conglomeration of varied and contradictory attitudes and motivations, all consorting together under one banner while they mutually confuse or cancel each other out. Much of the confusion in the Christian life with regard to its preferred goods and goals is held to stem from this fundamental ambiguity within its central concept. New Testament scholars have helpfully pointed out that even in the New Testament there are three levels or kinds of love, somewhat distinguishable by their respective Greek parent words, but whose various shades of meaning have been indiscriminately lumped together in translation into a single English word. Thus there is (1) love of the *erōs* quality, which implies ordinary human erotic and possessive love; (2) the *philia* type of love between equals and friends, institutionalized in the names of the Greek and American cities of brotherly love (Philadelphia); and (3) the highest of all loves, perhaps the distinctively Christian-religious love, which God sheds abroad upon all creatures alike, deserving and undeserving, called *agapē* in the New Testament.

It is most important to have these distinctions clearly in mind when we are speaking of Christian love, for there has indeed been great and confused ambiguity in its interpretation and expression. Nor should we seek to make of a linguistic accident a religious truth of great importance. Nevertheless, this very confusion of meanings is more than a mere linguistic ambiguity; it does, after all, bear witness to a most important truth about Christian love, namely, its essential unity at all levels. Or, to state the principle a little more fully and carefully, despite its varieties and levels of manifestation, love, in the Christian interpretation of it, is not of separate kinds but essentially all of a piece. The love of God does not war against the love of man; physically expressed love is not entirely unrelated to spiritual love. In the Christian sense, love is *not* a collection of contradictory qualities or mutually exclusive stages, but a continuum that stretches from the highest to the lowest forms (*agapē* to *erōs*) and back again in some kind of unity.[1]

The diagram on the opposite page may perhaps suggest what is meant.

A further word or two may be said about the interpretation of the diagram. That some other terms might have been chosen, or that those here used might be put in some other order, is unimportant for our present purposes. What the diagram is intended to convey is not a precisely accurate distinction between various synonyms for love or its varied manifestations; and most emphatically it is *not* intended to suggest that in the practice of the higher forms of love the

The God of Mystic Union

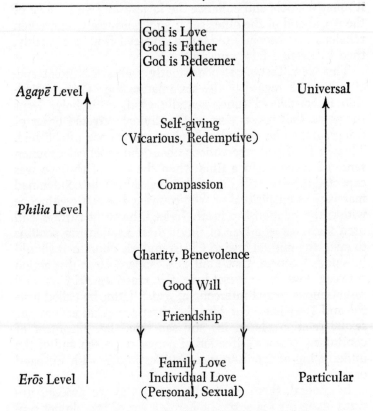

lower are left behind or renounced—despite some "super-Christian" interpretations to that effect. Quite the contrary, in fact. The diagram is intended to make only one central point: the *continuity* and *interrelatedness* of the various kinds of love in the Christian view. The diagram is intended to assert that something of the highest level of divine love may be found in the lowest level of earthly love, and conversely that even the lowest level of love may in at least a small degree intimate the nature of, and be a limited experience of, the highest. Or, still otherwise, the highest love

(God's *agapē* to man and man's wholehearted response to it) may ennoble and enhance the lowest level (*erōs,* love of the world and of the other sex); and, conversely, that when religious love becomes too much divorced from the earthly, then it becomes false and rootless.

The New Testament consistently makes this point specifically with regard to the sex relationship. This relationship is considered fundamentally good, even holy. Jesus suggested that it was part of the divinely created order of things, not to be denied or broken when once established. Though Paul had reservations about the practical common sense of marriage in a time when the end of the age was expected momentarily, he condemned those who condemned marriage as unspiritual or who counseled sexual continence within the relationship itself. Indeed, he went further and used marriage as a type of the highest relationship possible to man, the mutual love of Christ and his church. It should be said, of course, that Paul also made a clear distinction between love as expressed in the marriage relation and promiscuous sexual intercourse, which latter he called lustful and lascivious. For him the marriage relation was the sexual relation placed in, and sanctified by, a context of continuing personal affection of person to person and of the undertaking of family responsibilities jointly with husband or wife.

In general, then, we might say that as we proceed upward along the scale, the higher degrees of love do not represent a negation but an extension and elevation of the values of the lower level, so that the values of sexual-personal love are extended into family love, to friendship, benevolence, compassionate self-sacrifice, and even to the love of God. And in reverse the love of God provides motive and guidance, as well as strength and balance, to all the lower loves. So it is that the Christian finds it meaningful to use the language of human love for God, calling him Father, and seeks the blessing of God upon the sex relation itself in Christian marriage.

b. *Christian Love as Personal*

Implied in what has just been said is another quality of Christian love: it is, so to speak, always person to person. This personalistic vocabulary is often given a less complimentary name by those who disapprove of it: anthropomorphic. Particularly is this derogatory term applied to the Christian conception of the God-man relation. Here, say the critics—and Buddhists among them—is an example of the projection of the lowest order of term to the highest relationship, the personal category to the superpersonal, or of the personal to the nonpersonal. This is not the place to discuss the relative merits of the two positions except to say that there seems to be no compelling reason to evaluate the nonpersonal or impersonal as being superior to the personal, despite considerable religious and philosophical opinion to the contrary, nor to imply that the impersonal is necessarily more inclusive or real than the personal. But in any case the Christian must frankly confess that in one sense, in the sense of its being fully personal, his conception of love *is* anthropomorphic, drawn from his experience of other persons.

Theologically basic to this position is the Christian belief in God as in some sense personal. It is hard to see how this position can be abandoned, however much it may be qualified or refined in concept, without abandonment of the meaning of "Christian." It may well be that much Christian terminology about God needs to be more restrained and rendered much less emotional and sentimental; that there is, as I believe, a need for the re-examination of the terms "personal" and "impersonal" in religious language. Yet the Christian experience of God as manifest in the life of Christ and in the experiences of forgiveness and prayer is incurably personalistic. Its language will be that of interpersonal communion; and even its mysticism has always been set in the context of interpersonal love.

With regard to the expression of love for other human

beings, this too is most Christian when it is fully and concretely interpersonal. The Christian ministry of love is one that attempts to do good to specific individuals rather than to the mass of mankind, or to man as such. True, it seeks to spread its help as widely as possible, and must sometimes in cases of great emergencies think in terms of quantitative spread rather than qualitative depth of personal encounter. But basically and characteristically Christian love prefers the direct person-to-person fellowship and individually directed helpfulness.

c. *Love and Its Response*

Love considered as a mutuality of relationship, an initial move toward fellowship and an affirmative response to it, is likewise typically Christian and grows in the soil of the personalistic quality of the total Christian religious life. And because of certain apparent contrasts with what corresponds to Christian love in Buddhism, namely, loving-kindness and its related dispositions, it is most important to stress the mutuality involved in Christian love. For Christians often either take this basic interpersonal mutuality for granted or else frequently fail to realize fully its meaning either in understanding or in practice.

Mutuality comprises give-and-take, the give-and-take peculiar to genuine interpersonal relationships. And two things at least are implied by its nature. One is that there *is* both give and take—and that what is returned is not necessarily the same as what is given. Indeed, if it is genuinely mutual, the response will necessarily be different from the gift, the other person giving what he considers appropriate by way of response or reaction, what there is in him to give. The dull, stereotyped actions and reactions of persons who are supposedly expressing Christian love and responding to it, so frequent in institutionalized Christianity, would suggest that somehow true interpersonal mutuality is lacking. Love has become channeled in a rut of prefabricated forms and has lost its quality of venturesome personal encounter.

The other implication of Christian love as mutuality is that of an encounter in *essential likeness and freedom*. It is difficult to think of mutuality (and hence of love) between man and inanimate nature; a stone may respond variously to one's efforts to move it, but the encounter is neither between similar entities nor personal. Relations to animals can be limitedly personal in so far as there is a genuinely affective response; but again the difference is so great that there is no person-to-person encounter.[2] Also only in an uncoerced relationship, where each party to it is free to give to the other the gifts of his own fellowship, can there be true mutuality. This raises difficult, practical problems of the interrelationships of people on different levels or performing different functions in society. For how can the vastly superior or more powerful individual have mutuality with the socially weak and inferior? Here we can only answer that Christian love should always seek to moderate or bypass the impersonal distances that divide men, by means of direct personal regard; to keep kindness free from coercive response, yet at the same time to unashamedly rejoice in the spontaneous expression of fellowship, gratitude, and good will as integral parts of the personal exchange that love calls forth.

And if we ask how man can fellowship with God, the Christian has only one answer, that He

> emptied himself, taking the form of a servant, being born in the likeness of men (Phil. 2:7).

By the incarnation the Christian knows that mutuality of love is possible, even with God.

2. Buddhist Metta

a. The Quality of Loving-kindness

Metta, or loving-kindness, is much spoken of today as the Buddhist equivalent of, or better-than substitute for, Christian love. Yet its likeness or unlikeness to Christian love is difficult to grasp. It seems both similar to and yet different from Christian love; here is typified again the curiously mingled tale of Buddhist-Christian likeness and difference. One may well be impressed with the resemblance of some of its classic portrayals to like portrayals of Christian love (see below) and be willing to equate them across the board. But just when the Christian studying Buddhism has almost become convinced of the deep spiritual kinship of love and loving-kindness, he rather unwillingly becomes aware also of subtle dissimilarities of meaning, context, and application that lead him to withhold the simple equal sign for a while longer. For one thing there is the *Buddhist* unwillingness to make love and loving-kindness purely and simply equal; and despite all the difficulties of the translation of words from one language into another that might reduce this difference to a mere matter of semantics, this unwillingness should give us pause. Besides, as we shall see when we raise such questions as to *what* man is to be loved Buddhistically, and how and why, further difficulties arise.

We may begin by quoting two or three examples of the Buddhist interpretation of metta. From the famous Metta-Sutta, somewhat comparable in the Buddhism to the thirteenth chapter of First Corinthians in Christianity, we have the following description of Buddhist loving-kindness:

Whatever living beings there be . . .
May all beings be happy.

Let none deceive another
Nor despise any person whatsoever in any
    place.
Let him not wish any harm to another
Out of anger or ill will.

Just as a mother would protect her only child
At the risk of her own life
Even so let him cultivate a boundless heart
Toward all beings.

Let his thoughts of boundless love
Pervade the whole world,

> Above, below, and across without any obstruc-
> tion
> Without any hatred, without any enmity.
>
> Whether he stands, walks, sits,
> Lies down, as long as he is awake
> He should develop his mindfulness—
> This they say is the noblest living here.[3]

We may further note a contemporary description of metta by a well-known Buddhist monk of Burma:

> The Pali word *metta* means literally—friendliness—also love without a desire to possess but with a desire to help, to sacrifice self-interest for the welfare and well-being of humanity. . . .
> It is a dynamic suffusing of every living being . . . with dynamic creative thoughts of loving-kindness. If the thoughts are intense enough, right actions follow automatically.[4]

Such is the Buddhist account of what is meant by loving-kindness, and it is obvious that it closely parallels the Christian conception of love at several points. As does Christian love, it stands opposed to all ill will, either in deed or in thought. It goes further than this: It speaks in accents of respect for others (even though they supposedly have no immortal souls) and of right, i.e., charitable, actions toward them; and it uses near-Christian language about a love so self-sacrificial in quality that it may call for the laying down of one's life for another. Still further, it out-Christians the Christian in calling for a benevolence toward *all* living creatures, not merely toward man; it is an absolute univer-salization of love. Do we, then, have here in nontheistic, non-Christian Buddhism genuine crosslike vicarious suffer-ing?

It may be of interest to note one other quality of metta, or perhaps better, pattern of its application. Contrastingly with the spontaneous person-to-person manner in which Christian love is usually expressed, there is here a definite and carefully ordered methodology of the progressive direction of loving-kindness. Especially important in Buddhist eyes is the initial point of direction. For if a person first seeks to extend metta toward the wrong class of person, the whole enterprise may go astray. He will either end up in total discouragement, and consequently in spiritual stagnation, or else metta will become something quite other, and quite injurious.

For such spiritual purposes Buddhism classifies persons in the following four orders: oneself; dear ones (family and friends); neutral persons (those toward whom one has no emotional disposition, positive or negative, as well as strangers and all the multitudinous beings now in existence but unknown to him); and hostile persons or enemies. Should one try to extend loving-kindness to the enemy, this would be too hard. A neutral person as object would offer none of the initially necessary inspiration. And loving-kindness first extended toward a loved one might turn into a partial and affectionate personal attachment, or into lust in the case of one of the opposite sex. Therefore, one begins by extending loving-kindness to himself (charity begins at home) and from thence to others. Thus does Buddhaghosa put it:

If he develops it in this way, "I am happy. Just as I want to be happy and dread pain, as I want to live and not to die, so do other beings, too," making himself the example, then desire for other beings' welfare and happiness arises in him. . . .

So should he first, as the example, pervade himself with loving-kindness . . . , for "Who loves himself will never harm another."[5]

The preferred order from this point on is: extension of metta to a good and respected person (teacher, revered monk), then to a loved one, then to a neutral person, then to the hostile enemy as the climax. One seeks to establish himself in the loving-kindness frame of mind or disposition in the area where it is most natural, for

> I visited all quarters with my mind
> Nor found I any dearer than myself,[6]

and then, maintaining the same quality of affection, systematically extend it step by step to the uttermost and most difficult object, one's enemy.

Both the similarity and the contrast of this way to the Christian method of extending love to others will strike the reader at once. The end goal of loving the enemy is the same. And in some sense also the Christian begins with himself: only if his own heart is suffused with the love of God for *him,* can he extend love to others. (Or in psychological language, the man who is divided within himself and hates himself cannot love anyone else either, but will project on to others his own self-hate.) So also the Christian is exhorted to love others *as* he loves himself. Yet there *is* the Christian reference to God, a sense of being first loved by Another. And it is not absolutely certain that loving another as oneself is the same as extending one's will-to-be-happy first to himself and then to others. Of this we shall speak later.

b. *Metta and the Achievement of Equanimity*

Before we can fully understand Buddhist loving-kindness, however, we must study it further by noting the company it keeps. For though metta is predominantly emphasized today in Buddhism, it is actually only one of four related qualities, all of which are traditionally called the Divine Abidings, or Illimitables. The reason for this name is as follows, according to Bhandatācariya Buddhaghosa, the famous commentator of the fifth century A.D.:

The divineness of the Abiding should be understood here in the sense of the best and in the sense of immaculate. For these Abidings are best in being the right attitude toward beings. And just as *Brahmā* Gods abide with immaculate minds, so the mediators who associate themselves with these Abidings abide on an equal footing with the *Brahmā* Gods. . . . For the Great Beings' [*Brahmā Gods'*] minds retain their balance by giving preference to beings' welfare, by dislike of beings' suffering, by desire for the various successes achieved by beings to last, and by impartiality toward all beings. And to all beings they give *gifts* . . . without discriminating thus: "It must be given to this one: it must not be given to this [i.e., that] one."[7]

They are also called Illimitables or Measureless States because their development may be expanded indefinitely as to quality, and universally as to application. They represent the highest desirable states of mind or virtuous attitudes, a set of Blessed Dispositions like Christian faith, hope, and love. And we may observe that in their interpretation in the passage above there is a certain likeness in these Illimitables to Christian *agāpe*: a flowing out from the one who is thus blessedly disposed to all creatures without measure, and without limitation as to their worth.

We may now observe what the other Blessed Dispositions are, and their internal relations to each other. Besides metta, or loving kindness, there are: *karunā,* or compassion; *muditā,* translated as sympathetic or altruistic joy; and *upekkhā,* usually translated as equanimity. Together these four make a "team" whose chief is equanimity, as we shall note a little later.

Karunā, or compassion, is much the same in its root meaning as that same word in the New Testament when it is recorded that Jesus looked upon the multitudes and had compassion on them. It represents sympathy for the sufferings of others, be those sufferings mental or physical. And its peculiar Buddhistic flavor is that of fellow feeling on the part of the compassionator toward all other sentient beings who, like himself, are caught in the toils of *saṁsāra,* i.e., the endless birth-life-death cycle of individual existences that is under the iron rule of karma.

And what, then, is the order of the extension of compassion to others? Here the Buddhist method is to extend karuna first to *hostile* persons. The reasons for this are not so clearly outlined as in the case of extending metta first to oneself. Perhaps it is by the process of elimination that it is achieved, since equanimity begins most naturally with the neutral person, and sympathetic joy with a dear friend. Or it may be that in an enemy we most easily observe some specific failure, weakness, or misfortune; or that we can certainly reflect that even enemies also are caught in the same birth-death rounds as we ourselves. This is probably what Buddhaghosa means when he describes compassion-centered meditation as meditation upon the "helplessness in those overwhelmed by suffering,"[8] which includes all mankind.

And in a distinctively Buddhist emphasis he goes on to affirm that indeed the hostile person is to be compassionated *because* of his hostility. For hostility is more grievous than misfortune. It is indeed the basic cause of misfortune, since the hostile feeling or disposition of mind, and the unfriendly act, have their *primary* effects upon the actor and feeler himself. They set in motion karmic forces that will later bear evil fruit within the life, or subsequent lives, of the hostile person. This is graphically expressed in the following passage:

Now what is the point of your getting angry with him [i.e., anyone else]? Will not this kamma [karma] of yours that has anger as its source lead to your own harm? For you are the owner of your deeds, heir of your deeds, having deeds as your parent, deeds as your kin, deeds as your refuge; you will become the heir of whatever deeds you do. . . .

By doing this [getting angry] you are like a man who wants to hit another and picks up a burning ember or excrement in his hand and so first burns himself or makes himself stink.[9]

In fact, each person in his present character and situation is completely and only the result of his own deeds, i.e., his karma; whatever he does, harms or benefits himself far more than the supposed recipients of his deeds.

Sympathetic or altruistic joy (mudita) is the capacity to rejoice in the success or joy of others, without envy and without hypocrisy. It is somewhat related to the New Testament suggestion about rejoicing with those who rejoice, but it also goes somewhat beyond that level. Its highest form and limitless extension involve a state of experience in which one passes even beyond empathy (the feeling of oneself as though momentarily he *were* another) into the *complete identification* of oneself with other selves, so that the distinction between "my" joy and "your" joy actually ceases to be. I feel one as keenly as the other. Understandably, Buddhism considers this to be a very difficult attainment, even to a limited degree.

The order of extending altruistic joy to others, as noted above, is to begin with its extension toward dear friends. Here again, as in the case of metta, the most natural psychological order is taken. With whom is it more easy or natural to rejoice in success than with a friend? To be sure, there is a limitation even here: the friend must be of the same sex, lest sympathetic joy become in fact something quite other. Therefore, it is said that "a very dear companion"[10] offers the proper object for its initial projection. By immersing himself unenviously in another's joy one establishes himself easily and naturally in this frame of mind, which with further practice he may ultimately exercise toward the neutral and the hostile person, rejoicing in even the latter's joy as though it were his very own.

These three Abidings, then, form a kind of holy triad of Blessed Dispositions, a love syndrome, in which one compassionates with all suffering sentient creatures in their misery and rejoices in their successes and joys. Together they operate as benevolent, selfless loving-kindness toward all beings without limit and without distinction. These three saintly dispositions in their joint operation might well be compared with Paul's well-known description of Christian love:

Love is patient and kind; love is not jealous or boastful; it is not arrogant or rude. Love does not insist on its own way; it is not irritable or resentful; it does not rejoice at wrong, but rejoices in the right. Love bears all things, believes all things, hopes all things, endures all things (I Cor. 13:4–7).

But the fourth, and most important, of the Abidings is yet to be described. In the above-quoted *Path of Purification,* which has become the classic manual of the way to

Nirvana for Southern Buddhism, we have the following description of equanimity:

> It looks on . . . abandoning such interestedness as thinking "May they be free from enmity," and having recourse to neutrality, thus it is equanimity. . . .
>
> *Equanimity* has the equanimity of unknowing . . . since both share in ignoring faults and virtues. . . .
>
> When he [any man] abides in equanimity, his mind becomes skilled in apprehending what is nonexistent . . . having no further concern such as "May beings be happy" or "May they be released from pain" or "May they not lose the success they have obtained."[11]

The general quality of equanimity is clear: it is emotionally neutral, detached and disinterested—though contemporary Buddhists reject the translation of *upekkhā* as neutrality or indifference. Indeed, it rises far above the concerns expressed by other Abidings. Equanimity does not *care* whether all beings be happy (the concern of loving-kindness), or be released from pain (compassion), or enjoy the success they have obtained (the exercise of sympathetic joy). Equanimity has become skilled in "apprehending what is nonexistent" in the ultimate sense; and ordinary individualized sentient beings are nonexistent in the ultimate sense. Hence, for equanimity, their welfare, suffering, and joy are not matters of genuine concern. Equanimity is the achievement of detachment from all such interests, either with regard to oneself or others.

As we might expect, the natural place to begin the exercise of equanimity is with the neutral, i.e., strange and unknown, person. By achieving a settled, emotionally neutral equanimity of disposition or frame of mind with regard to the stranger, one gets to know the feel of equanimity; he can then turn this same disposition toward the dear one, then the hostile one, and finally toward himself; so that in reverse to the way of loving-kindness he again "breaks down the barriers" (a Buddhist expression) between selves and sees them all indifferently and equanimously as one and the same in nature and in interest to him.

c. *Equanimity as the Chief of the Abidings*

Such is equanimity. And the amazing and confounding feature of the total situation to the non-Buddhist is that according to Buddhism *equanimity is the chief, the crowning jewel, the climactic synthesis of all the Divine Abidings.* We may well ask, How can it possibly be that equanimity, which only detachedly observes the course of human life that "makes beings its object by simply looking on,"[12] deliberately disciplining itself to avoid any concern for the sorrows, joys, and welfare of human or other beings, can be called the *synthesis* of the other dispositions of loving-kindness, compassion, and altruistic joy that are the specific embodiment of that concern?

There is no simple, easy answer here for the Christian. For in this final placing of loving-kindness, compassion, and altruistic joy—so much like Christian love in their totality —in their proper context we come to one of those ultimate distinctions between Buddhism and Christianity over which, like a mountain pass among the cloud-high peaks, it is most difficult to make understanding flow. Here, in the Buddhist conviction that equanimity is indeed the crown of the other Blessed Dispositions, we come to what is most centrally Buddhist in the whole range of human interrelations, and perhaps in some ways farthest removed from the Christian's conception of the meaning of love.

We may begin an attempted explanation of the relation of equanimity to the other Abidings by adding two further observations. One is that even in the Buddhist conception of loving-kindness, compassion, and altruistic joy, there is a Middle Path to be followed, which term is rightly characteristic of the total Buddhist attitude toward life. But what is a Middle Path with regard to the cultivation of the Abidings? It is the avoidance of the extremes of attitude that might grow out of their improper practice and extension, an avoidance that finds its completion and perfection in the way of equanimity, which in turn is the way to Nirvana.

Thus our commentator, Buddhaghosa, in a summary of

these Illimitables tells us that loving-kindness must avoid both ill will *and* personalized affection. It is essential to realize that for Buddhism either extreme is as dangerous as the other; loving-kindness is of course opposed to ill will, but on the other hand should not plunge into (what it conceives to be) the abyss of personal attachments. At this point it criticizes the Christian concept of love as inevitably tending toward narrowly personalized relationships, easily confused with selfish attachment, or to sentimentality and emotional debauch. So, likewise, with the other Abidings. Compassion seeks to avoid and reduce cruelty, but it "fails when it produces sorrow"—even sympathetic sorrow, evidently, or emotional involvement. Sympathetic joy avoids both bored aversion to all things and likewise lighthearted heedless merriment. And equanimity, as before noted, is the perfection of this middleness between the extremes. From *its* exercise *all* emotional flavor is rigorously expunged; neither approval nor resentment is to be indulged. Yet, on the other hand, it must avoid sheer indifferentism, the indifferentism that grows out of ignorance. Thus it is a calculatedly deliberate neutrality.[13]

The other feature of the interrelationship of the four Abidings to be noted is that Buddhaghosa treats them in the context of *meditational devices* rather than practical working attitudes. These dispositions—or their symbols—are to be taken as bases for achieving trances, jhanic states, or absorptions, as they are also called. Each of the Abidings serves as a base, i.e., meditational springboard, for a specific absorption. Meditation on loving-kindness leads one to a state called "Liberation by the Beautiful," since beings are no longer repulsive but delightful; compassion meditation escapes materiality and leads to the absorption induced by the contemplation of boundless consciousness; and equanimity meditation is the basic support of the absorption of the contemplation of nothingness.[14]

And what is the significance of this? That such attitudes are *primarily* considered by Buddhism to be good *in terms of their effect upon one's own spiritual welfare, rather than upon others.* To be sure, such attitudes are sometimes viewed on the moral-social level and there construed as ideal ethical dispositions. But the classically Buddhist way to think of them is as contributing toward the individual spiritual advancement of the person who tries to perfect himself for Nirvana rather than as means to save the world. Of course, in so far as in saving oneself he saves the world —and it is Buddhism's contention that this is the best and only way to save it—world salvation may come as a side effect. But the difference between Buddhism and Christianity at this point must be clearly grasped, whatever our verdict on the two ways may be.

We may put this situation into a diagram:

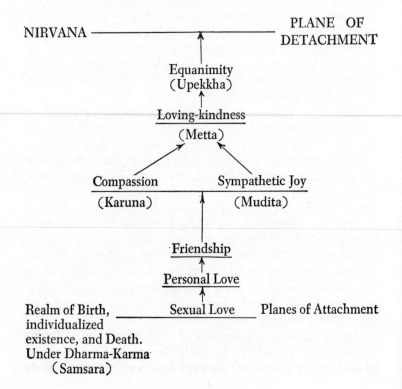

Compared to the diagram of Christian love, we observe one or two differences. In general, there is not the sense of the mutual and total involvement of all levels of love with each other. While it is wrong to think of each stage as radically distinct with regard to the others, especially in the case of the Divine Abidings, there is considerably more exclusion of one level of love by the other than in the Christian scheme. Quite different words are designedly used for the different varieties of concern. One would not say that metta had absolutely nothing at all to do with sexual love, but it would certainly be quite distinct and different from it; and if we think of following the Middle Way through each type of Divine Abiding, this Way would be contradictory and exclusive of the lower orders of merely human love and friendship. Certainly equanimity at the top, as a kind of vestibule to Nirvana, is of a *completely* different order from sexual love at the bottom.

3. *Contrasts in Motivation and Method*

We have now distinguished Christian love and Buddhist Blessed Dispositions as they are described in the respective scriptures and classical interpretations. We turn next to a somewhat more practical aspect as a further means of understanding likenesses and differences and will inquire as to the *motivations* and *methods* or *characteristic expressions* of love and loving-kindness respectively. At this level we are primarily concerned with the interhuman relationships and therefore leave largely out of account man's relation to God in Christianity and the role of Nirvana in Buddhism, though these aspects do condition the total situation and must necessarily be referred to now and again.

a. *Motivation*

Our first question to both Christian and Buddhist is simply this: *Why* should a human being love his fellow? And the answers that Christianity and Buddhism have historically provided will be revealing. The best Christian statement of which I know, one that succinctly and classically sets forth the basic Christian reasons for loving other men, over and above the range of natural affections, is the following passage from the First Epistle of John:

Beloved, let us love one another; for love is of God, and he who loves is born of God and knows God. He who does not love does not know God; for God is love. In this the love of God was made manifest among us, that God sent his only Son into the world, so that we might live through him. In this is love, not that we loved God but that he loved us and sent his Son to be the expiation for our sins. Beloved, if God so loved us, we also ought to love one another. No man has ever seen God; if we love one another, God abides in us and his love is perfected in us (I John 4:7–12).

The basic Christian reason for universalizing the expression of love to all men is the Christian belief in a personal God who has manifested his love to men, most particularly in Christ, who died that men might live more abundantly. To be sure, the redeeming God is also the creating God; the world and man's life in it are both evidences of divine love. Divine love, "all loves excelling," comes to clearest expression, however, for the Christian in the life and death of his Master. And it is continued in the sense of the permeative purpose and presence of God in human life that the Christian has called the Holy Spirit. Thus, in short, because God (the Supreme Reality) is love toward all his creatures, they are to love one another.

It may be observed here again that love of man through, or because of, God is not to displace or destroy the natural love of man to man, but to confirm and extend it. It is both to strengthen the force of natural associations and to extend human concern beyond its natural range. The writer of the above passage seems to suggest indeed that *all* love, of whatever sort, brings one nearer God; or, at least, lacking natural affection altogether, one cannot truly know God. There is no evident concern here about natural affection's being so great that it may crowd out the love of God, or vice versa.

Indeed, when such an interpretation is given to Christian love we may be sure that either strong mystical or ecclesiastical influences are at work. It may also be observed that this motivation of human love through the experience of divine love has the practical corollary that when the sense of the reality of the love of God declines in the Christian life, then that special quality of Christian love to man also grows weak. The two can scarcely live apart.

What, then, is the counterpart to this basic Christian motivation in Buddhism? Obviously, it will not be the experience of the love of God for man, for the Buddhist God-in-four-parts does not "love" man. Nirvana is not to be prayed to; dharma-karma is only to be respected and profitably used; and the Buddha's memory is to be venerated but he cannot be petitioned. (Actually, of course, Buddha-veneration often approaches theistic adoration in quality.) This leaves each man to be his own sole god so far as working out his salvation is concerned, or in finding the power to exert loving-kindness toward others. So it is that the practice of metta, like charity, must begin at home and is solidly rooted in one's own concern for oneself.

However cold such a portrayal of the reasons for other-love leaves the Christian, he must not accuse the Buddhist at this point of mere narrow selfishness. If one views the universe as does the Buddhist—as an impersonal, meaningless process in which are found separate streams of conscious being, each of which is the product of its own past deeds—how else should he react to it? It is of vital importance that *he* (one of these streams of conscious being) should purify himself to achieve his own salvation. Only then can he be of spiritual help to anyone at all; in helping and loving himself he helps and loves others in the only possible way. For he cannot directly change another's karmic character or destiny; but by purging himself of impurities he may provide some light for another who is ready to receive it and cease to be an occasion for another's stumbling through arousing his ill will.

One must keep in mind here also the strong Buddhist belief in the power of "suffusing" others with good will. (A more contemporary expression is "radiating.") This to the Buddhist represents an actual and positive force for good. Though its maximum benefits can be received only by those who are themselves men of good will, yet in an extra-sensory way, like the invisible radio wave, it impinges upon others, strengthening the forces of good will and purity in the world, turning aside hostility, and healing divisions between men. Thus it is that after every generous or pious deed the good Buddhist seeks to radiate or share the merit of what he has done by the fervent wish "May all beings be happy." This is the Buddhist "prayer" of love.

We may observe in both Christian and Buddhist patterns two other motivational factors, both derivative from their central propositions. With regard to the Christian we may say that he loves another person in the Christian sense be-cause that person is of worth in the eyes of God. The other person, a personality as such, is given genuine status in the Christian scheme of world order; he is significant within that order. It is often phrased in other ways: that each man is a child of God; that man is made in the image of God; that man has an immortal soul. Or, on more humanistic grounds, but ones that derive from the Christian view, each individual has that of unique dignity and worth within him. It should be noted that this is not genuinely counter to the *agapē* quality of the divine love that descends, like sunlight, and rain, upon all alike. For though, to use a Buddhist phrase, this love is expressed "without distinction" as to worthy or worthless recipients, the basic meaning of the figure is an emphasis upon the generosity of the love of God, not the meaninglessness or worthlessness of indi-viduality. Indeed, Jesus was at pains to assure his disciples both of man's greater worth than animals ("You are of more value than many sparrows") and also of the Father's special regard for those who loved him. Therefore, in loving man we love a significant and worthful creature.

In this connection Buddhism speaks in quite other terms, not fully negative but far from any positive assertion of man's worth. We may say that the Buddhist regard for man at this point is rather one of depreciation—somewhat akin in spirit to a certain Christian emphasis upon the congenital sinfulness and depravity of man. To be sure, according to Buddhism, it is only on the human plane that salvation can be achieved, which is a kind of backhanded means of conferring unique nobility upon human beings. But this is not because of his intrinsic worth but primarily because the peculiar mixture of pain and pleasure found on the human plane is psychologically conducive to a frame of mind that longs to escape it all. (The gods are too happy to seek deliverance; and those in animal form or in the hells, too miserable and hopeless.) As a sentient individual, man is a set of errors, i.e., he "exists" only because of ignorant past deeds; hopefully he is slated for disappearance as an individual personal being.

How, then, does, or should, one man regard another when he looks upon him in loving-kindness and compassion? Primarily as an object of pity. For all sentient beings are *caught* by their sentient individuality; individuality is not their glory, but their misfortune, a mark of their crime-laden status, so to speak. All living creatures, therefore, including oneself, are to be pitied because of their victimized state (even though they are self-victimized), not loved for any inherent nobility. And curiously the extension of the category of selfhood or life of essentially the same quality to all sentient beings has a partially *negative* effect upon the status of man in Buddhism. For while it raises the status of the animal of even the humblest sort to a kind of sacredness, so that it should not (ideally) be killed, in logic and somewhat in fact it disvalues *man*. For just as animals are ex-men, so men are only ex-animals.[15] In any case, the Buddhist view is one that distinctly plays down the intrinsic worth of personal individuality in the space-time world.

Yet by one of those curious twists of religious logic which

always leave one wondering whether he has truly understood another faith, even when he reads its specific and
emphatic statements on some subject, it is not true to say
that Buddhism writes man off as of little worth. Indeed, it
often takes Christianity to task for teaching that man is filled
with original sin, depraved by nature; it proclaims that the
Buddha took a more hopeful view of human nature; and
some Buddhists will even say that he taught that human
nature was basically pure and good. What, then, is the key
to the puzzle? It seems to be this: Buddhism makes a distinction between *individuality* and *spirituality* or *mentality*.
The former is evil, belonging to the world of birth and
death, and it is to be escaped in its narrowness and selfishness. Both the first and last step in one's salvation is to
realize that there is in reality no such thing as a substantial
self. Yet there is also a spiritual energy and capacity within
the human being sufficient to transcend the self; this is that
pure essence of goodness which individuality sullies. As it
is developed, it becomes more and more universal, able to
enter into other frames of mind and project its sympathy
to all beings so that it becomes one with them. Some in
Northern Buddhism are willing to speak of a "true" or
"higher" Self in this connection; but Southern Buddhism
leaves such a conception implicit only by its specific rejection of self-language, particularly with regard to the being of the saint and his "existence" in Nirvana. We shall
discuss this subject more fully in a later chapter.

A third reason is given by both Buddhist and Christian
for extending loving-kindness and love to others: to do so
will produce a better world in which to live. Sometimes this
reason is expressed very naïvely by both Christian and Buddhist. "If only everyone would practice the Golden Rule; if
every man would love his fellow man according to New
Testament standards, then world problems would be
solved," says the Christian. Says the Buddhist, "If everyone
would destroy the I-consciousness within him, root out ill
will and greed within himself, gain nirvanic peace within,

then there would be universal peace in the world." The Christian believes that the practice of love is according to the will of God and hopes for the coming of the Kingdom of Universal Love, usually called the Kingdom of Heaven. The Buddhist does not expect a Kingdom of Heaven, but there is the tradition of the temporary betterment of the world with the coming of a future Buddha (Maitreya). Or at the very least he hopes to improve world conditions sufficiently to enable men to seek salvation more successfully, as would be possible in a world of peace. This is worth doing, even though the world order cannot be permanently or basically improved and though Nirvana is man's proper destiny.

How different, then, in actuality is the quality of Christian love and Buddhist loving-kindness? Their statements of *motivation* are quite different in several respects, as we have seen. But before we can make a final answer, we should also briefly note the respective methods employed by each to express itself.

b. *The Methods of Love and Loving-kindness*

By method we mean the characteristic way in which Christian love and Buddhist loving-kindness seek to express themselves. Something both of the ideal and of the actual practice in each case must be indicated, for the proof and even the meaning of an ideal come to light only as they are joined in conflict with actual historical conditions.

(1) *The Expression of Christian Love*

It would be erroneous to speak of Christian love as having a method, at least in any thoroughgoing systematic sense. And it is both the weakness and the strength of Christian love that it *is* unsystematic. Practically this has often resulted in spasmodic, feverishly active, and ill-considered efforts toward doing good, alternating with periods of vague or gushing emotionalism. Yet, on the other hand, since love is conceived and practiced as a direct person-to-person relationship, flexibility and spontaneity must remain its essential features. In this sense love has no method but that of a consistent attempt to secure and practice maximum personal mutuality, and it must freely adapt itself to new situations.

In this attempt at mutuality there are two key words: *forgiveness* and *reconciliation*. Forgiveness represents the attitude of the Christian who in love seeks to break the walls that separate men from each other, and reconciliation represents the implementation and result of that attitude. Both root primarily in the Christian conception of man's relation to God. Man's reconciliation with God, i.e., the universe in which he lives, takes the form of the sense of his own forgiveness; as forgiven he is reconciled and the estrangement is overcome. In so far as the Christian finds men estranged by class structure, racial difference, national antagonisms, and on the personal level by past hostile deeds and attitudes, he seeks to break down the barriers and close the gaps by purging his own heart of ill will and by the performance of loving (reconciling) deeds. In this he is strongly motivated by the sense of God's prior and continuing great mercy to *him*.

For the Christian the work of reconciliation (the achievement of mutuality) is a very active and practical matter. Believing, as he does, that the concrete world order of space and time realities in which he lives, including the human individuals who live therein, is the creation of God and the continuing object of His love, the Christian thinks inevitably about *do*ing something tangible for, to, and with actual living persons. He thinks in terms of modifying physical circumstances of human life, of altering the flow of historical events, and of dealing with specific persons in the fullness of their individuality and in the concreteness of their individual needs. Sometimes, to be sure, there has been such an excessive emphasis upon the saving of man's "soul" that man's mind and body have been neglected. Yet the full Christian ministry of love is to the total man however we wish to describe him.

This leads obviously to a strong emphasis upon personal

fellowship within Christianity and to communal practice. It is true that some Christian mystics believed the highest expression of Christian love to be man's union with God— the alone within man approaching Divine Aloneness. Yet even this is a kind of fellowship. And the Christian can agree only limitedly with Whitehead when he says that religion is what a man does with his solitariness. For Christianity maintains that religion is also what a man does with his mutualities. Hence, in some sense the fellowship of faith and worship, of which the church is one expression, is absolutely essential even to the true love of God; and the attempt to achieve strong communal ties with one's fellows is an inevitable expression of Christian love. For the Christian, then, there can be no truly "higher" quality of religious or saintly life that, because it is "higher," leaves out as nonessential, or reduces to lower religious rank, the service and fellowship of man. For in loving man he also loves and serves God.

(2) *The Methods of Loving-kindness*

When we turn to the practice of Buddhist loving-kindness we are immediately struck by those basic contrasts which grow out of the very different Buddhist view of the universe and of the self. If Christian love might be described as spontaneously and intensely personal in spirit, practical and direct in its expression, historically and socially minded in viewpoint, Buddhist loving-kindness must be described as systematic and calculated, indirect and impersonal, and atomistically individualistic.

The calculated system of Buddhist loving-kindness has already been described in one connection: the methodical and carefully prescribed way in which the Blessed Dispositions are to be practiced. And this methodical quality is integral to the total Buddhist spiritual life. The spontaneous and the personal in themselves are to be distrusted; they must be pruned and regulated, even negated at times. While it is true that Buddhism seeks to achieve in its higher reaches of sainthood a kind of naturalness about being good, so that it becomes absolutely spontaneous to extend loving-kindness to all other beings with the same fullness as to oneself, this is a cultured and created spontaneity, a deliberately developed naturalness that produces few surprises and implements no reforms.

This gives point also to a characteristic noted earlier: the practice of the Blessed Dispositions as integrally related to meditation. Though the Dispositions may be limitedly cultivated in the layman's life, primarily and supremely they go with the methodology of the life of the (monkish) meditator. Consequently, it is only in the life of the Christian monastic mystic that we can find anything comparable, where sometimes elaborate prayer systems were worked out. But these assumed, because of their Christian context, that the ordinary mode of man-to-man love and charity ought to go on in general, and should go on even in their own lives in their noncontemplative periods—though such practical charity might be temporarily or partially sidetracked for the superior loveliness of union with God. With regard to Buddhism, however, we must say that what was in Christianity a somewhat unconscious or temporary sidetracking of practical humanward love for the higher varieties of divine love, in Buddhism is fully deliberate and permanent. The saint, to be a saint at all, must put his primary attention on the higher goods of inner realization and self-perfection; the lower life of ordinary ethical virtues and merely human kindness is only for the layman who is not yet spiritually developed enough to practice the higher life of meditation.

Obviously, then, interpersonal terms, values, and practices are less highly esteemed in Buddhism than in Christianity. Take the matter of basic concepts (terms), for example. Since the Buddhist conceptual world is nonpersonal—no personal God, but only Order; no real selves, but streams of karmic thrust that accumulate personal factors about them—the use of such words as forgiveness and reconciliation do not come naturally. Certainly the practicing

Buddhist, layman or monk, has the same practical problems of personal resentment and hatred to deal with as the practicing Christian. And among the monks there is a mandatory ritual in which each monk, somewhat as a Roman Catholic priest confesses to and seeks absolution from another priest, periodically confesses his failures to some fellow monks. Yet here the very act of confessing *itself* cleanses the confessor. There is no God whose forgiveness is sought; nor do the other monks extend absolution in the name of God. For of course the law of karma ensures that each evil deed will receive its reward. And in a parody of the Jewish psalmist, the Buddhist might "pray," "Against karma, and karma only, have I sinned, and done evil in its sight." But what is karma, after all? Not a Being who sees and rewards or punishes. It is only the power of completed deeds to bring future consequences upon their doer. Karma, so far as it affects me, is really myself. So the Buddhist confession in essence must be, "Against myself and myself only have I sinned, and done that which is evil."

Thus in Buddhism, as we have emphasized before, in the end a man can only do good or harm to himself. The walls of karmic isolation forever separate him from his fellow. He could not redeem him if he would. He can only redeem himself by his own corrective action and leave the other man to his own karma. Or better, he can only help the other person as he helps himself. Such indirect benefit as he can give will be that of example, of the calm detached radiation of harmless benevolence, and by avoiding occasions for fanning the resentment and greed of others.

What effect has this doctrine of seemingly cold aloofness from the plight of one's fellows had upon Buddhist practice in actuality? Has it meant the total destruction of natural humanward concern among Buddhists? Certainly not. In practice one finds Buddhist people loving, gentle, and helpful in many cases, apparently both because of and in spite of their religious beliefs. The doctrine that one builds up merit for himself by helping others fortifies the natural human desire to extend help and hospitality. And further, it should be remembered that the perfection of the Blessed Dispositions in the pervasive practice of detached equanimity is only for the saints, who are always few and far between. It is not the practical everyday rule for Buddhist monks or laity.

Yet the fact that systematically cultivated detachment and impersonality are the great ideals of Buddhist spiritual discipline has had its effect. This effect is not to be stated in the crude and grossly inaccurate forms of portraying Western-Christian culture as full of vigor, initiative, active social concern, and innately progressive, over against Eastern Buddhist culture as innately pessimistic, inactive, inhuman, and static. Too many other factors are involved to make such contrasts more than merely an exercise in exchanging epithets.[16] It may rather be put in terms of pervasive attitudes and influences that have stemmed in part from Buddhism. And the general principle involved is this: *Buddhism's depreciation of the worth and reality of human, space-time, physicomental individuality has subtly undermined most expressions of human mutuality.* For if there is no truly ultimate self, if space-time individuality is an evil and a burden to be escaped, if the world order in which man lives is neutrally impersonal and purposeless, then wherein lies the motivation for deeply mutual human relationships or for effective social and historical action?

Specifically we may note briefly three results of this principle:

1. *Fellowship and community are not natural to Buddhism.* The highest religious values in Buddhism are not found in this area, but quite apart from it. The saint is one who escapes (withdraws, detaches himself) from direct physicosocial involvement with others. To be sure, there is the Sangha, or order of monks among Nirvana-seekers, and its values of fellowship are real. And there is the association of laymen that gathers about the local monastery to assure its support. Yet in each case there is a pervasive atomism,

religiously speaking; the fellowship that is there is on the human level and not the religious. Each monk is a seeker for Nirvana; that is why he has left the householder's (layman's) life. And the way to Nirvana is a solitary way. His association with other monks is for necessity and convenience—instruction, discipline, living arrangements—not of the essence of his religious life. The highest ideal example even for the monastery is actually the forest dweller, i.e., the purely solitary meditator who only rarely descends again to human associations. And the laymen who frequent monastery or pagoda do not do so as a congregation, or in the fellowship of worship. This latter is essentially unknown in Buddhism. A group of pagoda worshipers is a group of individuals, each one of whom is seeking to improve his own karmic destiny, not essentially fellowshiping as the people of the Buddha. Such fellowship as arises is social and incidental.

2. *Ordinary ethical goodness is downgraded in the scale of Buddhist values.* This does not mean that the Buddhist saint becomes immoral by becoming saintly. Quite the contrary. Except in Tantric Buddhism, which had only a very limited career in Southern Buddhism, there has been much less of rising ecstatically and erotically above common morality in Buddhism as a whole, even than in Christianity. (Witness the periodic outbursts of free-love communities, the appearance of a Rasputin, and the physically innocuous but emotionally fervid eroticism involved in the use of the Songs of Solomon in European monastic communities.) The Buddhist saint is the essence of nonsexual otherworldliness and benevolent harmlessness. The downgrading of ethics in Buddhism is of another sort: it is a depreciation of the religious worth of the practical life of active moral virtue because of its attachment to values, causes, and persons. It is the elevation of the contemplative life, not as a counterbalance to the active, but to its *displacement* on the level of authentic sainthood. The fullest sainthood is the fullest detachment from the life and concerns of ordinary indi-

viduality and society. Therefore, in Buddhism a deed of physical charity is consistently regarded as of lower worth than a state of equanimity induced by meditation, or the "radiating" of impersonal (nondiscriminating) benevolence. The individual as an individual is not the primary target of Buddhist good actions, but the individual as karmic-stream-needing-to-be-ended, or sentient being qua sentient being.

This downgrading of practical ethics to the foundational, but nevertheless lowest, role in Buddhist spiritual life has been reinforced by the twin doctrines of karma and merit. Merit is actually only another name for the accumulation of good karma, of course; but its particular form accentuates a kind of nonhuman yet religious individualism. One must estimate every deed done in terms of what it does for the doer, karmically speaking. Does it add to his store of good or bad credits on the karmic books? And further, since every man is the author and keeper of his own karma, and his own karma keeps him in turn, why should one concern himself with another's self-induced good or evil fate? He is but reaping his own just deserts. That this reading of karmic influence has resulted in a current of indifference to human suffering running ambivalently alongside the doctrine of harmlessness to all living beings, and that it has resulted in a considerable degree of social passivity, is undeniable.[17]

3. *Sociohistorical activity has no primary or vital rationale in traditional Buddhism.* This is the inevitable logic of the Buddhist view of the world and of man. Man is a stranger and pilgrim in an alien order of existence; and the existence of both is a grievous mistake, though Buddhism refuses to assign responsibility for their existence or to speculate about the origins of either. It finds man involved in a restless career of sensuous craving that inexorably produces individuality, and involved in a world that only entices him on to endless more such existences. What boots it to try to improve one's status in such a situation? Man may indeed rise to the higher levels of this dharma-karma world by the ordinary virtues, and to the very highest levels of worldly style bliss and longevity in the heavens by prac-

ticing the lower grades of meditation. But even this bliss is limited in time and blessedness; sooner or later—and what difference does sooner or later make when it is all past, as it will be sooner or later?—it is ended, and even the once-god is now man again, or even beast. He must find a way out of the whole order by a totally different discipline from that of ordinary good character and ordinarily acceptable good deeds. Nor is there any way in which fundamentally to improve this world order. It is far greater than man, who is but a small eddy within its ongoing stream so long as he remains an ignorant, questing, desiring, acting individual according to its terms. Though good karma helps to hold the universe together, it can never permanently renovate and perfect the world order; this universe will have its ups and downs and then dissolve, and other universes will replace it. But to what end?

This does not in actuality mean that Buddhism has collapsed into a complete pessimism. It too, like Christianity, and even more consistently, decries war and violence, worldly materialism and insatiable greed. It too affirms that its gospel of the destruction of self-interest, of disinterested detachment, and peaceable benevolence, if practiced, would make even this evanescent world a better place. It would be better in any sense: in terms of immediate visible happiness and in terms of providing better conditions for man to pursue his proper goal of ultimate Nirvana. Especially is contemporary Buddhism most urgent in its insistence upon the need to improve the present order of society and change the dangerous trend of world affairs. The question that remains is whether Buddhism, considering its fundamental depreciation of society and history, has religious resources to achieve a social and political philosophy of any significance.

4. *Summing Up*

What remains to say? We have now sketched in some rather sharp distinctions between Christian love and Buddhist loving-kindness, both in their doctrinal and in their practical aspects. The over-all portrait that emerges is something such as follows:

Due to its personalistic conception of the universe as governed by a supreme God who is purposefully loving in his creation and in the maintenance of that universe in existence, a universe that is populated by uniquely personal individuals called human beings, Christianity thinks, feels, speaks, and acts in interpersonal terms. The supreme virtue known to Christians is to love God, in a sense not absolutely different from that of loving men. And correspondingly its highest humanward virtue is also the exercise of love, love toward each man in terms of his concrete individuality. Its hope is to achieve genuine interpersonal mutuality in attitude and in actual association under space-time conditions. Therefore, Christianity has sought social and communal expression, majoring in fellowship and proliferating its organizations; it has also sought to minister to the totality of the concrete individual as he belongs to the personal, social, economic, political, and historical orders of being. Christianity has therefore built church fellowships, attempted social orders, been abundant in physical deeds of helpfulness and healing, and been the author of countless attempts to achieve the Kingdom of God on earth.

By the same token Buddhism has been quite other. Because it conceives the universe as an impersonal and purposeless order of physicomental proportions, populated by streams of being that endlessly perpetuate themselves in newly individual forms, rather than by genuinely unique persons, Buddhism thinks, feels, speaks, and acts in what the West calls an *im*personal manner. Emphasis upon the uniqueness and value of the space-time individuality of the person, or even upon his immortal soul, is for Buddhism a delusion and snare that prevents man's true enlightenment and ultimate salvation. Buddhism views the Christian tendency to emphasize personal attachments and to act primarily in terms of concrete practical helpfulness to other individuals, as either fundamentally mistaken or at the very best repre-

senting a lower order of spiritual action than its own detached benevolence. It believes Christianity is misled in that
it attaches too much importance to individuality and to the
individual, and thus binds its efforts and loyalties to what
is not essentially real or enduring. And because it does this,
Christianity achieves a lesser order of spiritual good, even
to those it seeks to help, than does Buddhism, for it touches
only the fringes, not the heart, of man's basic problem. Re-
sultingly, Buddhism has no basic faith in the real possibility
of world improvement or a vital drive toward historically and
politically oriented action.

We may remark, however, that in practice and historical
actuality the sharp lines here drawn are somewhat blurred
by qualifying factors. For instance, there is in Christianity
as well as in Buddhism a distrust of this world, most sharply
expressed by the medieval mystic but never fully exorcised
from the Christian soul even in this most worldly of all
"Christian" eras. In the words of his own Scriptures the
Christian sometimes knows that he is "a stranger and a
pilgrim" who has found no enduring city here, and does not
know precisely where he will find it this side of some
heavenly order, in heaven or on earth. And conversely the
practicalities of life have not altogether passed Buddhism
by. Even in its often passive past, Buddhism sought to per-
meate the wordly affairs of the cultures that it encountered,
and in part formed, with its basic principles and values, even
while theoretically discounting the real value of those affairs.
Through the centuries the practical lay Buddhism of this
world has increased in importance over that monkish variety
that was once its *only* form.

But more suggestively for the present day we may note
that not only has there been some presence of both sets of
values in each religion, though in different proportion of
course, but that each of the two traditions has produced its
countervalues. Sometimes these have been the reverse or
excesses of its own peculiar values; again they have been
actually counter to its own professed standards and truths.

Such cases are not hard to find in Christianity; for the actuality of its presumedly spontaneous, person-centered, activist love spreading its glowing warmth throughout the world, has not always been lovely. Its love has often been inordinately possessive in personal relationships; it has wished to own those whom it loved. Therefore, these personal relations have often been hypocritical, contorted, and full of domination and hidden hostility. Because it has lost sight of its own deeper values and been cut off from the inward mystical forces within its own tradition, Christianity has frequently made its vaunted charity into a pure superficialism of external deeds. Its passion for fellowship has led to the formation of person-destroying organizations and oppressive ecclesiasticisms. Indeed, more than this has occurred. Its activism has not infrequently become aggressive, the more aggressive the more it has been resisted. Its confidence that the world is improvable and that there is a Kingdom to come has led it to force its values upon others by a variety of means up to and including military force.

On the other hand, it is not hard to observe the sins and failures peculiar to the manifestation of Buddhist loving-kindness. They are, in general, of the opposite sort from those of the Christian, sins of omission rather than of commission. For if a man is unreal, or only secondarily real as a physico-socio-historical individual, he may be, and usually has been, neglected as a person and body in Buddhism. (Here is a curious inversion by which no-soul Buddhism commits the Christian sin of valuing a man's no-soul so much that the tangible man himself is despised.) There has been that pervasive, centuries-old tendency, already noted, callously to let each man reap the fruits of his own past deeds karmically projected into his present existence, and feel no sense of personal responsibility for another. That gentle unwillingness to interfere with another's spiritual destiny, so attractive to so many Christians who are not sure of their own faith and who are tired of the unlovely coercions that litter Christian history, may also be a cover for a nearly com-

plete unconcern for the welfare of others in any form whatsoever save in the most general and impersonal terms of
"radiated" benevolence. Perhaps it would be both more
charitable and balanced to point out that historically some
of this unconcern has come not from the lack of good will
but from the lack of resources and knowledge of how to alter
fundamentally the situation of the masses; and, lacking
ability, the Buddhist did the next best thing: accommodated
to what he could not see how to improve. But in any case
Buddhist loving-kindness did not provide the necessary inspiration to change the social order, and thereby demonstrated a fundamental incapacity to deal with historical and
political realities.

Different as these ways are, hard as it is for one to understand the other, may it still not be suggested that Buddhist
loving-kindness and Christian love have something to contribute to each other, if only they can be engaged in meaningful conversation in which each will not try at the outset
to prove itself one hundred per cent perfect and sufficient?
For Christianity, such a review of its own love policy, so to
speak, in the light of the Buddhist witness would mean a
re-examination of its hard aggressive personalism that tries
so hard to be selfless and yet fears so much the loss of its
own selfhood. Perhaps something of the Buddhist attempt
to remain detached even in closest personal relationships
would be of value to the depth and vitality of Christian love
and enable Christians to live more happily with themselves.
In another area, it would mean the renewal of a conversation
that this-world, practical, ethical, and socially minded Jewish
Christianity once had with Greek-Oriental mysticism. While
that conversation in medieval Christianity may not have had
fully ideal results, it should not have been called off. In
losing contact with its own mystical deeps, Christianity has
made its love one-sided (hence not love) and lost that vital
sense of Divine Presence upon which depends the true depth
and quality of Christian love even toward man.

On the side of Buddhism it would mean a confession that

Buddhism has never had the courage to make up to this point: that however successful it has been in dealing with the inner man, it has not encountered the world in which he lives head on, but rather avoided it. It has historically taken little or no responsibility for that world in which men have heretofore existed, finding little lovely in it save in a non-religious way. Because it has despised the world in which it lives, it has not been able to redeem it. It has in reality evaded the problem of suffering, of which it speaks so fluently, by discounting the worth and reality of the individual and by refusing to deal directly with the problems of that individuality and its personal misery.

Is there any hope of such a fruitful contact? This is most difficult to say. The barriers are old and high: the traditional and usual Christian tendency to refuse to acknowledge anything of worth in any other religion; and the contemporary, nationalist-tinged tendency in Buddhism to claim that it is all-sufficient, as it stands, for the salvation of that world which Christianity has been too weak or too debauched to redeem. But there are some in each faith who are interested in such conversation. And perhaps the daunting problems of the present world will force upon both Buddhism and Christianity a new mood of humility and self-examination, hopefully before the fast-moving currents of world events make either's co-operation and sympathetic study of the other tradition futile or impossible.

(IV)

Christian Guilt and Buddhist Dukkha

> We know that the law is spiritual; but I am carnal, sold under sin. I do not understand my own actions. For I do not do what I want, but I do the very thing I hate. Now if I do what I do not want, I agree that the law is good. So then it is no longer I that do it, but sin which dwells within me. For I know that nothing good dwells within me, that is, in my flesh. I can will what is right, but I cannot do it. For I do not do the good I want, but the evil I do not want is what I do. Now if I do what I do not want, it is no longer I that do it, but sin which dwells within me. . . . Wretched man that I am! Who will deliver me from this body of death? (Rom. 7:14–20, 24.)

Such is a most vivid, yet characteristic, Christian statement of the human condition that has been echoed and re-echoed many times since Paul's day both in Christian tradition and experience. With it we may contrast the following famous passage from the Buddhist scriptures, which has been no less influential and characteristic in Buddhism. It is part of the famous "Fire Sermon" of the Buddha:

> And there the Lord addressed the monks, saying: "Monks, everything is burning. And what, monks, is everything that is burning? The eye, monks, is burning, material shapes are burning, consciousness through the eye is burning, impingement on the eye is burning; in other words the feeling which arises from impingement on the eye, be it pleasant or painful or neither painful nor pleasant, that too is burning. With what is it burning? I say it is burning with the fire of passion, with the

103

fire of hatred, with the fire of stupidity; it is burning because
of birth, ageing, dying, because of grief, sorrow, suffering, lam-
entation, and despair."[1]

Likewise, the Buddha goes on to say, the ear, nose,
tongue, body, and even "consciousness through the mind [a
separate sixth sense in Buddhist psychology]" are all on fire
in the same way.

Better than any other, these two quotations set before us
the differing ways in which Christianity and Buddhism conceive the human predicament. With Paul, it is stated in
terms of sin, guilt, a sense of alienation from God, and deep
division within the self. With the Buddha, the statement is
couched in terms of ignorance and burning dis-ease. This
burning dis-ease, with which all experiences of the self are
filled, is but a specifically vivid expression of the Buddhist
sense of all-pervasive dukkha—somewhat too narrowly
translated as "suffering"—that characterizes the Buddhist
consciousness as completely as the sense of sin and guilt
does the Christian consciousness.

The interest of this chapter then centers around this
basic contrast in viewpoint. Perhaps we cannot meaningfully ask *why* the two religions—each of which views the
human situation as one of dire human distress, and both of
which emphasize the same direful features of human subjection to mental anguish, physical pain and disease, feebleness of strength and intelligence, and finally of death—
should differ so radically in their analysis of the basic nature
of man's predicament. This roots in that fundamentally in-
soluble mystery as to why Semitic and Indo-Aryan views of
the world differ so radically even in their primordial forms.
But we may seek to *characterize* the basically divergent guilt
and dukkha views, and inquire as to how or from what
sources they arose and as to their religious results. Such a
description of the nature and context of each view should
throw some further light on the spiritual relation of Christianity and Buddhism to each other.

1. Man as Guilty Sinner

Every Christian and many a non-Christian is aware of the Adam mythos found in the Biblical "explanation" of the basic human predicament. In the beginning the *first* man— for Hebraic thought must needs think in temporal-historical terms—was created in pure innocence of nature and happiness of condition in a paradisal garden. But in a deliberate act of prideful rebellion against his Creator—pictured in primitive language as the eating of the fruit of the tree of the knowledge of good and evil—Adam disobeyed the divine commandment. True, he was persuaded to do so by his female companion Eve, who in turn had been corrupted in mind by the question of the ambiguously evil "serpent"; yet the act was essentially his very own for which he must take the consequences. Indeed, he had a guilty premonition of such consequences and hid behind the garden shrubbery when the Lord God, with whom he had been in happy fellowship before, next appeared. His guilty premonitions were fulfilled: he was driven from the garden with Eve, condemned to propagate his kind in lust and pain, sentenced to gain his bread from an unwilling earth cursed because of his sin. His sons were filled with anger and hatred against each other as well as rage against their Creator.

The story of Adam's sin and its consequences is told in naïve and primitive language. Adam eats fruit from a tree and like a naughty child hides when Father-God comes looking for him. Yet in its very form we have a basic clue to the whole Judeo-Christian pattern of thinking about man and his relation to the universe, one that has permeated all of Western culture down to the present day. It is a feature to which we have referred before, and to which we must necessarily return again and again in our understanding of the Christian viewpoint. It is this: man's fundamental relation to the universe is an interpersonal one. The basic context in which man has his being is an "I-Thou" relationship, to use Martin Buber's phrase. It is before a Divine Presence that man lives out all his days. "In the beginning is relation. All real living is meeting."[2]

The importance of this factor for the Christian conception of the fundamental situation in which man finds himself cannot be overemphasized. For one thing it places personal-ethical elements in the very center of the Christian perspective. Man's primary relation to the universe is conceived of in terms of faithfulness, righteousness, justice, obedience, or the reverse. It is true that this central ethical emphasis did not come easily, quickly, or fully to the Judeo-Christian tradition; for even through the screen of the fully ethicized, religious view of the postprophetic editing of the Old Testament we can sense strong elements of that impersonal and near-magical relation to God, characteristic of the early Hebrew religion. And saints of the Old Testament continue up till its end to battle against the nonethical superstitions of popular faith. But under the influence of the prophets in particular, what was intrinsic to, or at least implied by, the personal-God imagery was developed into the central Jewish and Christian conception of God as an irresistible power for justice and righteousness that moves in history and manifests itself in nature. Reciprocally man's relation to God must be conceived in personal-ethical terms. Man may "obey" or "disobey" the commandments that God has given him. He may "serve" Him "faithfully" or "rebel" against him. He may "love" or "hate" his Creator. Such a personal-ethical vocabulary and orientation is therefore as native to the Judeo-Christian as the air he breathes.

Once fully established at the core of the Judeo-Christian world perspective, this sense of a basic personal-ethical relation with God permeates all the other categories and relationships in which Jew or Christian may find himself. The Old Testament so conceives the meaning of *natural* events, for example: they are demonstrations of the wrath or favor of Yahweh; so also the historical event. Pestilence, destructive storm, flood, drought, defeat in battle, barrenness in women and cattle, and sudden death are God's punishments;

their opposites are his blessings. This way of interpretation was carried over bodily into Christianity where characteristically the same construction has been put upon like events. For example, the Black Death that ravaged Europe in the fourteenth century was considered to be evidence of God's great wrath upon that generation's sin and disobedience. How many a battle's bloody victory has been celebrated with a churchly Te Deum on the corpse-strewn field itself, or has been more privately viewed by the participants as a singular demonstration of divine favor! Such seems to have been the case with General Archdale Wilson who, after the bloody capture of Delhi from the mutinous sepoys in 1857, wrote to his wife: "The more I see of the strength of the place, the more I am astonished at our success. Most certainly to the Lord of Hosts can be ascribed the victory."[3]

Nor has this same sense of divinely based personal-ethical relationships been limited to the interpretation of natural and historical events. It became pervasive and determinant of the total Judeo-Christian sense of social structure and relationships as well. The final Old Testament version is that all the ritual and legal regulations of the five books of Moses (Torah), as well as the basic Ten Commandments, were given verbatim to Moses on Mt. Sinai by God. Thus did religious ritual, moral principle, and civil regulation all alike become the command of Yahweh to the devout Jew. Disregard of even the least of the regulations was thus sinful disobedience to God himself.

The fundamental thrust of this basic attitude, though with some dilution and variation, carried over into the Christian schema. Paul found something of God's ordering even in the legion-enforced Pax Romana of Nero's time, and the flicker of the lightning of His judgments in the brandishments of Caesar's sword of authority. A later writer, however, the author of the New Testament Revelation to John, could see in Rome only the great anti-Christian harlot drunk with the blood of Christian martyrs; and subsequent revolutionaries searched the Scriptures (successfully it appears) for a warrant to justify their rebellion against some civil authority or other as contravening the Divine Social Order —which latter they proceeded to establish at once upon the successful conclusion of their revolution. But whether for or against a given contemporary social order, the Christian has sought during much of his history to mold his societies according to his understanding and hope of the coming Kingdom of Heaven. And more often than otherwise, following Paul rather than the author of Revelation, he has considered loyalty to country and government as loyalty to God's order—particularly if there has been some semblance of Christian influence in its laws and institutions.

Now what more natural in a context so permeated with a sense of the Divine Presence and influence than that the Christian should think of failure as *sin?* How else could he think of it indeed? For sin has a twofold nature. It is always, properly speaking, against persons and not things or forces. And even more importantly it is against Deity. No mere social *faux pas,* or even a severe breach of moral principle, is per se a sin. *Sin* is rebellion against Deity; deliberate affront of Divine Majesty, or severance of the relationship of loving sonship. And *guilt* follows sin like its shadow. For objectively considered, guilt is the consequence of a sin that entails judgment upon the offender. And subjectively it is the feeling of personal responsibility for sin, mingled with premonitions of coming judgment.

If this is the case, then the occasions for guilt, both objective and subjective, would be manifold in the human context when it is Christianly conceived. For as we have been at pains to point out, the conviction of the all-pervasive expression of the divine will in every aspect of life—natural, historical, political, moral, religious, social—is fundamental to the Judeo-Christian world view. And such is in fact the situation in nearly all societies and cultures that have been strongly influenced by the Judeo-Christian tradition. The characteristic way in which a member of such society or culture reacts to his moral lapses, character weaknesses, religious lassitude or personal failures of almost any sort, is with a sense of guilt. It may be sharply channeled into a specific religious expression as with Kierkegaard, who for many years labored under the shadow of a sense of divine displeasure visited upon him because once in his youth his father had cursed God to His face; or it may be, as it increasingly is today, an oppressive and omnipresent guilt sense that yet remains obscure and ill-defined both as to cause or remedy. Especially is a sense of guilt oppressive among Protestant Christians who possess no sacramental apparatus, such as the Roman Catholic has in confession and absolution, to tangibly dissipate the sense of guilt.

Indeed, as most psychoanalysts and psychiatrists are deeply aware, guilt has become one of the major problems of Western man, whether he is religious or not. Though rooted in the Judeo-Christian context, though based on its religious presuppositions and experiences, guilt has by now overflowed its specifically religious channels. Once-upon-a-time-religious guilt has linked itself with many other forms of guilt and anxiety of purely psychological and secular origins. Indeed, paradoxical though it may sound, the very decay of the guilt-producing religious sensibility has contributed to a larger and more diffuse sense of guilt.

In any case, Guilt is now Here. Its causes are multitudinous and its forms of expression infinite. Modern Western man feels guilty because he breaks sexual taboos— though less so than in the days of Freud's original analysis of the libido. He feels guilty for failing to do well at his job; for not providing for his family as well as his neighbor does for his; for taking *any* time off from work; for smoking or drinking; for not being more active in community affairs or social welfare work; for not giving more to charitable causes; for not going to church more frequently; for the rottenness of politics; and for the generally sorry condition of the world. Or the causes and forms may be other and more deeply personal: long-ago rejected childhood religious beliefs and loyalties gone into the guilty underground of unacknowledged feeling; the experience of mingled love and hatred for the same person; the discovery in oneself of tendencies toward hostility and aggression against others—directly opposed to the explicit Christian teachings about love and forgiveness one nominally accepts; or even under cover of their practice. And the case is rendered the worse because most persons do not know the causes, either proximate or ultimate, of their psychological symptoms—an interesting Western form of what the Buddhist calls ignorance of things "as they are."

Into this jungly thicket of obscure motives and confusingly diverse psychological symptoms we cannot enter here. But it is one that is increasingly engaging the concern of the whole body of Western psychological thought and a great deal of psychiatric practice. And curiously enough it is also in this area that Christian West and Buddhist East seem to be achieving a more exciting and vital rapport than is often the case on the religious level. For on the religious level the tyranny of systems of doctrine, of theological formulations, of institutional and cultural habits, and of religious pretensions is hard to escape. Polemic claim ánd counterclaim seem to prevail here—or *religiously* disinterested scholarship. But in the area of the West's growing appreciation and study of the inner psychological dimensions of humankind it is the psychologist with a deeply existential interest in the matter who now studies and explores and expounds Eastern religious values to the West. Without being able at this point to more than mark out this area as one of greatest importance for future rapprochement between East and West, we must now turn to the interpretation of the Buddhist sense of dukkha.

2. *Man as Ignorant Sufferer*

We have now entered into quite a different atmosphere —at least as far as language is concerned. One has left behind the miasmatic swamps of human passion permeated by an overpowering sense of obscure guilt, where friend and foe can be distinguished only with difficulty, but only to find oneself alone in an infinitely complicated maze in which he, like a lost soul—or lost no-soul—is condemned to wander endlessly about looking for an exit from this dark and lonely misery but finding none. It is the world of Buddhist dukkha. In *this* world we seldom hear of "sin" and "guilt." Of course, a normal Buddhist has his ordinary, human guilt feelings that come from the neglect of social obligations, especially with regard to the family, or from his failure to observe social protocol. And it is also true that in the Sangha, or order of monks, there is a ritual of periodic confession of sin by each monk to his brethren. However, this is more a device for keeping before the mind of each monk the duties and standards of his calling than a deeply anguished expression of contrition. Indeed, the Buddha counseled his monks to avoid morbid self-accusations after the deed.

Now and then a sense of sin and guilt, with repentance to follow, is given a specifically religious expression, as in the following passage:

I did not remember even once, O Father, to worship your lotus-feet, because enshrouded as I was by the darkness of ignorance . . . thereby utterly disabled from developing wisdom in the proper way, likewise, remaining void of the knowledge of reality, although the moral laws of right and wrong were palpable in their clearness, so O Gotama, Lion among men, deign to forgive this failure of mine.[4]

There are many other like passages in this same work by a Singhalese monk in which the Buddha's forgiveness is asked for eternities of sins and forgetfulness. But such expressions are rare and atypical, especially in Southern Buddhism. The Buddhist mythos and philosophy of the human condition ordinarily find little or no place for sin and guilt, but give a dominant and central place to dukkha, whose detailed meaning we will explore later.

The Buddhist mythos of the human predicament is as

hard to grasp in its way as is the Christian, though for different reasons. For it is completely nonhistorical even in form; there was no moment in time when man fell into his present predicament, unless it was at his last birth, or at the birth of each new moment of his life. Man's plight is that his existence is endlessly repetitious; what happens now, and the next moment, has been happening for endless ages, and will happen for endless ages more in the ordinary course of events. Where, then, can we grasp the endless pointless tale of man's existence to unravel its meaning and now bring it to its proper ending?

Perhaps it is best first to describe the main actors in this human treadmill of ennui and suffering. And the first one to note is *Tanhā* or craving. Now craving is the vitalistic, mentalistic core or dynamic center of each unit of sentient existence. Every living being represents an eternally repeated thrust into new being, whether we consider it on a moment-to-moment, or life-to-life, or age-to-age scale of time. Sentient life is the frantic will-to-be, which the Buddhist views, somewhat as Schopenhauer did in the West, as struggling in perpetual anguish against its own dissipation or extinction.

There is also *Avijjā,* or ignorance, which is the fructifying condition for the endless rebirth of new forms, each one craving for at least *one* more birth. For craving's endless thrust into new being is blind. Craving has no knowledge of the real truth about sentient existence but is driven forward into *any* new form of existence rather than face dissolution. And so it reaches out with eternally unjaded appetite for new birth. Though it may be tragically unhappy at the moment, it is certain that the next moment, or a new experience, will bring enduring happiness. Though wounded and frustrated in this form of existence, it is certain with an unquenchable optimism that another existence will overcome its frustration and cure its wounds. Thus in its thoroughly blind drive to be, and its fear of nonbeing, craving clothes not only itself but also other selves and entities with spurious substantiality and fictitious being. And having so clothed them in its blindness and out of its fear, it finds them both real and desirable.

Obviously, there is also *Karma*. For it is karma that inexorably determines the course that each further projection of ignorant craving into new being shall take, what shall be its new form. As we have already seen, karma is no guardian spirit or just deity, but simply the power of a voluntary thought, word, physical action, or dominant attitude to produce a fitting consequence in the life of its author or possessor. Buddhist scriptures are full of stories of the fitting transformation of beings into new forms that embody their dominant attitudes in the past existence or result from their past deeds: the acting-like-an-animal ascetic who becomes the acted-like animal in his next life; the gluttonous man born as a hog; the rapacious man as a tiger; the stingy man as a ghost with giant belly and tiny mouth; one who has shed a saint's blood born into the deepest of hells.

Such are the great moving forces that generate the human predicament according to the Buddhist mythos. Two features of that predicament, perhaps already implied by what has been said, need further emphasis. One is the *eternity*, both forward and backward, of man's plight especially emphasized by Southern Buddhism.[5] Behind each individual stretches an infinite number of past existences; for each existence implies at least another before it and so on endlessly. This means that my present self is full of multitudinous good and evil potentialities (good and bad karma, forces of purity and impurity) that will inexorably produce their fruitage of happiness and pain in this or some future life. And the average man being what he is, it is more likely than not that the evil heritage in him predominates over the good—an analogue to Christian teaching about depravity or carnal nature. And in the forward direction there extends the prospect of another infinitude of similar future existences of restless, mixed pain-pleasure—much like this present one—into which the thrust of craving will carry him.

To be sure, the ordinary man, ignorantly enamored of this present life, totally unaware that he has been before and will be again, or perhaps only intellectually assenting to this truth and not fully realizing it, continues to yearn for more being; and thus every deed, being one that is attached to life and permeated with the desire for continued existence, will in fact produce such existence. Only those from whose eyes a bit of dust has been removed (to use a Buddhist metaphor), so that they apprehend even a little of the truth of things as they are, see the appalling nature of the prospect of future eternities of life dominated by craving and bounded by birth and death in each instance.

The other notable feature of man's predicament is his eternal *aloneness* so far as his spiritual destiny is concerned. For the mass of ignorant craving that characterizes the living world is not a great blind giant, but is divided into an infinite number of completely individualized streams or strands, i.e., sentient beings. Each one of these is eternally separate from every other so far as the course of its rebirths is concerned. Each one is governed by the thrust of its own karmic manufacture, for, as we have noted before, karma in this sense is completely individualized. I am my own karma. What I now am, I have made of myself by my past deeds. I am what the dominant desires and deepest cravings of my past existences—or moments of being in this existence—have made me. Thus I can shift the blame for my present condition on to no blind forces or malignant fate, but only on to "myself," i.e., past selves. And the responsibility for the future lies with no one else but my *present* self. *This sense of sole personal responsibility for one's own fate is essential to the Buddhist view of man's predicament.* Whether there is in fact a shift of significance and identity here in the meaning of "self" that allows for a kind of spiritual irresponsibility as between the discontinuous selfhoods of past, present, and future selves, despite such strenuously responsible language, remains open to question, however.

This, then, is man according to Buddhism: an eternally individualized, infinitely repetitive projection of the will-to-be into ever new forms, of which his present being is but one. The difference from the Christian view of man is obvious. The Buddhist view sharply qualifies or even undercuts the Christian sense of the "worth" of the unique human individual that grows out of the latter's historicity and personalism. Or, at the very least, it places the worth of man in a very different context. And since this so basically colors the Buddhist approach to man's problem and to human life and activity in general, it is most important to grasp its real significance. It may therefore help if the Buddhist view of man is phrased thus: *The fundamental root of man's misery is his existence as a personalized individual.* (And for whatever form of Buddhism we survey, this holds true.) The "fall" of man, according to Buddhism, was his "fall" into individualized sentient being.

And when and how did this "fall" take place? Not in history. Buddhism rejects any mythological tale of a first man through whom craving came into the world—though it has a myth of the cyclical deterioration of beings of radiant splendor into mere men. But the Buddha refused to speculate about the beginning of individualized sentient beings or whether there ever was a state of the world in which no craving and no karma existed. According to the Pali scriptures, he listed it among those like metaphysical questions whose discussion and whose solution (*per impossible*) were not essential to salvation, perhaps even hindrances to it. Presumably now-existent individuals, full of craving, governed by karma, always have been; their *absolute* beginning is a mystery. Therefore, the fall of man into individualized being really takes place every time a new birth occurs, or for that matter, at every successive moment of one's continued individual existence.

The Buddhist heritage from Hindu India at this point is both obvious and interesting. For this conviction of the misfortune and essential restlessness of individualized existence lies at the heart of Hinduism. It is given form in the Brahman-Maya doctrine. Brahman is the Absolute Truth-Reality, which in itself is an eternal union of existence-consciousness-bliss (*sat-chit-ānanda*). As Absolute, it is absolutely undifferentiated, having no parts, no individual forms, no opposite of itself in any other. While Brahman is therefore neither personal or impersonal in the full sense, being far beyond all such qualities and attributes, yet it seems to be a kind of mentalistic monism that is here portrayed. That is, the ultimate "stuff," or being of the universe, is existence of a consciously blissful quality.

Though undifferentiated and needing nothing for its happiness or perfection, Brahman from time to time produces a visible world of individual forms and beings. Some Hindu writings liken this process to the exhalation of a sleeping giant who in one agelong outbreath produces a universe, and in a subsequent inhalation withdraws it into himself. Other scriptures see it as the creative play of Brahman (or of one of his individualized forms among the gods) and then its destruction in ennui. In either case, what comes to be in visible individualized form is Maya. Maya is less real than Brahman, even though an expression of it. And because Maya is less than real in the ultimate sense, all its forms are restless and tormented even in their pleasure at being. Individual forms long, even though unbeknown to themselves, to return to their quiescent state in the undifferentiated Absolute. Especially is this true of the soul (*Ātman*), which passes through many forms until by spiritual discipline and insight it realizes that it is of the essence of Brahman, and in this realization regains the primordial unity.

A curious result ensues with regard to Buddhism, which was the rebellious (heretical) child of Indian religion: it inherits the basic Hindu philosophy of man's existence *under the form of its denial.* For Buddhism in its Southern form refuses to posit any primordial substance or reality, such as Brahman, that serves as the creative womb out of which come the universes and to which they return; and it denies the existence of soul in the Hindu sense, most explicitly in its doctrine of anatta. Yet clearly Nirvana inherits many qualities from Brahman and functions in many ways in Buddhism just as Brahman functions in Hinduism. For Nirvana also is the only and utterly Real;[6] it too is undifferentiated in itself; and for the Buddhist the final going out of the saint into Nirvana is a blissful cessation of individualized existence.

And now we come to the full Buddhist statement of the matter. *Individualized existence, as such, is essentially dukkha, or suffering.* Thus for the Buddhist the quality or experience of dukkha pervades life as completely as guilt does for the Christian—perhaps even more so, since dukkha can never be escaped completely as long as man is man, while guilt may. But to draw a proper comparison, we need to understand the dimensions and flavor of dukkha more fully. For the usual translation as "suffering" is too narrow and physical in its connotations. Thus write the authors of the *Pali-English Dictionary* in their long article on the term:

There is no word in English covering the same ground as Dukkha does in Pali. Our modern words are too specialized, too limited, and usually too strong. . . . We are forced in translation to use half synonyms, no one of which is exact. Dukkha is equally mental and physical. Pain is too predominantly physical, sorrow too exclusively mental, but in some connections they have to be used in default of any more exact rendering. Discomfort, suffering, ill, and trouble can occasionally be used in certain connections. Misery, distress, agony, affliction, and woe are never right. They are all much too strong and are only mental.[7]

Thus, dukkha feeling is hard to pin down. Many Buddhist scriptures do emphasize the physical aspects of dukkha —disease, pain, hunger, thirst, climatic discomforts, attacks of insects, and so forth, as integral elements. So also there are emotional stresses occasioned by the loss (or even prospective loss) of belongings by calamity, and of friends by alienation or death, the ups and downs of personal fortune, and the prospect of death—or even of another *life* of this same sort. Here the Buddhist is aware of a kind of suffering much mentioned also in Judaism and Christianity, those sufferings characteristic of this "vale of tears."

But there is a further, more complex, and peculiarly Buddhist, extension of the meaning of dukkha. Dukkha is seen, by the enlightened ones, as *characteristic of the total life of desire.* Such is the meaning of the statement of the Fourfold Noble Truth, according to which, (1) existence is suffering; (2) suffering springs from desire or craving; (3) the cure for suffering is the extinction of desire; (4) there is an Eightfold Path that leads to the extinction of desire. This is to say, To desire is to suffer. And this is true, the Buddhist holds, of *all* the life of desire on whatever level and in whatever form; and it is true of desire fulfilled as well as desire unfulfilled.

Now it is also a fact that *desire is the essence of individualized existence,* according to Buddhism. For to desire is to want or to lack. And this is precisely the condition of the individualized self, as self. It is never complete, and as incomplete it is always desirous. Self is per se the expression of desire and vice versa. It is brought into a new form of being by desire (or craving), and its life as a self is a continuous attempt to satisfy further desires. In fact, to live as a sentient being is to desire, neither more nor less. Thus a living sentient being is never at peace, whether as body or emotion or intellect. Conscious individualized experience as such is never better than bittersweet. For its sweetest sweets are always embittered by the prospect of their loss or passing; and their intensest enjoyment is always in its very intensity but a hairsbreadth away from, even mingled with, disturbing pain.

So it is that the Buddha said that all things relating to sense-life are on fire—with the fire of that desire which leads on to ever new birth-death experiences; and this is why he elsewhere called the body a "wound." The body, or our physical-sense capabilities, is a wound because it is a continual source of agitation and distress to man. Hence, he can never be at peace in the body. And it is also a wound because it is a breach in man's spiritual impregnability through which pour in the unspiritual infections of an order of existence driven by craving. Indeed, the total individualized existence of man is a wound. Mind-body individuality is an eternally bleeding, reinfecting, painful wound, producing a continual restless dis-ease in man, deeper and more pervasive than any of his specific ills. Thus did an early Buddhist writer conceive the fivefold grouping that constitutes a man:

> The five groups form the heavy load,
> And man this heavy load doth bear;
> This load 'tis misery to take up,
> The laying down thereof is bliss.[8]

One might well interpret Buddhist dukkha partially in the manner of contemporary Western existentialism. In fact with regard to dukkha, Buddhism *is* deeply existentialist. This self that I now am is threatened, partial and evanescent as it is, by the prospect of its own dissolution, either moment by moment, or finally by death. Though a new form ensues and though many Buddhists seem to derive some comfort from the thought of a new existence immediately following on this one, this is essentially immature, sub-Buddhism; the very comfort taken here is a hiding from the ultimate truth of anatta, no-selfness. For the self dies anew at every moment. It can hold on to nothing permanently, either as a body or in any kind of enduring identity. But because of this underlying anxiety about its own being, because of the continual threat of nonbeing, this shadow-self tries ever more madly to assure itself that it *is* real. Thus it indulges its appetites, searches out new sensations, asserts its own importance and reality at the expense of other selves, and intellectually affirms its independent substance by distinguishing itself from "non-selves" or objects to its subject, and by the multiplication of ideas and distinctions. And so does this shadow-self, this mere confection of five temporarily joined factors, jealously and fearfully guard its *un*reality by magnifying its specious reality and importance through a multitude of activities aimed at "self-fulfillment."

Therefore, in Buddhism the problem of salvation is the resolution of the problem of selfhood. Here we may draw a rough, theological parallel between Buddhist and Christian teachings about man. For Buddhism, man's "original sin" is his sentient individuality, incorporated in the very fiber of his nature as such by a primordial set of circumstances that he cannot deal with directly, or fully understand. This original "sinful" bent (craving individuality) manifests itself in his persistent attachment to unreality, particularly the shadow-self of the fivefold grouping. The fruit of this attachment tendency is deeds ("sinful" deeds, or "sins") that are done because of attachment, which because of their attached quality perpetuate the self in its individualized ("sinful," or dukkha-ridden) condition.

3. *The Remedies*

As the disease is, so must the cure be. And so it is not surprising that Christianity and Buddhism, each having diagnosed man's basic ailment somewhat differently, should prescribe for its cure in likewise different fashion. Here we shall deal with the *general* type of cure prescribed by each. In the three subsequent chapters, which are in some sense a more detailed exploration of these prescriptions, we shall describe the respective techniques of spiritual living, concern ourselves with the problem of selfhood and its remedy by selflessness (in both Buddhism and Christianity), and trace out the "theological" implications and qualifications of Buddhist self-salvation.

a. *Christian Redemption by Another*

In restating the human situation to which Christianity

seeks to minister, we shall quote the following words, which, though they are written relative to the condition of the hoping-to-be-reformed Christians of early sixteenth-century Europe, well express the problem and hope of mankind in general:

Their problem was rather how the reformation, the renewal, the regeneration of human life, was to be achieved. How can man, rebellious, full of suspicion of all powers including the ultimate power, full of anger and fear, become reconciled to life and to God? How is it possible for moral man, the incorrigible lover of self and continual victim of his passions, whether ruler or subject, whether exercising or obeying authority, to become a lover of God and of his companions? How can he become free, not of external restraint, but of those internal conflicts and that alienation from himself which justify external restraint and are increased by it?[9]

Why is man thus alienated? and divided within? The Christian answer is that the root, though not sole, cause is in man's alienation from God. What the Adam mythos of first sin and fall from divine favor does is to state in pseudo-historical terms a supposed primary act by which the perpetual experience of man's alienation from the universe and from his fellows was originated. But far more important than the mythos is the fact to which it bears witness: that by pridefully projecting its claims to be more and other than it is—actually a creature endowed with intelligence and conscience, i.e., a "soul," but yet feeble, full of error, and of creaturely dependence upon the life of God that gave it birth—this self has cut itself off from the sustaining life of God, and consequently both divided itself within and alienated itself from other selves.

Let us explore this further. Christianity holds that man's rejection of God, either consciously or by default of any conscious relation to Him, involves man in frustration and anxiety. And how is this rejection accomplished? In a multitude of ways, every man after his own private pattern; but most frequently in keeping with the Adamic pattern of the prideful magnification of the needs, claims, and pretensions of the self beyond its proper role of dependent creature-hood. But in so doing, man cuts himself off from his deepest spiritual resource, an anchorage in that Life in which he lives, moves, and has his spiritual being. For it is the sense of man's significance as a personal being in the universe, of that universe's support of his personal being and its responsiveness to him as a spiritual being, that makes him and keeps him a man in the full sense. (The New Testament terms it a loving fellowship with God.) And when this sense of inner responsive nourishment is lost, by whatever route, man as a person becomes subject to anxiety because of the threat of insignificance, meaninglessness, and death—or nonbeing, as some philosophers put it.

Thus alienated from the Life that environs his own, man cannot live in peace with himself or in mutual love with his fellow. His own existential anxiety as a man, ministered to by the constant threats to his selfhood and being that are intrinsic to human life, and further intensified by his separation from God, drives him into division within himself and to hostile, aggressive behavior toward other men. He must continually assert his own ego in a multitude of ways against all other beings in order to sustain his own sense of being, at least sufficiently for continuance as a functioning person. Yet in so doing he feels guilty. He is aware more or less clearly that his alienation from his fellows and his aggressive use of them is wrong; that where he *should* be finding rich community in human associations, he experiences only a burdensome sense of social obligation; that instead of love, he experiences and expresses indifference and hostility. And feeling guilty, either specifically or obscurely, he is both divided within himself and resentfully hostile to all about him as the "cause" of his guilt. It is to something of this that Paul refers in the "wretched man" part of the passage with which this chapter was begun.

We may pause here to make an observation and ask a

question. The observation is to note the peculiar *intensity* of the guilt sense in the Judeo-Christian tradition. Judaism massively expressed and centrally located the guilt sense in its tradition by its elaborate sacrificial ritual that contained the explicit assumption that there is no healing of the breach between man and God, or even between man and man, without the sacrifice of a life—in this case an animal's, though probably in earlier times a human life. And Christianity was indelibly impressed by the same mark with the death of its Founder, whose crucifixion became its central symbol—guilt for which was severally distributed to every living man.

Why should this be so—that the Jew and Christian are persuaded that a man cannot cleanse his own guilt and heal his separation from others save by the sacrifice of still another? Apparently it grows primarily out of the deeply personalistic version of reality found in the Judeo-Christian tradition. For if a person, full of the sense of his own self-identity, dignity, and uniqueness as a person, is wronged, or wrongs another, how can the deed be undone? How can a broken relationship on the deeply personal level be restored? How can one forgive another who thus wrongs him by deliberate action? or how can he forgive himself—especially if that other be conceived to be the Supreme Being of all beings? Therefore, the Judeo-Christian answer has always been: only through a most costly sacrifice. True, according to Luke, Jesus prayed about his crucifiers in rather Buddhist terms, "Father, forgive them; for they *know* not what they do." But ordinarily ignorance on the part of the sinner is not allowed as a primary basis for forgiveness in Christianity. The sin of person against person is assumed to be deliberate, and its full malevolent force must be received deliberately by some person before its effect can be dissipated.

There is another element, however, in the Christian teaching about the way in which the death of another (Christ, in this case) redeems man and keeps the sacrificial act from being a merely selfish ticketing of some other being as a scapegoat for *my* sin. This is the conception of voluntary, vicarious suffering of the consequences of another's sin. Hence, the death of Christ has always been conceived by the Christian—though under some very crude and awkward theological forms—as evidence, not only of Christ's voluntary death, but also of *God's* taking the vicious thrust of man's sin into Himself, and thus demonstrating His love for man despite man's prideful alienation and self-sufficiency. The cross for the Christian is the assurance that even alienated, hostile, unlovable, unforgiving, and unforgivable man is yet loved and forgivable. Such, indeed, was the goodness of the good news that was the early Christian gospel: that in the universe there was such a power of divine "grace," i.e., rich, continuing love for man, that if man would receive it, he might be reconciled with God, with other men, and with himself. And this remains the basic Christian conviction about man's deepest healing: If a man is convinced within himself that God loves *him*, then he is able to live at peace with himself and can love his fellow man, because that inner anxiety and insecurity which formerly resulted in hostility and guilt is now removed. Now accepting himself as he is, forsaking his prideful attempts to make himself, the creature, into a self-sufficient self-creator, taking his specific abilities and capacities to be the gift of God's love, he is no longer hostile to the universe. Now at one with the life that sustains him as a man, he can, in the power of this renewal of life-giving communion, live as a man should.

To many Buddhists, particularly those in the Southern tradition, this doctrine of dependence upon another for one's salvation, whether upon a Savior or upon God, is distasteful and immoral—though, as we shall see, Buddhism has its own deep dependence upon the "grace" of Buddha. But the very terms "dependence," "salvation by faith," and "Savior" make them overlook what is of almost equal importance in Christian salvation—the response of

the saved or reconciled man. Only a very few Christian extremists, fanatically bent on asserting the absolute sover-
eignty of God at all costs whatsoever, have denied man at
least a minor part in his own salvation. And even those
extremists have been forced to acknowledge the *appearance*
of a human role in salvation, no matter how false. But the
basically Christian teaching is that neither God's revelation
nor His proffered salvation from guilt and sin can be ap-
propriated without their voluntary acceptance on the part
of man through *his* faith and repentance. Nor are faith
and repentance merely passive attitudes. Repentance means
an active, resolute turning away from past known sins. Paul
is indeed most insistent that the new life of liberty under
faith and freedom is not one of continued sin in the generous hope of God's continuing and unlimited forgiveness,
but a life that is thoroughly amended and is "dead" to sin.
And faith is a hopeful response to God. It is a courageous
affirmation of confidence in the power of God to free man
from his past, to remake his character, and to mold the
future after a different model. There is a considerable likeness here to the Buddhist "burning up" of one's past bad
karma and the creation of new and good karma.

Paradoxically, therefore, the doctrine of salvation by dependence upon another—Paul's "when I am weak, then I
am strong"—has not led as the rule to supine resignation to
one's own weak sinfulness, the continuing in known sin
that hoped-for grace may abound, or unconcern about the
surrounding world; contrarily, it has more often been
fanatically active. *You Can Change the World!* (the title of
a recent book) has frequently been its mood. And why
should this be so? Simply and purely because the Christian
depends upon Another for his salvation? No, but because
that Other, who has acted for his salvation, is also the prime
mover in the world, and in man's history in that world. The
Redeemer is also the Creator. And though the fact that the
world must be redeemed by its Creator creates an intellectual problem, the Christian has always been convinced

that whatever the solution here, there *is* a redemptive power at work in the world order; that this order, as created by God, has that in it which is worthy of redemption.

Thus, in varying degrees and ways, the Christian has hoped and worked for the redemption of the world. In the first two centuries of its history the Christian church indeed depended upon the imminent Second Advent of Christ to remake the world without any human effort save that of personal repentance and instant readiness for the Kingdom's coming. But as that hope faded and Christians found themselves yet in the same evil world, more and more they took upon themselves the task of assisting God in the task of redemption. The Jewish prophetic root of the Christian heritage—an active concern to find and express the will of God in social and political forms—sent up new shoots that maintained themselves even during the long centuries when Christendom was almost overwhelmed by the inactivism of Eastern mysticism. And since the Reformation, this mundane concern and activity for bringing the Kingdom of Heaven on earth have become full partners with the mystical quest. Indeed, in our day such concern and activity have sometimes almost monopolized the spiritual resources of Protestantism.

One last observation: In his concern for the world the Christian has at hand a further means of completing the expiation of his own sin and dissolving his sense of guilt. By seeking to be an instrument of God's reconciling love he can share in the redemptive sufferings of Christ, can thus take some of that suffering into himself voluntarily. This sense of responsibility for the world *may,* in one form or the other, tend to intensify the Christian's sense of guilt. The heathen still remain unconverted; there are wars and rumors of wars; evil flourishes; the Kingdom is yet afar off. Where have I failed? What are my sins? Even the secularist in the West often shares this compulsion to save the world; and in the absence of any living sense of God's reality, struggling alone in his feebleness, he may be quite overwhelmed by guilt and frustration. But for one who still has some sense of a "power that makes for righteousness" in the world, his efforts, no matter how temporarily unsuccessful, are buoyed up by the conviction that in the end "the battle is the Lord's"; and so he turns to work again.

b. *Buddhist Self-salvation*

Certainly, if language means anything at all, the Buddhist remedy for man's condition is quite different from the Christian remedy. The Buddhist categorically rejects "blind" faith in the power of God, the services of a savior, and the whole concept of undeserved grace.[10] Enlightenment, if it is to come (and for obvious reasons the Buddhist prefers the term "enlightenment" to "salvation"), must come through one's own efforts. The Buddha was *self*-enlightened; and so essentially must every other man be, if he is to be enlightened at all. That this should be the case is quite evident from our previous discussion of the Buddhist version of man's spiritual situation. For karmic necessity pushes each being on into new forms without cessation. There remains, indeed, the fundamental, aboriginal mystery of the very beginning of karmic individuality; but Buddhism has no sense either of logical or of religious obligation to explain this. And once given karmic individuality—whose *present* existence is certainly indubitable—we have an infallible apparatus for the self-continuation of each self by its own deeds.

Thus, to repeat, if I am a wretched victim of life, at odds with myself and others, bored or hostile, this victimization has been of my own manufacture. I have literally made my present self; I am my own creator. Or, to state it more orthodoxly, what I now am is the result of a chain of past physicomental deeds causally connected with my present status. What kind of being my present actions will project into future existence is my present responsibility. How, then, can I feel *guilty*? For my misdeeds have been against no supreme moral order or supreme God, but only my own "sins" against myself. And the selves that did the deeds whose consequence I now reap are dissolved, save for latent consequences. Hence, there is no place for remorse, and only for so much confession as will enable me to cleanse myself of impeding impurities.

Nor can I really sin against my fellows. For they, like me, are immured behind their walls of eternal karmic invulnerability. I may influence them for good or evil, but their final act is their own. Essentially I can do nothing for or against their karmic progress or decline. All attitudes and deeds that come under karmic control are inviolably theirs. I can neither harm nor benefit another beyond what his attitudes allow him to *receive* of benefit or harm. Besides, he is no more a true self than am I, but only a causally conditioned set of forward-moving psychophysical events in the final analysis.

What a Paradise, therefore, so largely free from guilt or blame, in which each man is his own master, indeed his own Maker! Yet there is a serpent in this Eden too, else there would not be so many sentient beings in it, and so much dukkha. The serpent is Ignorance, and all who remain in the realm of dukkha have been bitten by it. For though I may indeed be my own maker, I do not *naturally* know it, nor easily realize it in a way effective for my own salvation. Most of those the Buddha came to "save," i.e., enlighten, had their eyes thickly covered with dust. They were blaming others—gods and men—or chance, or impersonal circumstance, or the evil stars, for their condition, and depending upon them for their betterment. Not only does the poison of ignorance hide from me my own responsibility, but it hides from me the nature of the world in which I live. I suffer from the delusion that the world of which I am a part is more real and permanent than it is. I suffer from the delusion that I am a real, identical, enduring self from moment to moment and life to life. And I conceive that life is good, at least good enough to carry on into further new forms. Perhaps I suffer from the (Christian) delusion that this world order can somehow be permanently improved! In a word, I do not at all see "things as they are."

Therefore, inevitably, if we accept such a portrayal of the human condition as the true one, the sovereign remedy for man's sickness is *knowledge,* usually called *enlightenment.* Once gained, this knowledge will lead to man's liberation in Nirvana—equivalent in its finality and completeness to the Christian Kingdom of Heaven, or to heavenly life individually conceived. But we cannot stop here. The contrast, such as is so often made, between the Christian call for a total re-formation of the person through repentance and faith (what Luther called the healing of the evil will) and "mere knowledge" does not touch the fundamental situation at all. To be sure, liberating knowledge does have an ordinary intellectual beginning, for "how are they to believe" in karma, anicca, dukkha, and anatta, those saving truths of Buddhism, if they have not heard of them? So right belief and right aspiration are the first two steps in the Eightfold Path to Nirvana. But this is by no means the end; it is only the merest beginning of knowledge. For knowledge in the liberating sense is not information or idea. The merely intellectual must penetrate below the cerebral to the visceral level of man's life and awareness; it must cease to be another's deliverance to us, even though it is the Buddha's, and become our own insight. It must be a full, firsthand, "felt-in-the-bones" kind of thing out of which attitude and action will flow.

So it is that Buddhism often prefers to use the word "realization" for this deeper-level awareness rather than "knowledge." And even when not specifically used, it is always implied when speaking of liberating knowledge. So far as Buddhism is concerned, one "knows" in this sense only when an item of knowledge or belief has become an integral part of one's awareness and the form of his living volitions. What I truly "know," I will embody, i.e., realize, in what I am. The truth that I know will become me, my self of thought, will, and action.

Now truth "realized" thus becomes also a process of remaking the self. And in Buddhism the self is remade through the retraining of the powers of attention and the presentation of the proper objects for it to intensively focus upon. As this new mode of attention is learned, and as the chosen objects or themes are intensively contemplated to the exclusion of all other objects and thoughts, the self that contemplates them is changed, sometimes into their image, as it were; but again by means of other themes the self gains a new, i.e., detached, attitude toward them, which after a time becomes habitual and natural to the total psyche.

Such is the purpose of meditation, which is to be considered in comparison to Christian prayer in the next chapter. Its aim is to change the intellectually received truths about man's condition into vital intuitions, feelings, and attitudes within the meditator. It seeks to change knowledge into realization, i.e., to transform the self from a stream of blind craving that pushes ever forward into further dukkha-ridden forms, into a clear intelligence that dispassionately views itself and the world about it, knowing them for what they are and able in the light of this knowledge to achieve its own spiritual liberation.

4. Conclusion

How, then, shall we finally compare the two ways? Perhaps nothing more clearly sets forth the essence of the two different views of man found in Christianity and Buddhism, and the consequent implications for a redeemed or enlightened life pattern, than the figures of Jesus and Gotama themselves. For the two of them respectively embodied in their own lives, ministries, and deaths these fundamental convictions about man that their followers have taken as normative ever since. It is not that all or many Christians and Buddhists have lived up to these norms in their fullness, or that they would be found to be always radically divergent in their approach to common human situations and ways of living life. Yet there is a distinctive difference that even the passage of centuries and many dilutions along the way have not washed out.

The outlines of Jesus' life are well known. Born in a humble carpenter's family in Judea, Jesus in his thirtieth year received a divine call to serve his people through the agency of John the Baptist. His message was that God's purpose of establishing his kingdom of righteousness and peace upon the earth was even then about to come to fulfillment. The Kingdom, said Jesus, is at hand. About him he gathered a small group of disciples, and with them he went about the countryside healing and proclaiming the imminence of the Kingdom. But the religious leaders of his day were not persuaded by his message and, along with their Roman rulers, saw in the preaching of an imminent Kingdom, even though of Heaven, a danger to organized religion and the civil dominion. Therefore, when Jesus presented his proclamation boldly and directly to the leaders of his people in their capital city, Jerusalem, in the hope of their responsiveness, he was taken into custody and put to death on the cross, only at most a year or two after his call to Kingdom proclamation.

It is therefore Jesus on his cross that remains the vital and central symbol of the Christian way of life. This cross is the final consummation of Jesus' (and the Christian's) supreme prayer: Thy Kingdom come! It was the voluntary taking upon himself of the cost of Kingdom-coming, of world-changing into harmony with the will of God, up to and including the price of his own life. In this cross the Christian sees a matchless example of the deliberate involvement of Jesus, the sinless one, in the suffering of sinful men; in it he also reads the unforgettable lesson that the Kingdom will not come into the world easily; and in it he hears a command to share in its self-sacrificial involvement in the lives of men about him for their salvation and for the renewal of that world in which all men live.

It is a curious paradox that one who counseled his disciples:

Do not resist one who is evil. But if any one strikes you on the right cheek, turn to him the other also; . . . and if any one forces you to go one mile, go with him two miles. . . . I say to you, Love your enemies and pray for those who persecute you (Matt. 5:39, 41, 44),

should thus die on a cross as a religious and political agitator. (Many of his presumed followers have died for less paradoxical reasons.) But it is a paradox central to the Christian view of life. For Jesus' great renunciation, which logically led him straight from his baptism to the cross, was a *renunciation by involvement,* a renunciation of private and exclusive individuality because of the extension of his deeply personal concern to include his fellow men in their personal beings and needs. So to minister to them, in the hope of achieving a divine, universal, human brotherhood of mutual concern and help (the Kingdom), was the driving power behind Jesus' life and mission. As such, though nonviolent in its statement and pattern of conduct, this projected brotherhood fundamentally threatened the established orders of society. For the world, then as now, did not wish to be changed. The inevitable result was the cross. But it was the cross that made Jesus into Christ, the Redeemer.

The sharply contrasting symbol of Buddhism is of a man, with legs crossed, hands folded in the lap, and eyes half closed, withdrawn into imperturbable inner calm, sitting under the Bodhi-Tree. (Indeed, the Bodhi-Tree was originally the great central symbol of Buddhism, and then later the Meditator under it.) But what is he doing here? What is *his* relation to the world about him? It is also one of renunciation. For he too, as had Jesus, has renounced the world. He was a princeling, raised in luxury, married and with a child. But even in the midst of family love and physical satisfactions he restlessly sensed their essential emptiness and unreality. Therefore, he renounced them and turned to the life of a "homeless one" who, like Jesus, had nowhere to lay his head.

When we see Gotama under the Bodhi-Tree he has come

at last to the end of the way of renunciation. He will sit here under the tree in meditation until he pierces through the veil of ignorance that enshrouds all human knowing and cuts every bond that binds man to dukkha-ridden existence. And he succeeds! He pierces through to a knowledge of things as they are, the knowledge that life in this world is full of impermanence, suffering, and emptiness; and in the coming of that knowledge all desire for that world of selves and things dies within him. Thus the physical renunciation of the princely life is consummated in the spiritual-mental quality of equanimity, a *renunciation by detachment*.

Thus does Gotama become the Buddha, the enlightened one, whose final counsel to his disciples, before his death forty busy but peaceful years later, was "Be a lamp unto yourselves." And the Man under the Bodhi-Tree, with the ineffably serene smile upon his face, has become the central symbol of the Buddhist way of life, world conquest by world denial. For the Buddhist way of changing the world is primarily that of changing the individual. Indeed, the individual's world is all the world that matters. The Buddhist saint will not involve himself in the sufferings of others or the mundane concerns of the world, lest he too sink self-destructively in the maelstrom.[11] His own best defense and the way in which he can best help another is to create within himself a calm, dispassionate, center of benevolence and equanimity. Thus does he "save" himself, since

> When a fool hates a man that has no hate,
> Is purified and free from every blemish,
> Such evil he will find comes back on him,
> As does fine dust thrown up against the wind.[12]

And from the stillness of his equanimity he can radiate to all other beings the healing of his own peace.

Yet curiously the contrast between the Cross and the Bodhi-Tree, and the Men whom we find thereon and thereunder, is neither so stark nor so simple as this. And the coercive forces of our own contemporary world may make the contrast in the divergent ways of life flowing from these two supreme symbols, even less. For there is in Buddhism also the tradition that the future Buddha consented to be born as Gotama in the fullness of time; and though inclining after his Enlightenment under the Tree to go on into his own Nirvana at once, yielded to the intercession of the heavenly spirits to speak his words to men in the hope that some of them, with less dust in their eyes, might penetrate to the liberating truth of detachment even as he. In Mahayana, or Northern, Buddhism this has become a major theme, taking the form of the doctrine of the Compassionate Buddhas who have sworn to remain outside Nirvana until all other creatures are redeemed. Thus even the cold-seeming dispassionateness of the One under the Bodhi-Tree is in actuality a mode of greatest compassion—though it is a compassion of resignation rather than of resistance, of impartial benevolence rather than of ardent love.

But in our time even Southern Buddhism is also modifying its traditional pursuit of the aloof equanimity of the enlightened arahat to the neglect of active compassion. One now hears much of the compassionate giving of his life by the Buddha-to-be, when even during his lives in animal form he laid his physical life on some altar or other of sacrifice for his fellows that they might live. For instance, the Jataka story of the Buddha's compassionate giving of himself to a hungry tigress to keep her from devouring her own young (immortalized in a Japanese painting) circulates with renewed popularity. And the scriptures are today assiduously searched for instances of the Buddha's practical helpfulness to fellow monks and lay people during his forty-year teaching career after his Enlightenment.

What has occurred? Mostly it is that the material values and needs of modern (Western) civilization are pressing in upon Buddhist civilizations with ever-increasing force. Both Western-born capitalism and communism are inciting peo-

ples of the world, directly or indirectly, to rise up in their
space-time concreteness as craving human beings to seek
the materially abundant life and cease to think of themselves only as slaves of misfortune and past evil karma. To
this pressing demand for democratic freedoms and higher
living standards, even though they belong to the realm of
samsara and not Nirvana, Buddhism must make some meaningful response. And this it does by emphasizing the latent,
until recently ineffective, elements of social concern, public
welfare-mindedness, and compassion within its own tradition.

But finally, to cap the paradox, just as this dynamic structure of values is moving in upon the East and causing it to
awaken the Meditator under the Bodhi-Tree to the world
about him, there is in the noncommunist West a deepening
uncertainty about the worth of those skills and accomplish-
ments in which it excels. Does the increase of scientific
knowledge inevitably bring healing? Does the attainment of
a high standard of living dissipate man's basic problems?
or does it create new ones as fast as it solves old ones? Does
increase of intellectual knowledge bring happiness and self-
mastery in its train? Can even the Christian be as sure as
he once was that *he* knows what God's plan in history is,
where his Kingdom is to be established, and in what form—
a Kingdom for whose presumed establishment in varied
forms at varied times, oceans of tears and blood have been
shed? Thus the Christian on his side is made newly aware
of a statement attributed to Jesus by John, "My kingdom is
not of *this* world," and of another from Luke, "The kingdom
of God is *within* you." He begins to remember again that the
cross is as much a question as an answer; to remember that
Jesus himself struggled beforehand to know the *meaning* of
the cross while still in Gethsemane. And so in a sense the
Cross and the Man on it move nearer the Bodhi-Tree, as
the Bodhi-Tree and the Man under it must perforce move
nearer the Cross, if man is to be saved from *both* guilt and
dukkha.

(V)

Christian Prayer
and Buddhist Meditation

Every religion that develops sufficiently to achieve its own peculiar way of life chooses a distinctive set of methods for gaining its desired spiritual goals under the conditions surrounding human existence. By these methods, which we may call spiritual techniques or disciplines, religions seek in varied form and proportion: some measure of practical welfare, inward calm and assurance despite all outward disturbances, certain feelings or states of mind that are conceived to be of highest worth, and contact with a transcendent reality of some sort. Therefore, if we can isolate and study the characteristic spiritual techniques of a given religion for achieving its desired results, we may learn in such a study some things about a religion that cannot be learned elsewhere, certainly not by a sheerly philosophical study of doctrines. For at the level of discipline or technique we are in the area where the ideal and theoretical values of a religion impinge directly upon the physically actual and individually practical situation. What happens there is both very important and most revealing.

When we come to consider Christianity and Buddhism in this connection there are, of course, two words that immediately spring to mind: prayer and meditation. Prayer is at the heart of all Christian piety and devotion; and meditation is the one and only way recognized by Buddhism for the attainment of its highest spiritual goals. Indeed, one can say of meditation in Buddhism, perhaps even more inclusively than of prayer in Christianity, that it *is* Buddhism in its essence. Its practice is what the Buddhist conceives to be unique about Buddhism; and what may have been added to this in existing Buddhism is nonessential or peripheral. But in any case observation of the Christian at prayer and the Buddhist at meditation will present in sharp focus some aspects of the differing geniuses of the two faiths as nothing else can.

1. *Initial Contrasts*

Immediately upon hearing the terms "prayer" and "meditation," two divergent images form in our minds. *Prayer* means petition; petition directed toward a superior being. Once popular, but now largely archaic, forms of speech use the language of prayer even on the human level: the subject "prays" his sovereign, the socially superior person, or the parliament to hear what he has to say. But the root meaning, of course, is drawn from the religious realm. Religious language of the usual sort is full of petitions to supernatural beings for all kinds of things: safety from danger or enemies, birth of children, healing and health of body and mind, long life, nourishment and riches, success in an undertaking, victory in battle, vengeance on foes. Or, in a more spiritual vein, there are prayers for forgiveness, justice on the earth, reconciliation of men, peace, courage, strength in adversity and persecution, insight, purification of heart, the vision of God, immortality, and the like. There is perhaps nothing in the whole category of human desires that has not been prayed for in the course of human history.

There are, of course, other forms of prayer that represent the other side of the petitioner's religious coin: thanksgiving and praise, for example, for any of the above items that have supposedly been received as the result of prayer. (In some cases praise and thanksgiving have only been ways of ensuring further benefits, and therefore types of inverted petition.) Whatever the content and form of prayer, however, it usually implies a personalistic conception of the

One addressed—though primitive religions have been long in separating impersonal coercive magic from true personalized prayer. This personalistic reference seems implicit, perhaps essential, in all prayer. Thus writes a contemporary:

Now what is the meaning of prayer's assumption that God exists? Is it not simply that there is a Reality over against us which yet responds to us, a "stupendously rich Reality," in the words of Baron Friedrich von Hügel? If no such reality exists, the whole business of prayer falls to the ground. It becomes autosuggestion, or worse, autohypnosis. It becomes a monologue, not a dialogue. *Prayer of the Christian sort stands or falls on the assumption that God is, and responds to needful, aspiring men.*[1]

There is one other form of prayer that is not necessarily antipersonalistic yet that strains at the boundaries of at least a narrowly conceived personalism, and that is adoration. Adoration is, in some sense, of course, the heart of all worship: the rejoicing of the worshiper in the presence, goodness, and love of God. Yet it may become a wordless regard of an intense order that reaches toward contemplation and the mystic vision and therefore is on the edge of something else than prayer. To this, and to its importance for our consideration, we shall return later.

The usual connotations of "meditation" are quite different. One that comes to mind at once is that meditation is a solitary experience, solitary in every way. It implies not only physical solitude—which may also be associated with prayer in its private forms—but also the fact that there is neither other nor Other to whom meditation is addressed. For one does not address meditation; it is not for or to something or someone, but upon something or someone in his absence. Meditation is self-inclosed, similar psychologically to a daydream—though carefully and deliberately directed and controlled in the Buddhist sense of meditation. Its basic presumption, therefore, is self's aloneness with the self, if possible, physically, but *necessarily* so, psychically.

Thus if one of the main purposes of prayer is the achievement of spiritual *fellowship*, a major hope in meditation is the achievement of *aloneness*, true and absolute aloneness with one's own self. Meditation seeks for the full self-control of body and mind, so that one can shut out all unwanted presences of men or gods—even the presence of one's own thoughts, even the sense of "I" itself! So it is that some forms of Buddhism speak of the final goal of meditation as "voidness" or "emptiness." It is "the mood of an experience free from the 'I,' and therefore disindividualized, whose substratum may, analogically, be compared to infinite space."[2]

The relation of prayer and meditation might therefore be diagramed as that of polar opposites:

PRAYER		MEDITATION
In public or private, but to a Spiritual Presence.	Undefined	Both physically and spiritually solitary.
Spontaneous; two-way communion; personalistic in nature; petitional.	Middle Ground	Disciplined; controlled; self-contained; contemplative; nonpetitional.

2. *Christian Prayer*

We shall begin with what is most familiar in the West: prayer. And in our consideration of prayer we shall begin with its more familiar form, termed "prophetic" prayer by Friedrich Heiler in his volume *Prayer,* but here called "classical New Testament" prayer. From there we may proceed to less familiar forms, meditational and mystical prayer.

a. *Classical New Testament Prayer*

New Testament praying is strongly Jewish in form and content in that it is concrete and personalistic. And this we may regard as the primitive form of all Christian praying.

It is well typified in the so-called Lord's Prayer, which has been classically formative of much in Christian tradition and practice whatever its original source. According to Matthew, it was first spoken by Jesus in these words:

> Our Father who art in heaven,
> Hallowed be thy name.
> Thy kingdom come,
> Thy will be done,
>   On earth as it is in heaven.
> Give us this day our daily bread;
> And forgive us our debts,
>   As we also have forgiven our debtors;
> And lead us not into temptation,
> But deliver us from evil
>   (Matt. 6:9–13).

We may briefly note the outstanding features of this prayer. Evident at once is the quality of *personalistic mutuality*. God is addressed in personal fashion as "Father" —intensified in English by the intimate form of the second-personal pronoun "thy." And a petitional form of address prevails throughout: "give," "forgive," "lead," "deliver." So also is the same personal-mutual quality extended toward men: "Forgive us . . . as we also have forgiven our [human] debtors." Human-divine-human mutuality is here a virtuous, life-giving circle of interpersonal relationship; that is, one cannot receive spiritual renewal (forgiveness) for himself without extending it to others as well.

There are other notable features. There is a deep personal-social-historical consciousness here embodied in the prayer for the coming of the Kingdom (to earth). From Jesus' other teachings about the Kingdom of God we know that it is inclusive of all the following factors: personal renewal and healing of mind and body; reconciliation of men with God, and men with men; immediate, present spiritual power *and* future historical embodiment in some form or other.

There is also a wide range of both spiritual and physical fulfillment sought here. It is indeed true, as many have urged, that the coming of the Kingdom is the overriding purpose of this prayer, and consequently perhaps of Christian prayer in general. Or on a more individual level it is deliverance from spiritual evil. Some would urge that the petition for daily bread is to be understood also in the sense of *spiritual* nourishment. Whether or not this is so, there is considerable in Jesus' other teachings that indicates his deep concern with the physical needs of men—hunger, thirst, pain, disease—and the coming of the Kingdom as to some degree ministering to the physical, as well as to the spiritual, needs of man.

The course of Christian prayer in the centuries since has quite generally kept in view all the concerns mirrored in the Lord's Prayer. If one goes through the public prayer books of various Christian churches, listens to the public prayers used in Christian worship, or knows what the average Christian prays for, the gamut of all the above interests is sooner or later run through—though the dominant emphasis will vary from church to church, time to time, and person to person. Prayers for physical benefit are not strange to Christians, and indeed various modern groups like Christian Science and contemporary American healing cults strongly emphasize physical healing as one of the to-be-expected results of prayer. Prayers petitioning for personal and national safety and welfare, for peace and prosperity, for victorious peace in wartime, continued peace in peacetime, and for guidance of national leaders, also appear. Mingled with these are petitions for spiritual benefit: illumination upon personal problems, strengthening of faith, dissipation of doubt, enlargement of loving concern, conversion of nonbelievers, and the coming of God's Kingdom on earth.

It should be observed that despite this wide range of subject matter there has been considerable concern within Christian circles as to the *proper* content of Christian prayer. That there has been and is a great deal too much unabashed petition for purely personal and physical goods in Christian praying goes almost without saying. No doubt even today the quantity of prayer for such goods would outrank the quantity of prayer for "spiritual" benefits, especially if we consider that some of the latter are as full of self-concern as many of the more crassly physical-benefit prayers. Such prayers rather directly follow from the basic Christian prayer assumption that God as Heavenly Father is interested in *all* his children's concerns and that God as God sufficiently controls the physicohistorical order of the world to effectuate such answers. And there have been weighty names put behind this opinion:

When Thomas Aquinas, following Augustine, laid down the principle, "It is permissible to pray for whatever it is permissible to desire," he only puts into a concise formula the Biblical and early Christian belief that there is no difference between prayers for spiritual and prayers for material things. Luther speaks still more specifically: "We ought to bring before God all sorts of necessities; first, spiritual needs; after that, common temporal needs of this life on earth."[3]

Heiler himself suggests a kind of desirable balance here with regard to prophetic (i.e., classical, Christian) prayer:

The object and "goal" of prophetic petition is the affirmation of a good, whether a personal one—belonging to one's own or another's ego—or a superpersonal one. The material values [however] which are the exclusive end of primitive prayer are less significant than the spiritual ones.[4]

But there is another current of thinking about prayer that would go far beyond Heiler's compromise position. It is the conviction that it is totally unchristian to pray for material and first-personal benefits. (We shall note later that the *mystics* go beyond even such questionings to affirm that any or all petition whatsoever is unspiritual.) Prayer should be limited, according to such, to the truly central spiritual concerns of the human soul. Thus:

Bunyan gave this rule upon his death-bed: "Before thou enterest into prayer, ask thy soul, 'is thy business slight, does it concern the welfare of thy soul?' " And under the influence of Jansenism, Pascal prays: "I know that I know but one thing: that it is good to follow Thee, and that it is evil to grieve Thee."[5]

Then does, or should, this spiritually minded "ban" upon prayer for externals extend to prayer also for *others*? This is not readily evident; for intercessory prayer appears to avoid the grossness of selfish and material interest, and perhaps even represents a lofty height of attainment in Christian praying. And besides this, it has been so central to the Judeo-Christian tradition and practice through the centuries that one can scarcely think of prayer at all in the Christian context without including its intercessory forms.

For example, take that Old Testament devotional collection, The Psalms. It is indeed true that many of the prayers therein show the pray-er praying primarily for himself—and it must be confessed frequently for unspiritual goods. So also even his prayers for others often have as their ultimate goal the personal benefit of the pray-er, even at the cost of the misfortune or destruction of others. Yet these prayers do unmistakably imply that petition for others, whether "positive" or "negative," is an integral and effective part of prayer. And in the New Testament this Jewish heritage of intercessory prayer is not only taken for granted but also, in its intensified and purified form, becomes central to the Christian practice. Jesus prays for the spiritual enlightenment and strengthening of his disciples, for the healing of the sick, and for the coming of the Kingdom of God—his central concern. Now prayer for the Kingdom's coming, of necessity, includes petition for the increase of God's direct activity among men other than oneself and implies a confident expectation that the act of praying itself will be an actual instrumentality toward that end. Paul specifically prays that his converts may be strengthened in their faith, guided in their Christian living, and healed in body and spirit—as well as for the conversion of the unbelieving.

And one may point out that in the centuries since, prayers for the purifying and empowering of the church, the protection of men from danger and destruction, their conversion to the truth, and the coming of the Kingdom among them, have engrossed a major part of the church's praying energies. Even for the mystic, prayer for others is perhaps the least objectionable of "external" prayers—though he does often suggest that the *best*, if not the sole, way even to pray for others is to pray for one's own purification in order that he, the pray-er, may become a channel of grace rather than a rock of offense to his fellows. And the mystic further suggests that the specifying of presumed direct benefits for one's fellows, however well meant, had better be left to God's discretion than to man's.

One other value of prayer, germane to its essence in Christianity and often paramount in actual Christian practice, must not be passed by without notice. This is the realization of a sense of the presence and fellowship of God gained through the practice of prayer. That such a hope should be found in the context of the Judeo-Christian sense of God as personal, a sense that expresses itself in the language of Fatherhood, is inevitable. The expressions of this desire in Christian devotional literature are multitudinous, but it would be hard to find a better one than the following, from a hymn attributed to Francis Xavier:

> Not with the hope of gaining aught,
>   Not seeking a reward;
> But as Thyself hast lovèd me,
>   O ever-loving Lord!
>
> E'en so I love Thee, and will love,
>   And in Thy praise will sing,
> Solely because Thou art my God,
>   And my Eternal King.

Before we come back at the end of the chapter to a further consideration of the implications of this position, or before we turn to the meditational and mystical forms of

Christian prayer, we may ask whether there is any identifiable *method* in the New Testament classical type of Christian prayer. Almost we can say, "No." For it is largely true to characterize such prayer, as does Heiler, as primarily a "discharge of emotion," as an "outpouring of the soul," a "crying unto God out of the depths." In prayer

simply and without restraint, the petitioner unveils himself to God; he confides to him the agitation and tumult of his inmost soul, his fears and troubles, his desires and hopes, even his doubts and rebellion.[6]

With regard to such naïve and natural prayer, uninhibited in its forms and unashamed with regard to the objects of concern, modeled on the likeness of spontaneous conversation, the word "method" scarcely has meaning.

Yet Christian prayer even of the ordinary sort has not been quite so unschooled and unmethodical as this might suggest. There is, of course, a general pattern for the form of prayer, loosely analogous to meditational techniques: kneeling or prostration, with closed eyes, in a place apart from others, or in a sanctuary surrounded by sacred and significant symbols in company with other worshipers. The same effort is made, as in meditation, to keep the mind from "wandering," though by less rigid means such as the initial reading of a passage of Scripture or another's prayer, or looking at or calling to mind some Christian symbol or theme, and focusing the attention upon it for a time. From this inspirational springboard the would-be pray-er seeks to launch himself into his own personal prayer. But once launched, though having been taught the ways of proper Christian prayer or ostensibly taking as his model the Lord's Prayer, the heartfelt pray-er tends to follow the direction of spontaneous feeling and thought rather than any method or model.

b. *Meditational Prayer*

This is not a traditional title for such prayer as I am about to describe, yet it seems to be better than any other that can be used in the context of a comparison with Buddhist meditation; for there are some elements here that are much more like meditational practice than the ordinary prayer described above, and that, therefore, tend to close the gap between them. I refer here to the pattern of prayer represented by the *Spiritual Exercises* of Ignatius Loyola, a pattern that has exerted a profound influence both inside and outside the Jesuit order founded by Loyola. Before considering the method of prayer prescribed by the *Exercises,* we should put them in their proper religious and historical context. Loyola was much influenced by the medieval monastic conception of the good Christian life. For though the *Exercises* were written with the layman in mind and though his situation is given specific consideration in them, yet the clear implication is that the best life is one of abstinence and self-denial; virginity and sexual continence; frequent fasting; meagerness of food, raiment, and worldly estate.

The other consideration to be borne in mind is that the *Exercises* are geared directly into the confessional system of the Roman Catholic Church. They are a kind of manual for the *director,* i.e., Father-confessor or chaplain, by which he is to be guided in his guidance of the exercitant, or practitioner, of this way of praying. The likeness of the work of the director, who must not pry into the private thoughts and sins of the souls he is directing but who must be given a periodic progress report by the one he is directing, to the work of the Buddhist guru or meditation master, is unmistakable.

The *Exercises* are well named. They are a species of spiritual calisthenics by whose title is meant "every method of examination of conscience, of meditation, of vocal and mental prayer . . . every way of preparing and disposing the soul to rid itself of all inordinate attachments, and, after their removal, of seeking and finding the will of God."[7]

They are designed for an intensive period of four weeks' practice, though this period may be altered as to length or content at the discretion of the director; and it is further quite conceivable that this general method was considered by Loyola as valid for *all* Catholic prayer. If the *Exercises* are practiced in their fullness, they require some five hour-long sessions per day during the four weeks: one at midnight, one upon rising, one during the day, one before supper, and one before retiring. The prescribed themes for each week are as follows: sin, particularly one's own, for the first week; the life of Christ through Palm Sunday, for the second; Christ's Passion, for the third; and his resurrection and ascension, for the fourth.

In general, the method of praying is this: The chosen theme is so fully developed by thought and imaginative elaboration that its content becomes almost visionary in its vividness and seeming reality. By the imaginative process itself emotional power for action is produced. In Loyola's terms of faculty psychology all "three powers" of the soul are engaged: *memory; understanding* of what is remembered, meaning elaboration of its doctrinal significance; *will,* i.e., the imaginative visualization of the remembered and understood materials until they come to an emotional boiling point overflowing into intention and action.

Two specific examples of the practice of the *Exercises* will give their flavor. The first example is from the second exercise of the first week, in which the theme is sin. After a brief prayer to God to direct the exercitant's intentions and actions, the latter proceeds to think of his soul "as a prisoner in this corruptible body, and to consider my whole composite being as an exile here on earth."

From here he proceeds on to five successive points:

First Point: A calling to mind of his own sins year by year, place by place. "Three things will help me in this: first, to consider the place where I have lived; secondly, my dealings with others; thirdly; the office I have held," i.e., work done or position occupied.

Second Point: Weighing the gravity of his sins, considering their loathsomeness.

Third Point: A humbling comparison of himself with other men, angels, saints, and with God. Contemplating the corruption of his own body, and himself as a source of moral and spiritual corruption to others.

Fourth Point: A detailed comparison of the goodness of God, His attributes, with the pray-er's own opposite qualities.

Fifth Point: "This is a cry of wonder accompanied by surging emotion as I pass in review all creatures. How is it that they have permitted me to live, and have sustained me in life! . . . How is it that the earth did not swallow me up and create new hells in which I should be tormented forever!"

There follows a final colloquy or prayer in which he extols the mercy of God, thanks him for granting him life, and in which he resolves "with his grace to amend for the future. Close with an *Our Father*."[8]

The other example, from the second week, has more concretely visual materials. Its theme is the incarnation, and in general it follows the same pattern as the above. In the course of the meditation the exercitant visualizes at several times the Trinity as They look down from Their heavenly throne upon the earth; he vividly endeavors to see

those on the face of the earth, in such great diversity of dress and manner of acting. Some are white, some black; some at peace, some at war; some weeping, some laughing; some well, some sick; some coming into the world, and some dying.[9]

He also beholds men as they blaspheme, sin, and descend into hell; he visualizes the Trinity as They plan for man's salvation, Their sending the angel to Mary, the conversation that took place and the physical details of the house where Mary lived. Then finally after some contemplation on what he has seen in order to draw some spiritual fruitage therefrom, he ends with a prayer for "grace to follow and imitate more closely our Lord."

c. *Mystical Prayer*

While that type of meditational prayer outlined by Loyola may seem a considerable step away from spontaneous petitional prayer, mystic prayer represents a still further removal out into the undefined, intermediate ground toward meditation pure and undefiled. It will be an important question indeed, at a later point, to inquire whether the higher reaches of mystical devotion can be called prayer in any meaningful sense. But for the moment we may turn to the stages of attainment in mystical prayer.

A term that is often used among mystics is that of "the ladder of prayer." This figure expresses accurately what the mystic seeks to achieve by prayer. He wishes to "elevate the soul" to God. In fact, the ultimate aim of the mystic is what he calls "union with God," which in this world means a complete oneness of will with God's will with frequent moments of such nearness that he can no longer sense any difference between himself and God. (Some mystics spoke of "deification.") And in the life to come the mystic hopes for the complete absorption of himself into God's being. With the outward world and its goods and goals, mystic prayer obviously has nothing whatever to do. The "ladder of prayer" is then a descriptive metaphor of the various levels of prayer each of which ever deepens into the next stage or level until gradually but surely the pray-er is brought to his goal. Or we may say it is a description of a continuing process of self-development by which the narrower and partial self is ever expanded and remade in the image of the Eternal Self that the Christian calls God.

This ladder has been variously described by different mystical writers. Here we shall follow Evelyn Underhill in distinguishing three main types of prayer along the way toward union with God.

(1) *Recollection or Meditation*

Recollection is here used in the sense, not of memory, but of the re-collection of the scattered and distracted forces of one's mind and heart from a multitude of concerns. It is the Christian analogue of what the Buddhist refers to, perhaps a little more sharply, as "one-pointedness of mind." And its method is that of meditation, meditation on one central theme which at first may seem narrow and meager, but which in the end will become an opening door into a new world and lead ultimately to a deep awareness both of oneself and of that God who is found within.

Isolation during such prayer is of course essential. One must "set a ring of silence" between himself and the outer world.[10] He must intensify this silence by steady concentration on his one chosen theme. And then he must wait quietly for something to happen, not trying to force himself, or make it happen before he is ready for it to happen.

Cease but from thine own activity, steadfastly fixing thine [spiritual] Eye upon *one Point*. . . . For this end, gather in all thy thoughts, and by faith press into the Centre, laying hold upon the Word of God, which is infallible and which hath called thee. Be thou obedient to this call, and be silent before the Lord, sitting alone with Him in thy inmost and most hidden cell, thy mind being centrally united in itself, and attending His will in the patience of hope. So shall thy Light break forth as the morning, ... the Sun himself, which thou waitest for, shall arise unto thee.[11]

During this stage the emphasis must be upon man's effort, even though it is only the effort to keep the mind attentive and though it is a patient waiting. How long this stage will continue one cannot say. But there comes a change at last.

(2) *The Prayer of Quiet*

It may be that the pray-er suddenly realizes that his prayer has changed in quality; but probably the change has been going on gradually, and it is only now that he realizes it. In either case he begins to be aware of a new naturalness and ease of prayer. The prayer seems to speak itself, as it were, almost without the pray-er's effort. This does not mean a fluency in the use of words. Indeed, quite the contrary. One becomes more and more aware that words are less and less needed in this kind of prayer. Hence it is often called the prayer of quiet, "a wordless breathing of love in the immediate presence of God." Or in the words of Madame Guyon, such prayer "is not a single act, or series of acts which the soul undertakes, but the essential state in which the soul lives."[12]

Increasingly the "quietness" of prayer deepens into what seems at first a bare aloneness or nothingness. Thus does Evelyn Underhill finely describe it:

> The state of "Quiet" . . . follows, generally, on a period of deliberate and loving recollection, of a slow and steady withdrawal of the attention from the channels of sense. To one who is entering this state, the external world seems to get further and further away: till at last nothing but the paramount fact of his own existence remains. So startling, very often, is the deprivation of all his accustomed mental furniture . . . that . . . he can but describe it as a nothingness, a pure passivity, an emptiness, a "naked" orison [i.e., prayer].[13]

But in the midst of his own self-emptiness the pray-er—if he patiently and devoutly waits—discovers a fullness.

> Presently, however, he becomes aware that *Something* fills this emptiness; something omnipresent, intangible, like sunny air. Ceasing to attend to the messages from without, he begins to notice That which has always been within. His whole being is thrown open to its influence; it permeates his consciousness.[14]

Thus does the prayer of quiet deepen into wordless contemplation of this Something. The demanding sense of I-ness that fills so much of our waking attention, or its substitutes, the things to which I-ness busily attends, fade to almost nothing. That Infinite Something, which the Christian mystic calls God and which is yet also something within himself, permeates the total consciousness.

(3) *The Prayer of Union*

Union with God represents the ultimate mystic goal. That

sense of separation between finite and infinite, subject and object, prayed-to and pray-er, is overcome. In the prayer of union there is no need of any words whatsoever. To repeat the words of Madame Guyon, prayer at this point is not an act "but the essential state in which the soul lives." To be thus at one with God, with the quiet waiting in emptiness become full of Divine presence, this *is* prayer.

> Better than best that ear hath heard
> Is uttered now without a word
> To loving heart and lowly.[15]

And at the same time that the pray-er has become aware of the universal presence of God, he himself has become something more and other than he was at the beginning.

In the midst of his active work, his incessant spiritual creation, peace and joy enfold him. He needs no stretched and sharpened intuition now: for he dwells in that "most perfect form of contemplation" which "consists in simple and perceived contact of the substance of the soul with that of the divine." . . . In that mysterious death of selfhood on the summits of which is the medium of Eternal Life, heights meet the deeps: supreme achievement and complete humility are one.[16]

3. Buddhist Prayer and Meditation

Strictly speaking, there is no prayer in Buddhism. Yet as a matter of fact various prayer forms have attached themselves to the Buddhist structure, particularly in Southeast Asia. We shall begin at the outermost layer with a kind of prayer practice that is condemned and disowned by many Buddhists, but is defended by others as not incompatible with Buddhism though perhaps not of its essence.

a. Prayers to Spirits

With the elevation of the Buddha to a status far above that of the gods but denying him any capacity to answer prayers, or indeed any interest in the usual concerns of petitional prayer, and with retention of a vivid belief in the reality of those same gods, a paradoxical situation has resulted in Buddhism. For those who take the high way to Nirvana, the monks, no-prayer Buddhism is sufficient. But for the common man who yet lives in this world and is not ready for the supreme quest, Buddha has little help. Hence, he has turned to the gods for the satisfaction of his material interests, even while he keeps alive in himself the hope of a sometime far-off quest of Nirvana.

Thus it is that alongside the Buddhist pagoda, sometimes even on its very precincts, a Buddhist may pray to the spirits from whom he hopes to receive health and long life, riches and honor; and a few paces away he offers to the Buddha image his flowers and genuflexions in the hope that *all* that he does thereabout will finally add up to progress toward Nirvana through the celestial mathematics of merit. In Burma the demoted Indian gods have blended with native earth, air, fire, and water spirits, and the spirits of departed relatives not yet made perfect who malevolently haunt the regions they once lived in. The result is a wide range of beings called nats, whose shrines are everywhere, often cheek by jowl with Buddhist holy places. And on occasion even high government officials make their offerings to these nats in the hope of securing material blessings for the national good. There follows a prayer offered on such an occasion:

Ye *Bummacos* [nats of earth], *Rokkhacos* [nats of trees], *Akasacos* [nats of skies], and nats of sun, moon, fire and rain, not excluding *Kandawshinma* [Lady of this great lake], *Komoyothakin* [master and lord of the nine towns], the whole lot of *Wizzas* [thaumaturgists] who happily dwell in forests, *Lokapalas* [guardian nats of the world], [all] other plentiful masters and lords, and also the offside thirty-seven *devatas* [gods] and the inside thirty-seven *devatas,* I [an official] and the multitudes of Burmese citizens hereby, in holy *puja* [worship] and seeking refuge in you with high hope and in great anticipation, offer you coconuts, bananas, and also [foods] of various sorts.

As a sure result of this holy *puja* and offering may the power-ful nats guide the citizens and act in such a way as to fulfill whatever they wish and long for! [I or we] pray that by the unhesitating aid of the [nattish] powers of the rejoicing [nat] king of the rains, with no mistake . . . and with great manifesta-tion of [undoubted] evidence, this great lake which is the grace of this town and whose name and fame resound throughout [the land], be filled quickly, immediately and within a short period from now with raindrops and hailstones falling in great numbers with great noise and thunder, and may it overflow with lovely streams of water of silvery hue for all to see, a pleasant view without delay![17]

But another letter to the editor in the same issue indicates clearly that for some Buddhists at least such prayers have nothing at all to do with *their* conception of Buddhism.

In your issue of the 14th instant, you mentioned that the Cabinet has decided to erect two Nat-shrines, assigning the Ministry of Religious Affairs to implement this decision. . . . Whatever reasons the Government may have for this measure, we should, nevertheless, analyze the conception of "Nat-worship" with a view to find out . . . the effect it will have on the teachings of the Buddha.

If we are to search [out] the meaning of nat-worship, it is in brief the same as the primitive conception of "god-worship". . . . Gotama Buddha (624–544 B.C.) was the First Teacher, who taught mankind to dispel the concept of "god-worship" (i.e., a Micchiditthi, or false view) and to work out one's own sal-vation with diligence. He expounded the highly scientific ex-position of the LAW OF KAMMA. . . .

How can a Buddhist, therefore, dispel the conception of god or nat-worship while at the same time indulging in the practice of nat-worship?

Yours truly, A student of Abhidhamma.

b. *Pagoda Prayers*

However, even though we utterly cast nat worship out of the fold as completely un-Buddhist, there still remains a more Buddhistic type of prayer devotion centering around the pagoda. It is significant in this connection to note that the Burmese word for pagoda, *payah,* is the same one used for the Buddha himself. Thus a pagoda, because of its consecration to the Buddha and its containing of his images and/or relics, is in a sense the Buddha presence itself; and prayers, i.e., "fervent wishes," made in these holy precincts are more likely to be effective here than elsewhere, whatever their substance. Some pagodas consequently acquire a considerable reputation for "answering" prayers:

There are many pagodas that are called Hsutaungbyi, or prayer-fulfilling pagodas. The Rev. Kyiganshingyi, in his Myittaza, writes a model prayer for a layman to a Hsutaungbyi Pagoda: "By virtue of the good deed I have done in offering Thee this food and cool water and this bunch of flowers, may I get all the things I have prayed for. May I be unparalleled in length of life, beauty, happiness, strength, readiness of wit, pomp, and fame. May I in all my existences be able to learn in an instant, without special study, the Pitakas and Vedas [Buddhist and Hindu scriptures] and the eighteen arts and sciences so that I may be able readily to instruct all men as though pointing out the full moon in the sky. And may men and spirits in the three planes of existence love me as dearly as a mother loves her son."[18]

But again there is the counterblast from the fully orthodox Buddhist. The above, says the Venerable U Thittila, is a *perversion* of Buddhism.

Understanding that neither a god nor ceremonies can help or save him, the true Buddhist finds no place for prayer; he feels compelled to rely on his own efforts and thus gains self-confidence.

What the Buddhist worshiper *should* think and say as he offers flowers before a Buddha image is this:

These flowers I offer in memory of the Buddha, the Holy One, the Supremely Enlightened One. These flowers are now fair in form, glorious in color, sweet in scent. Yet all will soon have passed away, their fair form withered, their bright hues faded, their scent gone. It is even so with all conditioned things which are subject to change and suffering and are unreal. Realizing this, may we attain Nibbana, perfect peace, which is real and everlasting.[19]

With this latter interpretation we come yet closer to orthodox Buddhism and its doctrine of meditation. Thus viewed, Buddhist "prayer" even in popular form is essentially only meditation upon the transience of human life and the beauty of the Buddha's character.

But before we come to full-scale Buddhist meditation, there is one further element to consider. And we may best do it by noting what one author has called the "Buddhist Common Prayer," which is a type of devotion often done before a Buddha image and/or in the presence of monks:

I beg leave! I beg leave! In order that any offence I may have committed either by deed or by mouth or by thought may be made void, I raise my clasped hands to the forehead and crouch down humbly to worship, adore, and revere the Three Gems [the Buddha, the Law, and the Clergy], once, twice, three times. As the result of this act of reverence, may I be freed at all times from the four planes of woe, the three scourges, the eight local faults, the five enemies, the four corruptions, the five ruinations, and quickly attain the Path, the Fruition, and the Noble Law of Nibbana, Lord.[20]

Here is a combination of self-help and Other-help elements, still somewhat in the prayer orbit, but also strongly attracted toward the meditational pole. The Common Prayer, and others like it, is only effective *after the doing of a meritorious deed*—often making of an offering at the pagoda, or feeding the monks—and in proportion to the magnitude of the deed. The good deed represents a certain power of spiritual capital or force in the hands of its doer. With this in his possession he has a certain control over its application and may direct it into a specified form or area, somewhat independently of either gods or the Buddha.

There are indeed stories in the Buddhist scriptures and tradition of the seeking of all types of goals through merit-powered prayer wishes, from curses upon others up to and including the pious desire for the quick progress of all living beings to Nirvana's peace.

It is obvious that this fits directly into the conception of the suffusion or radiation of benefit directly toward other persons that we have noted in the discussion of Buddhist loving-kindness. There is in it no necessary reference to gods, though of course it implies a kind of order in the universe that makes such influence possible. And such prayers are usually said in the presence of holy images or persons. But again, illustrating the variety of opinion in Buddhism, prayer may be considered as almost entirely an inner psychical force that depends not at all upon the presence of monks, Buddha images, or gods. Thus wrote a notable Burmese scholar, the late U Shwe Zan Aung:

A strong driving force of desire urges us from within and a genuine prayer prompted by such a feeling will help us to form a definite goal. Such a prayer, if repeated in earnest, will aid us in the concentration of our thought on the object prayed for. The concentration of our mind reacts on our will which grows. . . . With our developed will power, we would build up, or reform, our character so as to reach the end in view.[21]

c. *Buddhist Meditation*

We come now at last to what Buddhism considers to be the essence of its way of life and the true equivalent of prayer in other religions, no matter what perversions have occurred along the way or what concessions historical Buddhism has made to the masses. For classical, orthodox Buddhism completely denies the efficacy and value of petitional prayer, either as it is practiced in other religions or though it may be directed toward the Buddha himself. That spiritual technique in which it puts all its trust, and which it affirms in its true form to be unique to Buddhism, is meditation.

(1) *Method*

The method of Buddhist meditational practice offers both striking likeness and contrast to Christian prayer. We may simplify its progression into three major steps.

(a) *Withdrawal*

As in Christian prayer, so in Buddhist meditation, the initial step is withdrawal, both physical and spiritual-mental. Solitude is initially a primary requisite for the meditator, and is always *desirable* for meditators at all levels. In early Buddhist times the place was a solitary tree in good weather, and a cave, hut, or cell in rainy weather. The purpose of solitude is, of course, to reduce physical distractions to the minimum. One specific Buddhist feature must be added: proper posture. While not maintaining, like some Hindu yogins, that a given posture of itself produces insight, Buddhism considers posture important. Lying, pacing, or standing are allowed, but the recommended posture for meditation is sitting in the position made familiar by Buddha images: cross-locked legs, hands idle in the lap, spine erect, and eyes half closed.

Obviously, as also in Christian prayer, mental withdrawal is more essential than physical. Indeed, the expert may learn to shut himself away by a "ring of silence" even in a crowd. The goal is to be utterly alone with oneself and one's thoughts—and not too many even of the latter. For the weakness of the ordinary kind of attention, says the Buddhist, is that it jumps from interest to interest like a monkey in a tree, or flickers from item to item with lightninglike rapidity. Indeed, it is more than a mere weakness: this inability to keep one's mind concentrated is the essence of his inability to achieve salvation! Therefore, it is necessary to cultivate, through meditation, a special type of intense awareness, the one-pointed mind to whose description we now turn.

(b) *Concentration*

Concentration is the name for the method used to inwardize and perfect what physical withdrawal begins: the complete centering of the attention at will by the meditator. And it is also the name for the second stage of spiritual development, good morality being presupposed as the first.[22] For even though one be a good man morally, such virtue will not achieve that detachment in him which alone brings one to Nirvana; nor will merely physical isolation and a generally quiet frame of mind bring the highest insight. There is within each man a vast territory of diverse thoughts even though sense stimulation be held to a minimum, as when sitting with closed eyes in a cell. The pinpointing of attention on some one object or theme, its holding there without wavering, and its complete control by the meditator, comprise the quality of spiritual-mental power sought here.

To this end, some subject or object of meditation must be adopted. *What* it is makes little difference so long as it can be used to achieve one-pointedness of attention. Thus there are physical devices such as the *kasiṇas,* or variously colored discs, put just far enough away from the eyes to serve as a convenient focal point for them. Even a circular opening in the wall will do. Or various themes may be employed, such as the Buddha's virtues, the four Divine Abidings, peace, the repulsiveness of food, or the various stages of the decomposition of a corpse. There are traditionally some forty subjects for meditation that are variously suited to specific types of temperament and lead to specified types of absorptions. And their basic purpose is to *unify* and *simplify* the total field of attention so that only one type of sensation or feeling remains in consciousness.

And how does one decide upon which theme or object to meditate? This is the function of the meditation master, or guru, with whom the beginner in meditation is counseled to start. Out of his own experience and growing knowledge of the meditator's personality the guru prescribes for the meditator. And though a meditator may freely choose his guru, having once chosen his master, the guru's help will be of value only if he unreservedly trusts his guru and puts himself completely in his hands. Of course problems of personal relation may arise in the form of hostility feelings or unduly affectionate attachment. The meditator must be steered through these distractions and be led to find resources within himself for balance and insight—strengthening his own forces of purity or good karma, the Buddhist would say. He stays with his guru until the latter can teach him no more, or they mutually agree that they are not compatible, or the meditator is able to take up meditation on his own. How like this is to the efforts of the Western psychiatrist and his patient is of course quite obvious.

A classical device, now very popular in Southwest Asia, is yet to be mentioned: what is called body-mindfulness, or meditation upon one's own bodily processes. The advantages of this are obvious: one's body is always with him, and where more vividly than here can certain truths of Buddhism be realized, such as the impermanence and emptiness of all things and selves? Body-mindfulness takes several forms. One may meditate upon the act of walking as he paces slowly back and forth, analyzing each step into a lift-swing-drop rhythm. Or he may concentrate on the breathing rhythm, either in the abdomen or at the nostril—this being done while seated. In any case, the purpose is the same: to unify and simplify the area of consciousness-awareness till it contains only one item: the rhythm of walking or of breathing.

How deep does concentration carry one? He may, and this is the classical Buddhist pattern, seek to make it absolute, so deep that absolutely all other sights and sounds are shut out and he achieves a jhanic trance, or absorption. Or it may be at a lower level called access, or neighborhood, concentration, just deep enough to push all distractive thoughts and sense awareness to the subconscious periphery of attention, which is sufficient as a requisite for the most important kind of meditation, namely, insight meditation.

(c) *Insight Meditation*

This third level of meditative practice is fundamentally an extension of the second level. Or better, the technique of one-pointedness of attention achieved at the second level may now be applied in a way that will lead on to enlightenment. (For second-level concentration skill is a mere technique, not intrinsically valuable. And the absorptions experienced thereby are *not* nirvanic enlightenment.) As a beginning the now one-pointed attention may be turned to other body parts or processes than the breathing, until, by the tingling, burning sensations that follow upon such focused attention, the meditator increasingly knows-feels in himself that his body is indeed only a composite of physical factors, transient in nature. When one so sees himself as a "no-body" he is laying the basis for liberation from attachment. For how can one seek to serve and love a body that is truly a nothingness? This burning is also seen as a process of purification, in which past bad karma is "burned up" (the only way to escape its effects), and the forces of purity (good karma) within one are further strengthened. Like a man tending a trash fire, the meditator must, by concentrated attention, keep stirring his body-consciousness into the purifying fire of detachment. For Buddhism holds that mental and spiritual ills express themselves in body tensions and ills, are often, indeed, one with them.

This concentrated type of attention must also sooner or later be focused on one's own *mind-states*. Even the thrilling recollections of his jhanic absorptions (if he has experienced such) must be put through this acid bath of concentration until the meditator realizes that they too are impermanent and essentially worthless, no matter how pleasant. He must also know directly in his own consciousness that he is a "no-self," that selfhood is nothing to cling to in passionate devotion but is a harmful delusion.

This is the high plane of clear detached attention, Bare Attention it is sometimes called, in which, without any emotional excitement, in the absence of any consoling or inspiring visions, a part of oneself simply observes what goes on within—thoughts, feelings, physical sensations. The observing awareness (the real I?) is above all this, unaffected by it, though fully conscious of it. (Zen Buddhism speaks of this state as an emptiness, as do some Christian mystics of the state of quiet [see above p. 150], but *without* expecting another Presence to be discovered.) In this Buddhist awareness one truly knows that he is no self, either bodily or spiritually but only a series of processes and thoughts; that all other "realities" are also thus empty and transient. And he is not disturbed by what he sees, but experiences a sense of illumination, peace, and freedom from all bonds of any sort. A Buddhist exponent thus describes this type of awareness, or enlightenment, in its maximum degree:

Having destroyed the roots of the mania of the "I", for them [the liberated meditators] the net of illusion has been burned, their heart is transparent with light, they are divine beings, immune from intoxication, untouched by the world. . . .

Unconquered, supreme, he [an awakened one] has laid down his burden; he has no "home" and he has no desires. Passion, pride, and falsity have fallen from him like a mustard seed from the point of a needle. Beyond good, beyond evil, he is loosed from both the bonds and, detached from pain, detached from pleasure, he is purified. . . .

Since he knows, he no longer asks "how?" He has touched the depths of the element free from death. He has abandoned the human bond and has overcome the divine bond, and he is freed from all bonds.[23]

(2) *The Goal of Meditation*

The supreme and *ultimate* goal of meditation is, of course, Nirvana-attainment. And when Nirvana is thought of as that ultimate condition in which all birth-death individuality comes to an end, we can see that it is both a religious and metaphysical goal that is sought in meditation. Indeed, it is this hope of final Nirvana-attainment which gives all their basic value to the states achieved in meditation; they are sought after *primarily* because they lead Nirvanaward, not because they are delightful per se. Thus, to the extent that it envisages Nirvana as its final goal, meditational method goes far beyond those psychological and psychiatric therapies which seek primarily only to achieve a working harmony within damaged and disrupted psyches. Meditation as a way of salvation implies that *all* psyches, except those of the saint, are damaged and need the ultimate healing of Nirvana-attainment.[24]

But in terms of *proximate* goals sought by meditation we may speak of the peaceful, radiant quality of the arahat's or Nirvana-bound saint's life as that which is supremely desired. Or we might say that meditation seeks to achieve Nirvana *in its presently experienceable form.* Thus we may sketch the kind of experience sought in meditation in terms of the knowledge-experience achieved by the third and highest level meditation noted just above. Three defining qualities of this goal-experience can be distinguished:

1. *A comprehensive self-unity moved and determined completely from within.* In this context the saint may be said to be the fullest perfection of selfhood, a superself, as it were. Now it may seem contradictory to use such a description of the final result of a meditational process that seeks to *destroy* the sense of selfhood in the individual, root and branch. This will be more fully dealt with in a later chapter; but here we may say that within the seeming negativity of no-soul (anatta) doctrine, there is a deep and perhaps more fundamental positiveness. For the saint in Buddhism is the one who is not misled by *false* ideas of the self or distracted by the motions of partial and false selves within his own being. He denies that his body, or ordinary consciousness, or any combination of the two, is a self. But he does this in the interests of establishing a truly inward center of spiritual self-control, which, when established, makes him completely immune to all sensual lures, all gross appetites, all mental distractions, all ups or downs of fortune or feeling, all fears including those of pain and death. He becomes impregnable against all internal or external forces whatsoever, the complete master of his own spiritual

destiny. Whether we *call* this a "self" or not is perhaps immaterial.[25]

2. *An absolute equanimity and detachment.* This may be only another way of looking at that absolute self-determination of inward states that we have just described, but it suggests another dimension of some importance. Whatever is truly of myself—thoughts, feelings, attitudes—I can control. No disturbing outward circumstance, pleasant or painful, can move me one hairsbreadth from my intentions or shake in the slightest my utter self-control. Why? Because I am utterly *detached*. For only those things to which one is emotionally or intellectually attached can really move him. Therefore, even though I am bodily sawed in two by enemies or tortured in any of several ways, no slightest flicker of resentment or ill will can arise in me—if I have reached the arahat's state. So completely has the process of meditation cut the bonds of my attachment to individualized existence in any form that there is nothing left to respond in hate and anger, severe though the physical pain might be and fully malevolent though the intentions of my torturers.

This detachment carries over to persons, as we have observed in the discussion of Buddhist loving-kindness. The height of developed loving-kindness, as it is also the goal of meditation, is a detachment both from self *and* others of such depth and quality that one cannot distinguish between his own welfare and being and that of another. Absolute equanimity comes to pass. Indeed, the saint who has achieved jhanic powers, as well as meditating at the third and highest level, may at will enter into what is called *nirodha-samāpatti,* or "extinction of perception and feeling," in which state—it may last up to seven days—

the bodily, verbal, and mental functions have been suspended and come to a standstill, but life is not exhausted, the vital heat not extinguished, and the faculties not destroyed,[26]

—as they would be in death. To "outsiders," of course, such

a one does appear to be dead; but sooner or later he comes back.

3. *Universalized feeling-knowledge.* That the Buddhist calls his highest levels of attainment "wisdom," "insight," and "enlightenment," is significant. For in common with the Christian mystic the Buddhist saint maintains that however inexpressible the final truths he comes to know through meditation may be—so that silence is their best description —they are yet truths and not mere feelings or private emotions. This ultimate knowledge is, of course, no mere knowledge composed of intellectual information. It is of piercing intuitional directness, like physical seeing, that needs no thoughts or words by means of which to know. It is also more than intellection, because it involves the total person in the knowing-feeling awareness; it is a kind of knowing that is also a state of being and a mode of living.

This knowledge is of penetrating universality. It includes a complete knowledge of oneself, in the case of the Buddha extended to a knowledge of millions of past existences—a caliber of total recall far beyond the wildest dreams of the Western psychoanalyst! The saint too is promised something of these same powers. But however we interpret this recall feature, the essential significance is clear: one who is sainted by meditation knows himself inside and out so completely that there is no unknown unconscious, no hidden subconscious, out of which unexpected and harmful tendencies may arise to trouble his calm.[27] This kind of knowing has been also a means of becoming; the totality of his psyche has been unified and purified on the level of the highest terms of his experience—clear, calm dispassionateness. In him, knowing-feeling-being-doing have become one act, a continual state of existence.

The words of Delacroix about meditative contemplation, though spoken about the Christian mystic, exactly describe what happens here:

Contemplation installs a method of being and of knowing.

Moreover, these two things tend at bottom to become one. The mystic has more and more the impression of being that which he knows, and of knowing that which he is.[28]

But is there aught else that the saint knows besides himself? Of the Buddha it is said that by his enlightenment he came to "see things as they are." To the Westerner it will seem more accurate to say that he was able to see *through* things. He knew that all tangible, perceptible entities (things, persons, worlds) whatsoever, are ultimately unreal, impermanent, and tainted with suffering. "Things as they are" are empty, unsatisfying delusions by which men are ensnared to their own everlasting bondage—unless they too see through these mere appearances. And this seeing through the emptiness of tangible realities and ordinary satisfactions is of the essence of the saintly vision—though the saint does not achieve the omniscience of the Buddhas, which is a capacity to know all that is knowable. As one sees through the delusions of self or soul and real physical worlds, so he cuts the bonds of affection that hold him to them and gains the glorious liberty of the sons of Enlightenment.

This liberty must not be seen as purely individual detachment, even though the language used about it often suggests that it is, and though the type of human involvement envisaged by the Buddhist may seem thin and deficient to the Christian. For the universalization of knowledge into the depths and widths of the saint's insight is also a universalization of pity and benevolence. *Because* he sees through the emptiness of self-illusion and of appearances, he can extend to other sentient beings a nondiscriminating, completely inclusive loving-kindness. Their joys are his joys, friend and foe alike, insect or god equally. To them all he sends forth pure, unattached, disinterested benevolent regard to the end that the forces of their own purity within them will be strengthened and that they shall be speeded along the way to ultimate release.

But we must persist with another question. When things

are seen through, is there beyond their emptiness no Transcendent Reality to gladden the eyes? This is an almost unanswerable question, for its anwer lies in the unsharable depths of the nirvanic quality of experience; and because the only *words* the Buddhist will use about the ultimate vision of the saint are negative ones. Southern Buddhists still speak in terms of the illusions they have seen *through* even at the highest level of insight; the sublime vision is that there is no-self or that all is impermanent. And Northern Buddhists speak of emptiness, or the Void, or Suchness, i.e., an ultimate quality in which there are no distinctions whatever. Certainly there seems to be expected no ultimate vision of God, no Presence that gloriously fills the emptiness. And of course if we speak of a "vision" of Nirvana, this is most unsatisfactory, because Nirvana is held to be the contradiction of all that can be felt, seen, heard, thought, or imagined. In a figure of speech the saint has climbed to the top of the mountain, above all clouds and shadows; once there, only a Glorious Nothingness is to be seen; and Glorious Nothingness—calm, clear, cool—is delightful for itself.

Yet this Nothingness—another name for Nirvana?—has in it a kind of luminousness. Around the experience, and near-experience of it, hovers the aura of the Absolutely Real and Supremely True, besides which all other experiences of all other realities and truths are dwarfed to nothingness. How else account for the monk's low-breathed words (p. 30) describing Nirvana as "bliss unspeakable"? Indeed, men come back from the nirodha experience of seeming death, refreshed in mind and body; and those flashes of the the sight of Nirvana itself, vouchsafed to the saint in his last existence, though seeming blanks, are yet considered highest knowledge and ultimate reality. Indeed, a Buddhist now and then will say that the *un*reality of ordinary experiences and truths, so much emphasized in Southern Buddhism, is but the hither side of the truly Real, the Nirvana-Element; that in the discovery of the unreality of the ordinary, the fullness of the supremely Real shines through.

Only to the worldly-minded who grasp greedily at the shadows of selfhood and thinghood does it seem nothingness or emptiness!

4. *Final Considerations*

In conclusion, what can now be said about the comparability of Christian prayer and Buddhist meditation? Can Buddhist and Christian meet even on the opposite ends of a common platform of similar goals and methods? Is any cross-fertilization possible here, or are the two forever separate?

With regard to the polarity of what Heiler calls "prophetic" prayer—the emotional, petitional outpouring of the heart to God for the changing of natural and historical circumstances and events—and pure meditation, there can be no meeting. The two are irrevocably, undeniably separated in nature. This does not mean, of course, that Christian and Buddhist *practice* are that far apart. Indeed, as earlier indicated, it may well be that the vast majority of Christians *and* Buddhists regularly practice this kind of prayer. But there is this difference: for the Christian, such prayer is embedded in the heart of his central tradition—though the mystics have protested some of its features; but for the Buddhist, praying in this sense is a completely un-Buddhistic perversion, or at most a dubious concession to human weakness. Thus, in praying, the Buddhist denies the essential nature of his own spiritual tradition. The most that a Buddhist can grant in this direction is the efficacy of the fervent wish which, made upon the basis of meritorious deed and in loving spirit, may influence the outside world. And though materially efficient power has been attributed to such wish-force, or will-force, in the past—such as turning away wild animals and vengeful foes, harmless and subdued— today's Buddhism tends to speak more cautiously in the vague generalities of extending loving-kindness to all sentient beings rather than in specific influences.

Now this raises an interesting question, at least by implication, about Christian prayer. Is the Christian also losing *his* confidence in the power of his peculiar spiritual discipline (prayer) tangibly to change the world? Not that there lack those who still pray convincedly for rain, for success in personal undertakings, for safety in danger, for national prosperity, and for health. Yet by and large, with the growth of scientific knowledge and theory about the mechanical regularities of the world order, there are fewer Christians who pray petitions of a world-altering intent. We may here quote from a contemporary scientist of Christian persuasion:

An indispensable element of worship is, or should be, prayer. What is happening to it—because of the effects of new knowledge?—Are we able to pray more meaningfully because of the new things we know? or more fervently? with a keener sense of God's presence? In particular, what is happening to *old* prayers? In the light of natural law, can we still pray as did our forebears, with the confidence that prayer makes a difference, say, in the outcome of physical processes as well as of spiritual ones, in nature as well as in history? . . . A distinguished theologian recently said to me: "I could never pray specifically for rain, or food, or physical healing. For spiritual healing, perhaps. In the last analysis the petitionary prayer I pray is for the presence of God in my life, with all this implies."[29]

That this is an increasing tendency among Christians can scarcely be doubted. And that lessened confidence in prayer for world alteration likewise affects the same Christians with regard to their prayers for other *persons* cannot be doubted either. Many postscientific Christians may still be willing to "pray" for others with a kind of telepathic faith in the exertion-at-a-distance of spiritual or even psychosomatic influences, but it is a rather thin shadow of the robust intercessory petitions of their Christian forebears.

Now there is a double-sided anomaly here. One side is that it is precisely with the practice of intercessory prayer that the Christian *experientially* draws nearer to the Buddhist than he does at many another point. For though the Buddhist does not believe in a God who answers prayers, even unselfish ones for others, and though he does believe, as do most mystics, including Christian ones, that the primary and perhaps only effect of prayer or meditation is upon the pray-er or meditator himself, and through him indirectly upon others and the outside world, he also believes, as we have seen, that one who is purified by meditation becomes thereby capable of radiating a powerful godlike benevolence out upon other creatures in a genuinely objective way. Might we not call it *intercessory meditation* in which he engages?

But the other side of the anomaly is that Christian prayer seems to be moving toward Buddhist meditation in its quality, and in its sense of primary efficacy for the pray-er, *because* the Christian has lost some of his confidence in the power of his intercessory prayer to help others. Thus as prayer moves toward meditation in its subjectivity on the one hand, it does so in a *negative* sense that takes it farther away from Buddhism on the other. Should Christian prayer become like Buddhist meditation in form, i.e., nonpetitionary, it would by the same token lack the Buddhist confidence that the pray-er, now become a meditator, can in actuality directly affect others. Thus we should have the resulting paradox of a nontheistic Buddhism that has more faith in the efficacious exertion of spiritual forces upon others at a distance and unknown to them than does a theistic Christianity that has a God to pray to for such results, but is less assured of His power to thus respond to prayer and hence has moved toward Buddhist meditation in its practice of prayer.

That some such movement is taking place in Christianity, let it be repeated, can scarcely be doubted. Whether when it gets "there" it will find contemporary Buddhism likewise less assured of the power of its "intercessory meditation" because of the same scientific influences is an interesting if unanswerable question. But it should also be remembered that as Christian prayer tends toward conceptualizing itself as a process of inward personal transformation rather than world change (the Buddhist pole) it also moves toward its own mystical tradition, by which it was asserted that truly spiritual praying is entirely for the purpose of inward transformation, and perhaps even nonpetitional altogether. How far Christianity will go in this direction remains to be seen. Whether this will become in fact a movement of increasing strength toward the rediscovery of its own mystical resources is likewise yet to be determined. What appears *more* likely than a reinvigoration of the Christian mystical tradition in theological terms is perhaps a renewal of mystical prayer or meditational practices under secular psychological stimulation.

For it is quite obvious when we speak in terms of the inward transformation of selves—as do Buddhism, Christianity, and psychiatry alike—that we are on some sort of common ground. What the nature of that common ground is, and whether divergent values and methods found respectively in meditation, prayer, and psychotherapy will achieve anything but confusion is not at all certain. In some sense their various goals are one: the healing of the human spirit. For all assume that many human spirits are in need of healing: Buddhism and Christianity on theological and experiental grounds; psychiatry on the basis of the empirical observation of many cases of psychic wreckage. And all work in the hope that demons of inner disturbance (however described) can be exorcised, and that broken psyches can be restored to health. So, too, there is some likeness of method, even though in quite different contexts. In each case there is an attempt to ventilate and free the subconscious potencies of the psyche and to unite them with the conscious life in a dynamic unity. And all are agreed that bodily health is deeply dependent upon spiritual-mental health.

By and large, the Western Christian is much closer to psychiatry than he is to Buddhist meditation, partly because he is geographically closer to its centers and partly because psychiatry has grown out of his own culture, either as a "help" to religious processes or as a secular substitute for them. In another context, however, Christian prayer and

Buddhist meditation must be set over against psychotherapy. For they are per se religious, and psychotherapy is not. What does this mean practically? That, as religious, prayer and meditation assume embracing world views and transcendent values in whose context the human healing must take place. The Christian says that through prayer a man repents of his sin, i.e., his rebellion against the will of God, and is thereby healed within and reconciled with the basic order of reality. He thereby becomes a new creature freed from bondage to his past. No less a reconciliation can solve his basic problem and creatively relate him to his fellow man. And the Buddhist maintains that only by meditation is one's subjection to the order of individualized existence (karma-dharma) overcome; that as a man sees through the unreality of this present self and this present world, he becomes capable of apprehending the only ultimate reality, Nirvana; that only an apprehension of this magnitude frees man from his basic illness.

By contrast, psychotherapy is secular, or neutral, in nature. Per se it recognizes no ultimate values in the religious sense nor necessary world views. Intelligent psychiatry must indeed be aware of the social, cultural, and geographical realities of the world in which renewal of the broken self is to take place in order to adjust it satisfactorily to its environment. But beyond this general kind of environmental orientation, psychiatric method demands nothing. It has no interest in bringing the patient to a specific world view, or particular theological beliefs and moral convictions. Quite indifferently, quite pragmatically, whatever adjustment "works" for the individual is "good." A functioning self-unity, sufficiently acceptable to the environing society to keep the patient from hurtful collision, is psychiatry's basic value and reality. This is probably closer to the Buddhist meditational pattern, where there is less emphasis upon theological belief and rigidly moralistic goals, than to Christian prayer. Yet the fundamental contrast between the nonreligious and the religious viewpoints remains even here.

This is a field of tremendous interest and future potential —as also of considerable confusion of statement, method, and goal—that is being developed and explored from all sides today, as the many volumes on religion and psychiatry attest. Into its breadth we cannot go here, but may conclude with some basic questions that the situation poses for Christian devotion. Presuming that Christian devotion will continue to move more in the direction of prayer as a vehicle of self-transformation than of world change, what effect will this have upon Christian practice and life? Is the description of prayer given years ago by George Santayana (much more like Buddhist meditation in spirit than like classic prophetic prayer) sufficient and desirable for Christianity?

In rational prayer the soul may be said to accomplish three things important to its welfare: it withdraws within itself and defines its good, it accommodates itself to destiny, and it grows like the ideal which is conceives.[30]

How will this development affect the richly personalistic and ethically oriented devotion of Christianity? Will such a change unrecognizably dilute and weaken the strong sense of divine-human fellowship and communion that has been the fountainhead of Christian devotion in the past into a theosophical-mystical type of impersonal awareness and contemplation? How shall the Christian keep his concern for the world about him vigorously alive within his piety if his prayer becomes almost entirely a matter of self-examination and inner spiritual development? Will he find himself caught between two Gods, or rather the *God* of the inner life and the *Force* that moves the world, and thus split into two ineffective halves that religious unity of inward ideal and vigorous historical action achieved by the prophets and Jesus, the peculiar hallmark of Christianity?

How these questions are to be answered is not a matter of futuristic prediction but a matter of such development as the future course of Christianity makes *possible* to it.

(VI)

The Conquest of Self

In a previous chapter it was suggested that for Buddhism the essence of liberation (Buddhist salvation) is the resolution of the problem of selfhood. Indeed, more than any other major religion Buddhism gives itself directly and specifically to this problem. The scriptural canon of Southern Buddhism gives an overwhelming amount of its attention to questions that have to do with the destruction of false ideas of the self and with the weaning of man away from the delusions clustering about "self." Much attention is given to the development of a "true" self, the self of enlightenment. But language betrays us here, since Southern Buddhism seldom if ever speaks of a true self even when describing methods of self-control necessary to liberation. Even these latter are spoken of in the context of the total destruction of all selfhood, the achievement of complete selflessness. It sometimes takes considerable penetration to find the lineaments of that "positive" selfhood which comes to light only through the negation of all selfhood.

Yet Buddhism is not alone in its concern about selfhood, even though it may be distinctive in its negativistic approach to the problem. For in some sense selfhood is a major problem in all religions, even those of theistic and metaphysical nature like Christianity. Even here it is the concern of the faith to save selves. And while Christianity saves selves in the context of divine power and grace, yet the evidences of salvation and the meaning of salvation are to be found in the transformation of the self from less worthy forms into the image of its Creator. And Christianity too is concerned to distinguish the self that must be "lost" from the one to be "found." And it too, as Buddhism, speaks of selflessness as the prime quality of the saved and liberated life in Christ.

It will be the interest of this chapter, then, to explore further the ways in which Buddhism and Christianity deal with the self. We have already in previous chapters made many references to Buddhism's doctrine of no-self and its classification of all ideas of a personal, continuing identity as illusory. We have also noticed in the foregoing chapter something of the meditative discipline of the self. Here we shall try to penetrate more deeply into these areas, particularly the Buddhist conquest of the self under the banner of selflessness, and to relate it to that Christian emphasis upon selflessness which Christianity has come to regard as peculiarly its own.

The use of the conception of selflessness as a bridging term between the religions offers difficulties. It is an English word and deeply tinctured with Christian meanings. For when the Christian speaks of selflessness he has in mind his own version of self, and a correlated type of self-denial. Therefore, his bridge word—even when accepted and used by the Buddhist as it often is today—may not actually cross the chasm as intended. It may be a circular walk out and back to the user's own side, not even in hailing distance of the other shore. Hence, the term must be used with due caution, but profitably perhaps, since the very differences in the connotations of Buddhist and of Christian selflessness may throw as much light on the problems of interfaith understanding as any area we might discuss. We may at least learn something more of the width and depth of the chasm that separates Buddhist and Christian.

1. *Christian Selflessness*

The classic Christian statement concerning selflessness is found in these words of Jesus:

If any man would come after me, let him deny himself and take up his cross and follow me. For whoever would save his life will lose it, and whoever loses his life for my sake will find it (Matt. 16:24–25).

These words were shortly given their definitive demonstration in Jesus' own fatal cross-bearing in Jerusalem.

And under the banner of selflessness we can assemble a family of related meanings that will here be, as they have before been, used almost synonymously: "unselfishness," "self-sacrifice," "sharing," "self-giving," and of course the gospel term of "losing" oneself or one's life. Selflessness may then be taken to stand for *all* these terms, with occasional lapses into the use of these others for the sake of variety.

If we shall ask what are the defining characteristics of Christian selflessness, what first comes to mind is perhaps the practical manifestation of helpfulness. Sometimes we call this self-sacrifice or sharing. By this we mean that the sharing man deliberately includes the needs and concerns of others within the totality of his own needs and concerns; and by thus reducing the monopoly that self-interest usually exercises upon his time and efforts he "sacrifices" some part of his own self. This is also the general meaning of *un*-selfishness—taking from oneself to give to others. It is unnecessary to belabor this point of which Jesus gave many illustrations both by parable and in his own living. The obligation to share is also found in Buddhism, it may be remarked in passing, in what is called *dāna sīla,* the morality of generosity and almsgiving. What is distinctive in the Christian usage is the fact that such a limitation of self monopoly is not, as it is in Buddhism, considered to be on the lowest level of the conquest of the self, one that must be transcended, but is often portrayed by Jesus as *of the essence* of self-conquest.

We may also remark that this quality of practical helpfulness has been outstanding in the Christian interpretation of the faith. To be sure, the actual manifestation of such helpfulness has had its ups and downs, its ins and outs, in

Christian history. And often its adequacy as a full or dominant expression of Christian selflessness has been questioned; but never its essentiality or legitimacy. The real question for the Christian has not been whether or not, but how much? What proportion of his individual time, physical strength, and material resources should he give to religious establishments or to the unfortunate? How *un*selfish should he be in actuality? And the answers have ranged anywhere from the giving of what one "can afford," through some stated proportion of income such as a tithe, to include those who, like St. Francis, have personally owned nothing at all and therefore technically have been *completely* selfless.

But there is a deeper level of selflessness in which not only is there a sacrificial sharing of material elements but the sharing of one's own *self* in friendship and personal mutuality with others. To be fully Christian, such mutuality must cut across the bounds of caste, group, race, and religion; for "if you salute only your brethren, what more are you doing than others?" Here selflessness manifests itself in direct personalized involvement with other individuals in all their specific individuality. It is neatly summed up in the "second" great commandment: "You shall love your neighbor as yourself," i.e., in the same concerned, first-person sense in which one regards himself.

It should be pointed out here, near the farthest limits of self-sacrificingness, that there have been some radical interpretations which maintain that Christian selflessness means self-erasure, and such self-erasure, not in the romantic-mystical merging of two selves into one, but in the practical sense of trying completely to destroy within oneself all self-regarding motives or thoughts. By some this has been expressed in ascetic hostility to the body; such have believed that to humiliate, torture, or reduce bodily needs to the barest minimum consonant with the maintenance of life is to "crucify" the self. A *theological* form of this is represented in the dichotomy set up by Anders Nygren, in his *Agape and Eros,* in which all self-love or human-love (*erōs*) is eternally separated from true Christian love (*agapē*).

There is also the social form in which the individual from semimasochistic motives, apparently, seeks utterly to efface himself as an individual of preferences, personal desires, or personal rights, and to "give" himself completely and absolutely for the spiritual and material welfare of certain others.

This will always remain an area of great practical tension and uncertainty for the practicing Christian. He may well affirm that in order to give of himself to others there must be a self of some consequence to give to others, not a washed-out, nonindividual self; that the essence of Christian mutuality is the coming together of selves in their particularity and uniqueness. He may also point out that some forms of supposed selflessness are either forms of securing attention for the selfless individual, or actually an obsession with oneself under the form of self's destruction. (Such is his dark suspicion of the techniques of Buddhist selflessness.) Yet it seems hard to believe that there is not a radical difference between self-love and other-love, between *erōs* and *agapē,* and to believe that one can serve another in serving himself. The actual balance between the two, and the form that other-love shall take, cannot be solved by any easy spiritual arithmetic.

This brings us to consider a concept or image that has played an immensely important role in Christian theology, art, music, and devotional life; it is on the border line between the practical and the theological-mystical expressions of selflessness. I speak of the theme of vicarious suffering, first expressed in The Book of Isaiah in the portrayal of the Suffering Servant, and then (in the Christian view) fully and supremely exemplified in the death of Jesus on the cross. Two or three verses from the former passage, and one verse from the New Testament, will give the essential quality and meaning of this concept:

> Surely he has borne our griefs
> and carried our sorrows;

yet we esteemed him stricken,
    smitten by God, and afflicted.
But he was wounded for our transgressions,
    he was bruised for our iniquities;
upon him was the chastisement that made us whole.
    and with his stripes we are healed.
All we like sheep have gone astray;
    we have turned every one to his own way;
and the Lord has laid on him
    the iniquity of us all.

                            (Isa. 53:4–6.)

For the Son of Man also came not to be served but to serve, and to give his life as a ransom for many.

                           (Mark 10:45.)

The questions raised by modern Biblical scholarship as to the original meaning of the Isaiah passage and whether Jesus himself used the latter words about his own lifework cannot be entered into here. Suffice it to say that it appears that Jesus was greatly influenced in his own conception of his divine call by the imagery of the Suffering Servant, and that the church immediately put Jesus' own death on the cross into the same context.

To state the exact meaning of vicarious suffering is much harder than to say that it expresses, perhaps supremely, the Christian doctrine of selflessness and has been of immense importance in the Christian tradition. Christians themselves have been radically disagreed on the *theological* and *sacramental* significance of vicariousness. One has only to remember the wide range of theories of atonement, i.e., theological formulations of how the death of Jesus on the cross can save other men, and the various theories of the Eucharist—transubstantiation, consubstantiation, and symbolic significance—to become acutely aware of these differences. Still further, it is even more difficult to state this doctrine in a meaningful way to a Buddhist *self*-salvationist. He will almost inevitably be misled by the extreme literalism of some interpretations of the self-sacrifice of Jesus, or by the metaphysical theories that have been developed from it with regard to the relation of God and man and the interrelations of the "Persons" of the Trinity. And the Southern Buddhist inclines to see in this approach to salvation the absolute antithesis of all that Buddhism stands for. To him it will indicate that according to Christianity one person can be saved by the deeds of another; that cheaply and easily he has only to call upon that Other for such merits and powers as make this salvation possible—all of which Buddhism categorically denies as efficacious for salvation.

We cannot here make a definitive and comprehensive statement of the meaning of vicarious suffering and the atonement of Christ. We shall briefly state something of its central significance for the Christian. The doctrine means and implies at least the following:

1. Both sin and goodness are in great part interpersonal and social in nature. (Sociologically, this may be termed the fact of social solidarity.) Not only are the forms of virtue given to one by his society and culture, but more basically each person, both in his vice and virtue, is organically related to others. There is no such thing as being morally good or bad, saint or sinner, all by oneself in the complete inwardness of his own self. Each one lives by and is helped and injured by the goodness and badness of others respectively; and in turn his own moral success and failure affect them as well.

2. One's own suffering bears little or no integral or apprehensible relation to his sin. Such is the negative contention of Job; such is implied in the portrait of the Suffering Servant in Isaiah—one who in spite of, or even because of, his own innocence suffers the results of the sins of others; and such is the fully explicit manifestation in the voluntary death of Christ on the cross. The Christian teaching is that knowingly and consciously he there died for, and because of, the sins of others. Indeed, the cross reverses the verdict of much of the Old Testament—Job and the Suffering Servant part of Isaiah excepted; sinless-

ness may expect more, rather than less, suffering. There is no room here, of course, for the Buddhist contention that this life's suffering is the product of a previous life's sins.

3. In view of the above, suffering must be *accepted,* at least for one's self, as an integral part of life. The Christian cannot explain it. Jesus did not explain it. He sought to lessen the suffering in other lives, and as the price of this lessening of others' suffering he took upon himself *more* suffering. His death upon the cross was in full identification of himself (though innocent) with the suffering of other men (though guilty).

4. All this implies that man cannot save himself by his own efforts alone. He needs the help of his fellow men with whose sins and virtues his own are so intimately intermingled. He needs the help of a structure of grace and strength in the universe (which he calls God) to which he must relate himself organically in order that its fullness may enter into and redeem his own emptiness and limitation of love, i.e., his sin. This is scarcely to be thought of in terms of "Christ paid a price to that evil spirit, Satan, who rules the world, and thereby freed me," or "Christ accumulated so much merit that I can draw upon it to balance up my own sadly unbalanced merit account." It is, rather, the recognition of the finiteness of each man when taken by himself or working only within himself, and a call to him to open out his being to the wider spiritual universe of which he is an integral part, whether he recognizes it or not.

We may pass on from this statement, adequate or inadequate, to the more theological aspects of the Christian conception of selflessness. In the Christian context, this is, of course, a matter of the relationship of the individual to God, the Christian ultimate truth-reality. With relation to God, what does human selflessness mean? Is the goal here the complete submergence of finite self in the Infinite Self? to "lose" one's being in God, in mystical trance in this life and in loss of personal identity in the next?

Paradoxically, it is on the theological level, where the

Christian is speaking of a God to whom Buddhism denies existence, that Christianity may be said to have come closest to Buddhist selflessness. It might be put thus: Only in God does the Christian find the possibility of, even the temptation of, completely losing himself—in the sense of self-destruction. So long as he thinks only in human social terms it will always be in the manner of mutuality, self confronting self, and hence not in terms of the absorption of one self by another. But at the level of the God-relationship such a possibility exists, most pronounced, of course, in the mystical forms of Christianity. Therefore, we shall spend a little time with one mystical Christian work to note its striking similarity in some respects to Buddhist teachings.

We may take as our example, though there are many others that might be equally well chosen, the *Theologia Germanica,* an anonymous mystical treatise of fourteenth-century German mysticism much influenced by Eckhart and Tauler. It is true that this little devotional, mystical work was never considered orthodox by the Roman Catholic Church; and there are more extensive and original expositions of the mystical life. Yet in its frequent emphasis upon the necessity for the destruction of Selfhood, I-hood, Me, and Mine in the living of the Christian life the *Theologia* admirably illustrates our theme. And because it is still firmly within the Christian context of personal communion with God and practical charity for man, it serves better than some more extreme mystical writings.

According to the *Theologia,* human life must be "deified" if it is to be truly Christian. And what is a deified life? It is a life in which man is in mystical union with God, as fully as it is possible for him to be while yet embodied in individual form. The goal is that a man

should be [so] possessed of the Spirit of God . . . that he should not know what he did or left undone, and thus have no power over himself, but the will and Spirit of God should have the mastery over him, and work, and do, and leave undone with him, what and as it would. . . .[1]

This theme of the complete possession of man's will by the Will of God is found over and over again in the *Theologia*. And always it is described as the complete loss or destruction of selfhood, i.e., achieving absolute "selflessness." Selfhood, I-hood, I, Me, Mine, We, are to be "forsaken and departed."[2] Man must come to the point where he has "no will to be or not to be, to live or die, to know or not to know, to do or to leave undone and the like; but I am ready for all that must and ought to be."[3] You are to be "simply and wholly sundered from [your] self."[4] The author of the *Theologia* indeed cannot be hard enough on self and self-will: for "nothing burns in hell but self-will."[5] The choice is clear: God or Self. It cannot be both. But how shall a man destroy self? Clearly he cannot do it all by himself. It is a work of Divine Grace. Yet it is man's work also, for God does not *force* his ways on any man, says the *Theologia*:

Likewise it is God's property that He does not constrain any [one] by force to do or not to do anything, but He allows every man to do and leave undone according to his will, whether it be good or bad, and resists none.[6]

Somewhat as in Buddhism, a man must come to "see things as they are" before he can destroy the self, or surrender his self to God's Self. He must see that there is nothing good in himself, as a separate, partial self, apart from God. On this theme the *Theologia* dilates repeatedly:

Man, of himself and his own, is nothing, has nothing, can do and is capable of nothing, but only infirmity, evil, and wickedness.[7]
No one shall dare to take goodness to himself, for that belongs to God and his Goodness only.[8]

When one understands the vileness of human nature as it is, then begins the negative work of self-destroying humility. And it is then also that the positive work of the

will of God begins. As the darkness of selfhood is destroyed,
so the light of the Eternal Goodness enters in. And he learns
to will and love the Good

for the sake of the Good, and for no other reason than that it
is good, not because it is this or that, or pleases or displeases
such a one, is pleasant or painful, bitter or sweet. . . .[9]

We may let the *Theologia* itself describe the quality of
that "deified" life in which human selfhood has been totally
destroyed and Divine Goodness put in its place, in this final
passage:

What is true obedience? I answer: A man should understand
and be so free from himself, that is, from selfhood, I-hood, Me,
Mine, and the like, that in all things he should no more seek
and regard himself and his own, than if he did not exist, and
should take as little account of himself as if he were not, and
another had done all his works. Likewise, he should count all
creatures for nothing. What is there, then, which is, and which
we may count for somewhat? I answer: Nothing but that which
we call God.[10]

Thus in the end the message of the *Theologia* is that
there is nothing truly good, nothing indeed that is truly
real in the final analysis, but God—which is what the Buddhist says of Nirvana. And it is assumed throughout the
length and breadth of the mysticism of the *Theologia*—
though seldom explicitly stated—that the earthly union of
human and divine selves will ultimately deepen into the
complete metaphysical unity of man and God in the heavenly life. Yet the fact that the *Theologia* never fully states,
or at least seldom emphasizes, that man and God become
absolutely one in metaphysical union, is perhaps significant.
Where it most specifically describes "union," that union is
a union of wills, man willing the Divine Will; or indeed,
as it is sometimes put, the Divine Will willing through the
human will. And even though this is the language of total

"self-destruction," we must remember again that God "does not constrain any by force to do or not to do." Thus, even when God wills through man's will, it is still man that is willing. He is a deified self, but not an annihilated self.

This retention of individual selfhood, even in the context of mysticism, whose *logic* is the metaphysical destruction of the self, represents the specifically *Christian* influence. It puts a brake on the headlong plunge of that non-Christian mysticism—absorbed from outside sources—toward self-annihilation in the Absolute. Even when it speaks of the absolute destruction of the Self, we can observe that it is only that partial and separated-from-God Self upon whose death it is resolved. But that dead Self is clearly to be resurrected in the form of a united-with-God-in-willing-Good Self, that even as it wills God's will, is willing its own purified will. And this purified Self becomes God's instrument in the world. The *Theologia* makes the bold statement, indeed, that "since God *cannot* will to do his works and accomplish changes *without* the creature, therefore it pleases him to do this in and with the creature."[11] So it is that though a man is possessed by God, indeed because he is possessed by God, he continues to work actively and meaningfully in this world of time and space in concrete deeds of loving-kindness.

Thus we come full Christian circle and combine the theological-mystical and the practical types of selflessness in one unified life, a life that can be neither unified nor Christian without both aspects. Man must expend his time, energy, and resources on his fellow men, in sharing and self-sacrifice. He must also share his very being as it were, with God, losing his will in the Divine Will. Yet in thus losing his own will he makes it ever more active in that world in which the Divine Will has placed him; that self which is "destroyed" in God comes back to him through God; and *he* comes back to the world as a "larger" self, one that can include the total world in its sympathy and redemptive loving-kindness.

2. *Buddhist Selflessness*

We turn now to the radically different Buddhist statement of selflessness. Its language—except for this sometimes shared English word—will seem to be in complete
opposition to most or all that Christianity means by "selflessness." Here is no statement of the losing of oneself in
loving service to others, nor of the identification of one's
will with a divine will, nor of the final metaphysical union
with Deity. All this is not only missing, but perhaps anti-
thetical to the very essence of the Buddhist principle of
selflessness. Here we shall find only, or apparently only,
the sheerest statement of a total negation of the self, not
only of the smaller and partial self, but of all self at all
levels. It is, of course, to the anatta, or no-self, doctrine that
we are referring. It is the core of the Buddhist teaching
about self and in Southern Buddhism is so central a part
of the tradition that many affirm that it is *the* basic Buddhist doctrine, absolutely fundamental and absolutely
unique. We have already stated the essential meaning of
this term (cf. p. 21) and referred to it on various other
occasions. Here we shall examine it somewhat more exten-
sively, particularly in its relation to the Buddhist interpretation of selflessness.[12]

Anatta (Pali *anattā,* derived from negative *an* plus Sanskrit *ātman*) has been variously translated as no-self, no-soul,
no true self-nature, emptiness of reality, and insubstan-
tiality. It is a companion statement, or negative formulation, of the truth of *Dependent Origination.* That doctrine
states that every item of experience is a compound structure
or confection made up of other elements. One may positively
emphasize the interrelatedness of all beings and things by
means of this doctrine, whereby it becomes really the truth
of *Inter*dependent Origination. Or he may negatively emphasize the fact that there is no true identity, unity, or
metaphysical reality in any being or thing of any sort. When
this is applied particularly and specifically to the human

self, we have the anatta doctrine in its most important and characteristic role of defining the nature of Buddhist self-lessness in a moral-religious context.

We may begin with the anatta analysis of the human being. He is a product of dependent origination and is composed of five factors or khandhas (Sanskrit *skandhas*). These are as follows:

1. The physical or material factor in the human constitution, called *rūpa,* i.e., form or shape. This is mainly but not purely physical, since the mind is held to have a *rūpa* also.

2. The mental or immaterial factors, which are four in number and are known collectively as *nāma.*

    a. *vedanā*—feeling, sensation, emotion;

    b. *saññā*—awareness, perception of sense objects;

    c. *sankhara*—mental formations or elements of consciousness in general, some fifty in number, which result from the activity of feeling and awareness;

    d. *viññāna*—consciousness, which is fundamental to the other three formations.

This latter factor is present in a double sense: as ordinary consciousness whose materials come from sense experience, which we often call simply "mind"; and in its subconscious or subliminal form, in which it is the karmic link between successive existences and contains the essential character pattern of the newly born being.

Now the important aspect of this analysis of the human being is not so much the nature and number of its constituent factors; with this analysis we may or may not agree. But it is essential to note two further features of the combination. First, the above elements are not, properly speaking, attributes or powers of the self; they are literally and only its *constitutive factors.* A self *is* physical form, feeling, perception, mental formations, and consciousness, rather than something possessing these attributes and features. A human self is a physicomental event analyzable into the above factors. Second, and corollary, Buddhism considers this analysis absolutely exhaustive. There is no self, soul, or being over and above these factors, beyond them, behind them, or within them as a reality within mere appearances. The "self" is a connected and continuous flux of psychosomatic elements that never remains the same for any two moments together. Thus an eminent Burmese monk, U Thittila, states the Buddhist conclusion after listing the constituent factors of the human self:

Is any one of the five aggregates Atta, the Self or Soul? The Buddha's answer is "no." Then is what remains to be called Atta, the self or soul? As it has been said above, *apart from the five aggregates there remains nothing to be called Atta.* Here then [in the human being] we have *one* of the three fundamental characteristics of all existence, namely, the characteristics of Anatta, the absence of a permanent unchanging self or soul.[13]

It follows directly and explicitly from this that there is no immortal soul or self that persists from one rebirth to another. The five factors are dissolved absolutely and completely. The individual person ceases to exist. His bodily elements return to the dust from which they came. There will be no resurrection of his body in any form; its elements will go to make other bodies or into the structure of the universe at large. And even those immaterial factors which compose the mental or spiritual side of man will likewise decompose. Consciousness without sense stimuli cannot exist; when those stimuli, along with the body, are gone, so is consciousness. So, likewise, with feeling and perception. The whole structure called a person simply falls apart upon death.

Yet this falling apart is perhaps not simple. For the force of its falling produces at least an echo as it were. Indeed, it is more than a mere echo. It is in some sense the continuation of this structure that was a self or person, and results in a new self, or at least sentient being, of some sort. What the nature of this ongoing impulse is in actuality raises a considerable philosophical problem. Into that much-discussed problem we cannot enter fully here. We shall only note the orthodox Buddhist answer to those who persist in perplexity. "That which passes on from one birth to another is not identical with itself." Indeed, what passes on even from one *moment* of our present existence to the next is not the same in terms of identity. The Buddhist is fond of saying that the new self is neither the same (identical) nor different (wholly other), yet is *connected* with the former self as its result. The following analogies are often used to illustrate this different but connected relationship: milk changes to curds to cheese; a tree produces a seed that produces a tree (of the same kind) that produces a seed—and so on ad infinitum. This is the "self" from moment to moment, or from life to life. Or we may quote a direct answer to the same question in more philosophical language:

If there is no Atta, the self or soul, what is it that moves from life to life, changing all the time until it enters into the state of Nirvana, which is the only unchanging Reality?

The answer is the uninterrupted process of psychophysical phenomena or the composition of the five aggregates which is called a being. The process of this psychophysical phenomenon called a being is constantly moving and changing like a river. . . . What is constantly changing cannot be restful, peaceful, or satisfactory.[14]

This element, or force, or energy, that passes from existence to existence is then distinctly *not* a self or soul in the sense of a self with a memory of the past or a fixed immortal quality. It is but a current of "personality-producing energy," as we have elsewhere termed it. It is that thrust of ignorant craving, craving for new delights, new sense experiences, a new individualized existence which we have described above. (Cf. p. 112.) This urgency-to-be, manifest in the tendency of a physical state to maintain its present condition, in the biological will-to-live and reproduce, and in the mental-emotional desire to continue to be aware, is the great motor force that pushes individuals and indeed the whole cosmos forward into new states of being, life after life, age after age.

The metaphysics of this conception we shall leave aside and confine ourselves to its moral and religious bearing. This is suggested in a phrase in the above quotation: "What is constantly changing cannot be restful, peaceful, or satisfactory." That is, salvation for the Buddhist consists in escape from this round of perpetual becoming, in cooling the fever of the ardent desire to exist in some form or other, to the absolute zero point. And the key point for this release, the vulnerable link in the chain of continual becoming, is, as before noted, to be found in the *ignorant* nature of the craving for being. Once dispel the mist of ignorance, once see the facts of life "as they truly are," and one has in his hand the power to unlock the chain that binds him to renewed becoming.

Now that light to dispel ignorance, that key to unlock the chain, that sword to cut the fetters that bind, is anatta. Actually it might be more correct to say that it is the threefold sword of anicca-dukkha-anatta that must be used. Yet the three are so interlocked that we can epitomize them in anatta. To know that the self is impermanent (anicca) and that even its sweet joys are but suffering (dukkha) in a thin disguise is to know that nowhere in the life or consciousness of the "self" (anatta) is there even a fragment of that unchanging and satisfying essence of true reality. The self is empty of reality, in what*ever* way we may choose to consider it. And when we fully realize this, and only then, can we break that otherwise unbreakable chain of desire which binds us to the ever-renewed misery of the whole birth-death cycle—or for that matter, to the restless craving fever of this *present* existence.

Thus it is that the Buddhist makes relentless war on the self in all its conceptions, forms, and manifestations. He does not believe that one can defeat self by treating the symptoms of the disease, that is, by moral exhortations to be unselfish, to consider the welfare of others, or by ascetic measures that restrain and limit self-centeredness. One may indeed limit his self-indulgence by giving away his substance and therefore having less for himself. One may discipline himself by exercising control over his passions and appetites. Yet the only successful operation will be one in which the illusion of self is destroyed in all its forms. When one beholds the emptiness of all selfhood, its absolute and utter unreality, *then* he will be able to dissolve his emotional and intellectual attachments to existence as an individual, and achieve in its place the utter detachment of the selfless, the saintly, the nirvanic life. Salvation begins with an intellectual apprehension of anatta; it continues and is completed by the firsthand realization of the reality of anatta, i.e., the unreality of the reality of the self, through meditational discipline. Thus the central importance of the anatta, or no-soul, doctrine of Buddhism.

If this is the discipline of mind and emotion that a follower of the Eightfold Noble Path must impose upon himself in respect to his own self (or not-self), what about other selves? They too are as totally unreal as he is. One must not believe in their unity or continuing identity any more than in his own. They are mere collections of psychophysical factors, nothing more.[15] Hence, one must beware of attachment to other not-selves (as though they *were* selves) as well as of attachment to his own not-self. He may remind himself when he is tempted to feel anger toward them, for example, that they *are* such mere collections and are not *worthy* of being the subject of angry feelings. (So Buddhaghosa.) They are not worthy of being the subject of *any* strong emotion, in fact, whether of anger or love or any of their derivatives or relatives. The spirit of equanimity that radiates its impersonal, nonindividualizing quality of harmless benevolence to all beings alike is the perfectly saintly and selfless attitude toward other selves.

We must say something here also of the final goal of the human self or not-self in Nirvana. Nirvana too partakes of the negative character of the anatta doctrine; indeed, it is the climax and perfection of no-souledness. It is the final "extinction" of the factors that constitute the human being; when once a being attains to Nirvana, the karmically powerful thrust toward renewed existence that has sustained his existence thus far will cease, and no new set of formations of sentient existence will take place as far as he is concerned. It is a "going out" into a trackless, signless, non-individualized dimension that is so different from existence as we now know it that one cannot properly call it existence at all. It is, of course, not physical in even that rarified manner of the Fine Material Spheres. And while some would say that it is therefore more like the mental pole of our being than the physical, this cannot be taken as a positive description; for in Nirvana even consciousness ceases. So it is that even the pseudoexistence of a self or soul here comes to an absolute end; Nirvana is Absolute Anatta. And in the light of Nirvana's absolute selflessness even the highest Realms of Immaterial Existence are full of gross self-delusion.[16]

Thus it is that Buddhist selflessness achieves an absolute negativity in its every context: metaphysically there is no self, only a temporary collection of elements about the persistent karmic impulse, cemented to it by the glue of ignorance. Religiously speaking, every effort must be bent toward the destruction of Self, or of the illusion of the Self, both with regard to intellectual belief in it and emotional attachment to it. Complete impersonal detachment from one's own and from other selves is the practical goal of this discipline. And in the end, my anatta is to find its eternal home in the final dissolution into nothingness of that fitful, feverish, dream-existence sometimes called Life.

Is this, then, the end and fullness of the doctrine of Buddhist selflessness? In terms of explicit doctrinal statement and religious discipline in the Southern tradition, it *is* the final word. As such, it represents what is perhaps the most baffling form of that negativity so characteristic of

Southern Buddhism. It is perhaps the extremest form of the *via negativa* to be found in all the world's religions. And it becomes the more baffling as we try to relate it to a way of ultimate salvation embraced by millions of people. Part of this bafflement is only on paper, since, as we have seen in an early chapter, most of these many millions practically speaking *deny* the denial of self by immersing themselves in the pursuit of better self-rebirths and by consoling themselves with the fellowship of devas and a personalized and living Buddha. But there still remains the problem of the orthodox *via negativa* of anatta, which leads somehow to a joyous and ardently desired salvation.

That there *is* such an expectation and a related experience cannot be doubted. When a complete negation (no-soul) is so vigorously negated by intellectual denial and disciplinary destruction, one can be as sure as in mathematics that two religious negatives make a religious positive of some sort. And so it is here, both by implication and by direct statement. Beneath the negations of Buddhism, especially its negation of the self, just as beneath the negation of Selfhood and I-hood of the *Theologia Germanica,* there is a nonnegated Something in whose positive interests the not-self is negated. I use the term "Something" rather than "Self" or "Soul" because the latter terms are completely unacceptable to Theravada Buddhism.

What is the nature of this positive Something hidden behind the negations? Though no "self" passes on from moment to moment or from life to life, there is yet a cumulative spiritual-mental potency that does. Though successive moments of existence do not make a self in the Buddhist sense (they are literally "selfless"), yet in such a series of moments that progressively frees itself from the illusion that it is a self, there is an almost infinite building up of spiritual power and "self" control. To speak in more personal terms, the saints and the Buddhas are at one and the same time those beings who have completely destroyed Self-illusion in themselves and with regard to others, and yet who have achieved an almost infinite quantity of personal virtues (*pāramī*), absolute self-mastery, and penetrative thought power that, in the case of the Buddhas, becomes an omniscient intelligence. This height of the Buddha's positive achievement represents the cumulative result during millions of existences of the continuous and deliberate will to virtue and wisdom.

There is besides this power of penetrative intelligence the power of universal benevolence already described as the universalization of loving-kindness (Chapter III). The saint (arahat) and the Buddha are characterized by their capacity to extend the spirit of harmless good will to all beings, including the stranger, the enemy, and the infinite multitudes of completely unknown beings. No attachments of positive or negative emotion impede the flow of this universal benevolence to them. The saint becomes unable to distinguish between the welfare of another and that of himself; they are absolutely one, without the slightest clinging of preferential emotion to "self" or "other self." Thus are all the walls of separating selfhood broken down in the experience and knowledge of those Super-Selves, the arahats and Buddhas.

And finally, and climactically, it is these same Super-Selves, supremely developed in all their innate powers of absolute self-control, who are ready for Nirvana. It is they who will enter directly therein after the wearing out of this their last set of khandhas. Thus in a supreme paradox of paradoxes, these Super-Selves, who represent an infinite spiritual capacity, are enabled at last by enlightenment to see that they are No-Selves, and to enter into their final reward—the utter cessation of their Super-Selfhood. Here is nearly perfected Atta (self), perfected in its self-mastery save for its last body, now achieving complete Selfhood by freeing itself of that body and entering into its full perfection of Absolute Selfhood in Nirvana; yet here also is Nirvana, the same Nirvana (since there is only one Nirvana) which is also the perfection of Absolute Annatahood, or No-

Selfhood. Thus in the end the Perfection of Self equals the Destruction of Self, and Anatta and Atta are the same.

3. *Some Comparisons*

How, then, shall we relate these two attempts, the Buddhist and the Christian, to conquer the self by means of selflessness? We may begin by observing that though "selflessness" is indeed to be used cautiously, its use by both religions does indicate some true similarities between them. It is evident from our past discussion, for example, that the *experience* pointed to by the term "selflessness" is more important in each case than the language. This sometimes is hard to believe, as when we find Christianity in its most militant theological-metaphysical-dogmatic mood; and Buddhism in its most antimetaphysical mood which would out of hand reject all theological and philosophical categories about ultimate realities. Then words and technical distinctions seem all-important to each. But in more mellow moods, or in terms of the quality of experience aimed at (and sometimes attained by the saints of each tradition), the two are nearer together than they seem; and the language of each is to be interpreted as symbolic of the experience rather than theologically descriptive.

It is certainly obvious also from the previous discussion that both Buddhism and Christianity are determined to conquer self in its many forms and different levels. Both are at war with self to the very end of self. We find in each a deep concern with that form of the love of oneself (called selfishness or idolatry by the Christian, and attachment and delusion by the Buddhist) which hinders the larger spiritual life and binds a man narrowly to his own limited being and interests. And there is in each tradition a full awareness that evil or false selfhood, when defeated in one form, can easily change itself almost imperceptibly into another. Thus it is possible to be proud of one's humility as a Christian, or for the Buddhist meditator to think in himself: "See how far *I* have come in the destruction of the illusion of self," or wish to remain in the self-enjoyment of the jhanic absorptions forever. The Christian may indeed feel that the total Buddhist meditational discipline is subtly and completely self-centered, but he should remember that the Buddhist is quite as aware as he of the dangers of self-worship even while self is presiding over its own demise.

We may also note that both religions do have a sense of the enlargement of the perspective of the self, the gaining of a larger selfhood. This is more positively explicit in Christianity due to its personalistic nature, according to which the redeemed life of man is thought of as the life of a "true," a "higher," a "larger," a "new," or an "immortal" self. For Christianity, redemption means salvation from a narrower or lesser self into a selfhood after the divine image, not a transition *from* selfhood into something else. But in Southern Buddhism such language is suppressed, though as we have noted above, there seems to be the hope of a realization of a spiritual Something or other within a man that is freed from the narrow limitations of self-concerned egoism. This larger Something is capable of including all beings whatsoever in its benevolent regard and has ceased to be moved by anything concerning its "own" condition. It is a state of attainment in which the spiritual quality in a man is completely master in its own house, in full charge of its own destiny.

This raises an interesting question for the Christian. So conditioned has he been by his personalism, so accustomed to thinking of selfhood as a tight, compact package of mind-soul stuff, so afraid of the diffusion of selfhood in what he calls *im*personalism that he can see nothing but "emptiness in the Buddhist view of the self—a term that, as we have seen, the Buddhist in fact uses about all the higher levels of spiritual attainment. But cannot it also be said that the higher levels of awareness *do* have less of direct self-awareness in them; that the highest spiritual capacity of which man is capable *is* that of becoming so absorbed in that Other which he contemplates and worships, or that

Goodness which he adores, that thought and awareness of self (as such) are forgotten? If this be so, the Christian need not be so deeply concerned at the negative emptiness of Buddhist terminology but may find here a profitable means of criticizing and re-forming his tightly contained Western selfhood.

There is still another important likeness between the two versions of selflessness: the similarity of the final result. This is not to say that the Buddhist and Christian saint would necessarily respond in the same manner to the same situation, or follow identical patterns of conduct. Perhaps even the contrary. But what is achieved in each case is a complete *spontaneity in goodness*. (Cf. pp. 91 f.) The saint, Christian or Buddhist, is so unified within himself, so purified (of carnal nature or bad karma), that he instinctively responds to every situation that confronts him in a fully Christian or Buddhist manner. In one sense of the word, he *can*not do evil. That goodness which he has so long loved and so ardently sought in one form or another has become incarnate in him. But having said this much, there is more to say. For there are also differences between Christian and Buddhist selflessness, fully as obvious and important as the similarities we have just noted. We may say in general that after all qualifications have been made with regard to differing language, all discounts of language in favor of experience, Buddhism pushes its no-soul selflessness further and more metaphysically than the Christian. This is a curious situation, of course. For Buddhism tries very hard to be nonmetaphysical and experiential; and Christianity usually becomes metaphysical at the drop of a phrase. Yet it is the case. For when the Christian speaks of the "destruction" of the self—some of the more radical mystics in their radically mystical moods aside—he does not mean it in the full literal sense. He is speaking only metaphorically of the "death" of selfishness in the self, but not actually of self's destruction. The self is to be raised from its "death" in newness of life, with more inclusive concerns and higher goals. It is the

transformation of the self, i.e., the preservation and enlargement of that which is good within the original self.
But it is still a self.

Of course, there is also much of this in the Buddhist
discipline of the self. And discounting the literalism of language, as we legitimately may, we can maintain that this
same conserving-enlarging transformation is also essentially
what occurs in the Buddhist "destruction" of the self as well
as in the Christian. Yet Buddhism does so vehemently and
persistently insist that it does not mean merely this; it so
dogmatically asserts down to the very end that there is indeed no soul or self; it so uniformly maintains that the last
and highest attainment of the saint is precisely his freedom
from self-delusion, that we cannot with confidence maintain that *no matter* what the Buddhist says, he does in fact
mean the same as the Christian. His words point to a quality
in his selflessness that is perhaps fundamentally different
from that of Christian selflessness.

A clue to this difference is given in the different starting
points of Christian and Buddhist as they seek to achieve the
conquest of the self. Here, as in the practice of love—and
what is Christian love but the conquest of self-love by God's
love?—the Christian almost instinctively begins his warfare
by attempting to extend the range of his love to include
others besides himself. This at least is his preferred and
usual way. He does not, of course, neglect the interior means
of grace through meditation, prayer, and self-examination.
But he considers the real test, the effective actualization of
his will to conquer the self, to be found in his extension of
loving regard actually and specifically to other selves. Love
that cannot, or at least does not, do this, both in spirit and
deed, is considered bogus; the self has not yet been conquered, or even attacked.

In Buddhism, as we have seen, one begins with his own
self. Of course, it is to be emphasized again that this does
not mean sheer selfishness, but only the rational Buddhist
response to the world as he sees it. Yet this approach to the

conquest of self is deeply significant. It further emphasizes and expresses a certain spiritual atomism in Buddhism. Each man is separated from all others by the impenetrable walls of his separate karmic identity. Nor is there any overarching Presence or Purpose to bind him together with his fellow. Inevitably his first and last thought in spiritual matters *must* be toward himself; even those actions done to others must be primarily evaluated as good or bad in relation to their effects upon him, the doer.

Obviously, this heavily discounts the sense of community and involvement with others and the practical ethicosocial helpfulness in which the Christian finds the best antidote to *his* self-love. In conversation with a noted Buddhist monk I pointed out that sometimes thoroughly self-centered people upon whom family cares descended became, by force of involvement with others, less *self*-concerned. I urged that while this did not always occur, it did seem to give some substance to the Christian claim that other-involvement was one effective means of attaining selflessness. The monk termed this situation "an exception," however; and he went on to say that if a person were not self-purified within, his love to others might be defective, love in name only, and actually full of self-regard. From this impasse there seems no logical way out. It is obvious that each side has something to offer. The Christian must confess that much of his "selfless" do-gooding *is* impure in its motivations and unfortunate in results. Yet a cautious self-inclosement for which specific human individuality is a distracting impurity and the values of involvement in the lives of others are accidental and exceptional is somehow deficiently selfless also.

We must recognize at this point that there *is* a fundamental difference of viewpoint and experience here that may be partially understood and appreciated but not easily bridged over. For the Buddhist approach to, and expression of, selflessness proceeds from the basis of the *depreciation* of the worth of *concrete* human individuality. This is the thrust of all its teaching about the endless rebirths to which man is subject, of its conception of man as only a fivefold grouping of elements each one of which is more real than the total "person," of its persistent attribution of "impermanence" and "unreality" (no-souledness) to the human individual. In view of this, what is man, after all, that one should be mindful of him? or what am I that I should value myself above others? Thus, quite characteristically, when a sorrowing mother with dead child on her hip came to the Buddha for consolation he sent her to find a proper Buddhist medicine—a few mustard seed from the house where death had not yet taken anyone. After many fruitless visits she returned, chastened and quieted; her grief was but a small drop in the infinite ocean of endless human grief. Thus, by a sense of the insignificance of its own individuality of concern and need is restive self to be quieted. And it is to be finally conquered by the meditative discipline of breaking its actions, thoughts, and states of consciousness into fragmentary bits without unity or identity and in no sense "selves."

Christian words, at least, about the source of its humble selflessness are quite different. They spring from the enhancement of the sense of human worth, not its depreciation. "What is man that thou art mindful of him?" queries the psalmist; and not in a sarcastic vein either, but in a wondering mood. Why should *God* care for man and so richly bless him? This remains the *basic* Christian source of confidence in the worth of selfhood: that selfhood is given by God, brought forth and sustained by the universe in which a man lives. But it is also the ground of his humility. It is indeed God who creates and sustains man, not he himself; and not only this man, but all other men as well. They are as precious in God's sight as he.

Does this have a practical effect in the mode of selfless living that is inspired by each of these two visions? I think that it does. And this is well expressed in a distinction made by Father Lubac in his little book *Aspects of Buddhism*[17] between *generalized* and *universalized* love. *Universalized*

love, he writes, is the *Christian* variety of selfless love. It
remains a particularized love directed specifically to individuals as such, in their full human concreteness of situation and relationship, but extended by each Christian as far
as humanly possible to *all* individuals. Thus everyone must
be loved in terms of helpfulness and mutuality in his own
particular circumstances and needs; and the Christian thinks
and acts always in the hope of the *maximum responsive
mutuality*. But *generalized* love, which is the *Buddhist* form
of selflessness, tends to be unspecific, impersonal, and non-
mutual. It is not that individual differences are unnoted in
Buddhism—and perhaps Father Lubac does not sufficiently
recognize this fact. For the Buddha did suit his remedies to
individual situations; and meditational discipline specifically
gears its subject matter to individual capabilities. Yet the
main tendency is certainly toward detached nonmutuality.
The following eloquent contemporary description of Buddhist selflessness in action will express this quality:

Unhindered goes the calm and majestic stream of consciousness, pure and radiant. . . . These . . . inner faculties have
grown into inner forces. . . . These inner forces emanate from
the mind and act upon the world but being guarded by mind-
fulness, *they nowhere bind themselves,* and *unchanged they
return.* Love, Compassion, and Sympathetic Joy continue to
emanate from the mind and act upon the world; *but being
guarded by Equanimity they cling nowhere, and unweakened
and unsullied they return.*[18]

And a companion piece, likewise contemporary, describes
in luminous words the height of the realization of freedom
from the self (selflessness perfected) by the Buddhist saint
as he stands ready for Nirvana:

In the same measure in which I succeed in liberating myself
from my personality, in outgrowing it, I also outgrow the world
and its sufferings; and after having entirely freed myself from
the components of my personality, I look down upon it as something entirely alien to me, and thereby in the same manner

upon the world and upon suffering. All of them have nothing more to do with me, for I have withdrawn myself from them. I am indeed still in the world, but I am no longer of the world. I tower above it, and look toward the approaching decay of my personality with cool indifference.[19]

Now if words mean anything at all, here are portrayed both an ideal and an experience of selflessness far different in its solitary godlike emotional immaculateness from the Christian selflessness of bruised and broken sharing. Yet for all its quiet lucid clarity and strangeness it is profoundly disturbing to the Christian. In his moods of depression, filled with distrust of the self-willed efforts he has made to redeem the world, this Buddhist picture of calm, imperturbable joy attracts him with the vision of a spiritual Shangri-La geared to his *own* mystical tradition. Perhaps this is, after all, the final way! an ultimate solution to the problem of self-conquest!

Yet his Christianized conscience will not let him rest here. He is somehow disquieted by a sense of spiritual irresponsibility. What self is here conquered? According to Buddhism, past selves are dead; future selves are not yet born; and the present self, save for this instant of flickering consciousness, is a partial no-self, aiming at Perfect No-Selfhood. Truly this is an open-ended, flexible view of the self that shatters all the tight, precious little circles of self-protection that we spend our lives in building. But the self that is left seems exceedingly vague, belonging in reality to no recognizable world at all save as a detached spectator-consciousness. And the shattering of old selves seems to have left their shattered fragments still within the confines of a vaguer and vaster, but yet isolated, Self that remains my own self, indeed my very own—so much my own that this larger self can scarcely hear the call of other selves for practical aid and mutual fellowship—unless it descends to a lower and less spiritual plane of existence and thereby works against its own final liberation.

In all likelihood, the Christian must choose a different

path. For it seems that in the end the only vision of selflessness that can engage the fullness of the Christian heart and
mind is the selflessness of mutual involvement with men in
the heat of their strife and in the depths of their present
spiritual and physical needs. For him, Buddhist detachment
as a full way of life must remain the siren temptation of a
far-off peaceful Haven wherein the sight of Christ on his
cross would be well-nigh lost to view. *His* Shangri-La cannot
be imperturbable and inaccessible; its seclusion must always open out easily to those among whom he lives. *His*
devotions must constantly include the concern for others.
His selfishness is judged by God, as known in Christ; and
Christ's cross condemns his apartness save to gather new
strength and the power of new love. The Buddhist warning
of the frequent shallowness of selflessness by involvement
must always be heeded and taken to heart by the Christian.
Yet, rather than desire to "tower above the world" of suffering in solitary and unruffled equanimity, he will feel the
pull of Father Zossima's dying counsel to his fellow monks:

Love one another, Fathers. . . . Love God's people. Because
we have come here and shut ourselves within these walls, we
are no holier than those that are outside, but on the contrary,
from the very fact of coming here, each of us has confessed to
himself that he is worse than others. . . . And the longer the
monk lives in his seclusion, the more keenly he must recognize
that. Else he would have had no reason to come here. When he
realizes that he is not only worse than others, but that he is responsible to all men for all and everything, for all human sins,
national and individual, only then is the aim of our seclusion
attained. For know, dear ones, that every one of us is undoubtedly responsible for all . . . mankind and every individual man.
*This knowledge is the crown of life for the monk and for every
man.* For monks are not a special sort of men, but only what all
men ought to be. Only through that knowledge, our heart grows
soft with infinite, universal, inexhaustible love. Then every one
of you will have the power to win over the whole world . . .
with your tears.[20]

(VII)

Grace and Faith in Buddhism

The title of this chapter might seem strange or even re-pulsive to a Buddhist. It would represent to him perhaps an attempted Christianization of Buddhism. For strictly speaking, Buddhism totally denies the operation of grace in its discipline and, as we have seen, contends that a man is saved sheerly by his own efforts. It uses the word "faith" very cautiously for fear of confusing its own "reasoned con-fidence" with the "blind belief" of all other religions. Yet our interest in this chapter is to observe whether there *are* in actuality some elements of both grace and faith hidden beneath the grace-faith-denying Buddhist vocabulary.

1. *The Buddhist Rejection of Grace and Faith*

We may first set forth very briefly the nature of grace and faith according to Christian understanding and the flat Buddhist rejection of both. Grace is generally defined as that help, strength, forgiveness, or spiritual insight which is given to a man by powers beyond himself, and apart from any direct relation to his own deservingness or his own efforts. It may be viewed as a kind of unearned dividend on any spiritual endeavor that he may undertake, or as a totally unexpected and undeserved mercy. Thus many Christian theologians would say that God's forgiveness and his renewal of the human heart are *always* and *completely* works of grace, for no man "merits" forgiveness or "de-serves" renewal. They are the free gift of God to sinful men.

It might be said, extremely perhaps, *wrongly for sure* that it is actually man's *sinfulness* that "merits" God's grace, i.e., calls it forth, not his goodness. *└ total mis-use of this word*

To be sure, grace is not absolutely independent of any relation whatever to human effort, not at least in the deeper and more spiritual sense. There are, of course, those general mercies like the rain and the sun which come to all alike without preparation or response of any sort. But spiritual grace in particular can come only to those who are ready to receive it; it flows out most fully to those who make response to such light as they already have even if it is only to recognize that they are in darkness. And this response which enables one to receive grace is called faith. In this context faith may be related to spiritual desire. It is a *responsive openness* to receive whatever of goodness or truth there may be beyond one's ordinary self and its understanding. It is also an *appropriative* desire for what is truly good and a trust in the capacity and disposition of reality to fulfill this desire. Thus, without a faith response there can be no grace received; and so it is that there is no fortuitous sainthood nor accidental purity of heart even in religions of grace.

But all this talk of unexpectedly receiving goodness from beyond oneself is summarily rejected by Southern Buddhism. The whole faith-grace viewpoint and vocabulary are foreign to its structure of ideas and values. We may recall, for example, the context of dharma-karma in which all human life is lived. This is conceived to be a strict cause-effect relationship rigidly governed by moral justice, in which without fail every good or evil deed produces its precisely deserved effect in the succeeding lives of the doer, so that every one of us at every moment of his existence is the product of his own deeds. And we should recall also that there is no "confusion of substance"—to use a Christian theological phrase—between individualized karmic streams. Each presently existing individual is a flowing stream of thought-emotion-word-deed that has been flowing onward through infinite time, but in all that time has never spilled or gained a single drop of good or bad karma-result to or from any other stream. Obviously, in such a structure there is not the slightest room for the slightest penetration of grace, at least in the full-scale Christian sense.

We may note in passing that if there is thus no meta-physical possibility for the operation of grace in Buddhism, it is also considered completely undesirable on the religious and moral side. We may emphasize again in this connection how firmly Buddhism rejects the idea of a savior who will redeem us by his grace. The Buddha is no savior who saves us by his merits or his sacrificial death; he is no god to whom one may now pray for help; he was only the Supreme Wayshower that every man himself must follow. And indeed a man should follow the indicated path not because the Buddha said it was the right way or because he has faith in the Buddha, but because he finds as he follows the way marked out by the Buddha that it is progressively and increasingly self-evidencing. Thus he comes by reasoned confidence and proved experience, not "blind credulous faith," to a full trust in the Buddha's word.

The whole spirit of Buddhism here is that of proud self-confidence. It glories in the ability of a man to save himself by his own efforts independently of the help of gods, of whatever sort they may be. If he does not achieve his glorious destiny of self-perfection, there is no dark mystery about it, no arbitrary withholding of divine favor from his life—he himself and he alone is to blame. And herein is all the more reason to reject the doctrines of faith-grace on *moral* grounds. For to depend upon the favor or merits of a god or savior, says the Buddhist, is to become less self-reliant and less energetic. Faith in the saving power of another is a moral and religious depressant, so to speak; it is a religious opiate that progressively weakens one's religious vigor and self-discipline.

Since it is not our purpose here to expound the Christian doctrine of grace except in so far as to give some tangible meaning to the term before we apply it to Buddhism, we may leave aside from discussion some of the perversions and inaccuracies in the above portrayal of the nature and effects of grace. We shall turn, rather, to the question of whether, despite the fully specific rejection of grace and faith in Buddhism, there is here anything at all equivalent to, or functioning religiously in the same manner as, faith-grace does in other religions. Now it is obvious that if there *are* such workings of grace in Buddhism, they will be implicit rather than explicit, sometimes peripheral rather than central, and often disguised under antigrace terminology. Therefore, we shall need to modify slightly and expand the meaning of "grace" to make it do service in the Buddhist context, and be prepared to recognize it even in disguise. Perhaps what we find in Buddhism may in the end turn out to be a relative of Grace rather than Grace itself; but perhaps it will be a very *near* relative.

Let us then modify our initial definition of grace in two directions. One will be that of considering it in its miniature form, as it were, that variety of "grace" which one sentient being can extend to another. For Buddhism, this will include all sorts of beings—gods, human beings, animals, disembodied spirits—for all beings are of the same essential quality at whatever level of present existence. They are ex-human beings or prospective human beings, or both at the same time when we consider all their past rebirths. Of course, this definition of grace may not appeal to the Christian theologian who may consider that only Divine Grace is worthy of the name. But it is surely at least a reflection of that Grace. And we may perhaps be allowed this modification if we keep it in the context of help toward *salvation*— not just any helpful action—and if we remember that devas or gods are included in this context. Our question here will be: Despite the Buddhist denial, is it possible for one individual, confined as he is to his own particular karmic stream of being, to help another being in any respect whatsoever toward that other's salvation in Nirvana?

The other interpretation of grace suitable for application

here is what we may call the grace of situation, context, or environment—in order to avoid the use of the word "God," which by definition is unallowable for the Buddhist. Here we shall ask whether there is not (1) substantial environmental help toward salvation in the *structure* of reality, and (2) whether there is not also a *transcendent positive potency* that breaks through the rigid negativity of the Buddhist spiritual discipline at its highest stages in particular. The term "transcendent" will be defined at the time of its discussion.

2. *Creature-grace*

We shall begin with small-grace and qualify it by the non-Buddhist term of creature, not to introduce theistic implications but simply as being neater than some such phrase as "sentient-being-grace." In any case, it is of the help toward salvation that one sentient being can render another that we speak here.

We may note first a partial and indirect manifestation of creature-grace—indirect in the sense that it does not directly conduce to Nirvana. This is to be found in the context of merit. Now merit, briefly defined, is the cumulative credit of one's own good deeds toward his own better future birth. Two aspects of merit should be noted here. One is that some types of good deeds are more meritorious, i.e., capable of more and better rebirth results, than others. But the difference is to be found in the character of the recipient, not of the donor. A good deed done to a worthy man, and especially to monks, saints, and Buddhas, rates the highest because of their superior virtue. After the analogy of sowing one's seeds in the richest soil possible, they are called the "worthiest fields of merit."

One striking illustration of this doctrine is to be found in the *Vimāna Vatthu* (*Stories of the Mansions*), part of the *Minor Anthologies of the Pali Canon*. It is related that two devis (goddesses), who had become devis because of good deeds done as human beings, were conversing (woman-

like) about a third devi who outshone them both in the
size and splendor of her heavenly mansion and in the general magnificence of her estate. Replies the questioned one:

> She who of yore was your sister, Bhadda, by Dhamma
> outshines you because she bestowed her giving
> upon the infinite Order.[1]

The "infinite Order" of course is the Order of Buddhist
monks; and it is infinite in part because of the infinite richness of the Order as a merit-producing field. In the same
context, though about other inequalities of heavenly estate,
another devi chants:

> A monk making mind grow was by me seen of yore,
> so I asked him to dine, Revata, with seven others.
> He, in compassion, Revata, devoted to good,
> Said to me, Give to the Order. I obeyed his behest.
> That gift to the Order was established in the infinite.
> *Your almsgiving to individuals* brought no great reward.[2]

Other passages of the same work promise very rich and
specific fruitage from a judicious sowing of good deeds in
this most fertile field of merit. A morsel of food given to the
Order will provide the giver with all sorts of delicious food
in a heavenly mansion for one thousand years; a handful
of cloth given to a monk on earth will produce a fabulous
array of splendid garments in the sky, and a bowl of water
so given will produce four lotus ponds in the compound of
the heavenly residence without fail. It is perhaps legitimate
to suspect a slight bias on the part of the writers of these
verses in favor of the Order. Nonetheless, the basic principle of the superior field of merit is central in all orthodox
Buddhist doctrine, even though such luxurious particulars
of imagination are seldom indulged in today.

The second grace-filled aspect of merit is the act of sharing merit with others. Here the situation is partially re-
versed from the above case, since it is primarily the recipient

that is benefited rather than the donor. The recipients are the *petas* (Sanskrit *pretas*), or miserable disembodied spirits that wander in the waste places of the earth due to their past evil deeds. These petas seem to be actually dependent upon the merit that human beings are willing to share with them for any improvement of their lot. One story in the *Peta Vatthu,* companion piece to the *Vimāna Vatthu,* tells us of a whole crowd of petas who howled so loudly in their misery outside the walls of a capital city that it was impossible for the reigning king to sleep—though he did not know why. Upon consultation a wise man told him that he (the king) had forgotten to transfer to the petas, some of whom were his former relatives, the merit of the gifts he had made the previous day. The next day he *did* remember to transfer the merit accruing to him from his good deeds and assuaged the suffering of the petas. So great is the effect of such sharing that in another case a king, by transferring the merit of his good deeds to the account of a peta, enabled that peta to be reborn as a deva almost immediately.[3]

Again we may say that though such claims about the efficacy of good deeds for the rescuing of petas are seldom made today, the doctrine of sharing merit is still very much a part of the living Buddhist tradition. To share one's merit with others is an integral part of many standard rituals, the water-pouring ceremony in particular, in which earth spirits are called to witness the good deeds of those present and their wish to share their merit with all others, while water is being poured drop by drop from one vessel to another. There are limits, of course. There is here usually no explicit sharing merit with souls in the hells as in Mahayana Buddhism; and, contrastingly to the tone of the *Minor Anthologies,* there is seldom if ever any *specific* direction of merit to given persons, but rather a general sharing with "all beings." Yet such help seems to be considered as genuinely efficacious, much deeper in meaning than a mere casual "God bless you."[4]

We must pause here to make two comments about this

variety of creature-grace. First, it is an act of grace on the part of those who are worthy of gifts and good deeds thus to allow themselves to be ministered to. The monk "graciously" offers himself before the layman's door in order to give the latter an occasion to plant his karmic seed in a superior field of merit; for the Order of monks, or the Sangha, as the fellowship of those devoted to the quest of Nirvana, stands perpetually there as a means of grace for the layman, who by generous gifts to it may immeasurably increase his own good karma. Of the Buddha's supreme act of grace in presenting himself to the world we shall speak in a moment.

In the second place, it may seem that this kind of help is not grace as we have previously defined it, even with a small g; for none of it is specifically directed toward helping the other soul on toward Nirvana, but only toward better rebirths in another world at the very most. Yet we must not forget that in *contemporary* Buddhism, whatever may have been the case in original Buddhism, it is most strongly affirmed that progress along the road even toward better rebirths is also, somehow or other, progress toward Nirvana. (Certainly a slipping back to animal purgatorial rebirth is a net loss in *every* way.) In accord with this, we may then say that even this creature-grace of the above sort, which helps only to achieve a better rebirth on some higher plane of individualized existence, is also real grace because it also helps toward the final goal of Nirvana. That this often is assumed in practice is made evident in the following encouraging exhortation in which the help of the devas or gods—whose help is ordinarily restricted solely to mundane affairs and seldom considered efficacious for progress toward Nirvana—is promised to the Nirvana-farer also:

Pancha Sila [i.e., the Five Precepts] is YOUR only protection from misery, pain, and grief. . . . If you obey these Precepts, the glorious devas will help and protect you, and you will have a happy life now and in your future birth. *This is the first step toward attaining Supreme Nibbana.*[5]

The supreme instance of creature-grace and the highest possible degree of help that one sentient being can offer to another along the way to salvation is, of course, to be found in the life of the Buddha himself. His whole life, beginning with his birth, was a sheer act of grace. When living in the Tusita heaven, where he had arrived by innumerable deeds of merit in past lives, he yielded to the entreaties of the devas and consented to be born in human form as one ready for Buddhahood. And again after his enlightenment (i.e., achievement of Buddhahood) when, it is traditionally held, he *could* straightway have entered Nirvana, he again yielded to deva-entreaty and remained on the earth to expound his saving truth to such as were ready for it. Probably we must view the emphasis placed on the devas' entreaty as intended to magnify the great significance of the decision, not to indicate the Buddha's unwillingness. But at any rate both decisions are acts of grace: he need not have been born in human form or remained therein after attaining Buddhahood; but out of compassion for mankind he decided to do both. Indeed, the act of grace goes even farther back than this if we remember that time, aeons and aeons ago, when the Buddha-to-be, then the monk Sumedha, made his original compassionate vow to become a Buddha.

Now having become a Buddha, what was the further quality of "grace" that he could grant to his fellows? In answering this question we must make one or two careful distinctions. Strictly speaking, even a Buddha cannot help another being to salvation unless the latter's karmic merit is already ripened to such a degree that he can respond to a Buddha's teaching and influence. (He must provide his own faith-grace, so to speak.) It must have been that Ananda, Moggalana, Sariputta and all the other disciples who attained arahatship under the Buddha's ministry were already ripe for attainment. So also even in the case of Angulimali, the notorious robber and murderer who was converted instantaneously by the Buddha: his past good karma was so tremendous that the merest contact with the Buddha brought it to full fruition. In keeping with this, it is often said today that the Buddha's only power over men is in the dharma, or teachings, that he left behind him; that a man can gain salvation only as he follows its directions and works out his own liberation for himself. Thus his sole assistance on the way to Nirvana, in the final analysis, is his own past good deeds.

Yet there are special qualifications to be made in the Buddha's case. One might say that the level of the creature-grace of help, counsel, and inspiration that *he* could offer was of such infinitely superior quality that it really surpassed the bounds of ordinary creature-grace and became a species of Supramundane Grace. (Such is the received tradition, at any rate.) For the Buddha's teaching of the truth had a power that no one else's proclamation of the same words had. Large numbers of persons, and some of them the most unlikely ones—contentious quibblers, thieves, prostitutes, murderers—were immediately converted and even brought to arahatship by the power of his words. Here indeed is genuine capital-G Grace in which the disciple is suddenly brought all the way to full salvation by the power of his Master. And if we accept the tradition that the Buddha in his omniscience was able to perceive any soul that was ripe and ready for conversion anywhere in a multitude of worlds and go there to his aid, we truly have Grace in every sense of the word.

A very interesting recent development—if indeed it be such—in connection with the life at some meditation centers is a faith that the power of the Buddha is still available to modern man, though the Buddha is long gone into Nirvana. It is held that there *is* a response to a man's spiritual SOS. Sometimes in moments of high devotion a "prayer" that the power and purity of the Buddha will come down upon his followers there assembled is uttered. The underlying concept seems to be that of an inexhaustible store of Buddha-merit yet available to men; or of the continuing spiritual potency or force of the Buddha's earthly lives for empowerment of the believer.

However, we must remind ourselves that in these latter

interpretations of the Buddha's life and present potency we may have a degree of exuberance of devout phrasing that would not be accepted by all Buddhists. The strictly orthodox would rejoin that even the Buddhas, past or present, can help only those who help themselves. And that only those can help themselves whose past karma is good enough to make them able to appropriate the Buddhist's truth. Orthodoxly speaking, we may say that there is only one sense in which a Buddha's help is absolutely essential: no man save a few Pacceka or "silent" Buddhas, can be saved without the historical proclamation of the Buddha's truth. Without that proclamation no one's ripened good karma would have anything to which to respond. Hence, the historical proclamation of the Buddha dharma by an incarnated Buddha is the absolute *sine qua non* of human salvation for even the most orthodox. And let it be noted again that both the "incarnation" of a Buddha and his proclamation of the saving truth are sheer acts of grace.

3. *Structural Grace*

Leaving behind the realm of creature-grace and the Super-creaturely Grace of the Buddha himself, we may turn to a second and perhaps more fundamental form of the operation of the faith-grace factor in Buddhism. And we find it obscurely embedded in the most forbidding anti-grace context that it is possible to imagine: the realm of karma.

Let it be noted in the beginning that karma itself is a matter of faith pure and simple, whether we call it "blind" faith or not. There is absolutely no proof of its operation, or at least not on the scale and of the sort that makes it "scientifically" proved or provable. That in many instances the individual reaps the result of his deeds everyone knows. The drunkard drinks himself out of successive jobs and into ill health; the liar is not trusted even when he tells the truth; the man who lives in the spirit of hatred brings hatred back upon himself; children suffer for parents' sins, but also for their own; and so forth—all things being equal. But there is precisely the difficulty. All things are *not* equal. There are the many exceptions in which evil dispositions and cruel deeds do *not* bring their deserved results and in which virtue goes unrewarded or is even apparently penalized. Now it is precisely to cover these exceptions that the Christian invokes the inscrutable providence of God and the Buddhist trusts in the law of karma. Both are creations of faith. Neither can be proved in the absolute sense, for *present* evidence is equally against both. Yet also in both cases there is the human insistence that there *must* be justice on some level, sometime sooner or later. Hence, faith in Providence and karma ensues.

But passing on, we may observe that even in the rigorous operation of the karmic law there is a species of grace. Or, to put it slightly differently, and more fundamentally, *karma is itself a grace-perforated structure.* We may first observe in this connection that the operation of karmic law is not so absolutely watertight as some statements seem to suggest. There is a kind of loose-jointedness about it that keeps it from being a sheer fatalism—which latter interpretation of karma every contemporary Buddhist emphatically denies. To quote:

Admittedly we are born to a state created by ourselves. Yet by our own well-directed efforts there is every favorable possibility for us to create new favorable environments even here and now. Not only individually but collectively we are at liberty to create fresh Kamma that tends either toward our progress or downfall in this very life. . . .

Is one bound to reap *all* that one has sown in just proportion? The Buddha provides an answer: If anyone says that a man *must* reap according to his deeds, in that case there is no religious life, nor is an opportunity afforded for the entire extinction of sorrow. But if anyone says that what a man reaps *accords* with his deeds, in that case there is a religious life, and an opportunity for the entire extinction of sorrow.[6]

This we might term the *negative condition* for the opera-

tion of grace, that there are loopholes in the karmic structure that permit of the entrance of the nondetermined. And
here we are arrived at the question of free will. For free
will is one aspect of grace; if a man can do only what he
had been predetermined to do by preceding conditions,
there can be no "work of grace" or hope of salvation in his
life. To be sure, there are some who deny free will, or at
least its meaning. Thus wrote the late author of the *Buddhist Dictionary*:

The problem "whether man has a free will" does not exist
to the Buddhist, since he knows that, apart from these ever-
changing mental and physical phenomena, no such entity as
man can be found, and that "man" is merely a name not relating to any reality. And the question, "whether will is free" must
be rejected for the reason that will, or volition, is a mental
phenomenon flashing forth only for a moment, and that as such,
it had not any existence at the preceding moment. . . .

The only admissible question would be whether the arising
of "Will" is independent of conditions, or whether it is conditioned. . . . And the answer would be: . . . the arising of anything whatsoever is dependent on conditions, and without the
condition nothing can ever arise or enter into existence.[7]

But the usual view, possibly on a less philosophical and
more practical level, is that man does and must have free
will. And how is this to be related to the cause-effect se-
quence in the law of karma? Even this more practical answer would agree fundamentally with the above quotation:
All acts of will, free or otherwise, are *somehow* included in
the karmic causal series. It cannot be that there are exceptions, else irrational chaos would result. *But*—and this is
most important—the act of free will is not *directly* related
to any *immediately* previous action or cause, as is the
coerced action. Its ancestry is located vaguely somewhere in
the unknown past; the free action springs from some deed
or thought, word, or physical action done perhaps many
lives ago, so-called latent karma that is just now come to

fruition. Thus is the law of karma kept inviolable in theory. But practically speaking, free will bypasses it: for (to repeat) not every action produces its result immediately, nor is every action the direct and immediate result of specifiable chronological predecessors. Thus the exceeding vagueness and indeterminacy of "latent" karma opens a wide, wide door for present free will.

Were this *not* the case, we should necessarily have to adopt the rejected interpretation of karma as an ironclad determinism of fatalistic proportions in which one *must* reap *all* that he has ever sown world without end.

But we may go still farther and observe that it is not only by virtue of its loopholes that karma is a grace structure— which would be making the essence of a doughnut to be the hole in it—but also by virtue of its integral nature and manner of operation. Karma is moral law. And when we say that it is a *moral* law that "judges" men, or operates in their lives in terms of ethical desert, we have something different from that sheer mechanical succession with which science deals in its laws. (Cf. Chapter II.) For when the terms "ethical" and "moral" are used it is always assumed that they embrace the possibility of voluntarily altered action and attitudes. An action can be called good or bad only in case it has within it the *possibility,* if not the actuality, of more than one response. So it is that I, as the product of my past karmic deeds, *could* have been different from what I am. My present being was not determined solely by a set of physical, mechanical circumstances over which I had absolutely no control, but by "my own" deeds. And if they were "my own" deeds for which I am responsible, rather than the mechanical results of previous states, they must have been to some extent free or voluntary. And most emphatically, as asserted on all sides, in my present existence I *do* have power deliberately to mold my future.

Thus because it is ethical in nature, karma is a grace-structure, i.e., one that offers the possibility of voluntary action, the direction of action in a self-chosen way. The present *could* have been different; the future *may* be variously directed into any of several channels. The degree of choice is not complete, but the possibility of choice exists to some extent. And indeed this is much emphasized in modern discussions of karma. "Do not despair," it is said, "because of your past karma. Present karma now lies in your hands, flexible, malleable. Mold it according to heart's desire. It is within your power. Karma will establish all your virtue without loss, inviolate within your own being."

And here appears another facet of the grace-quality of karma. Not only does it imply the freedom of the individual to choose his deed, but it guarantees that deed's persistence. Or should we say that it guarantees the persistence of the essential quality of the freely chosen, voluntary deed? (For the coerced deed has no karmic consequences whatever. If I am forced to rob at the point of a gun, the deed has no evil karmic result for me.) And any structure of reality that preserves the essential moral quality of my free deed and brings it to full fruition without fail is surely a structure of grace rather than of pure law.

Here we may observe especially the form of that preservation. One's moral or immoral deeds are stored *in the person himself*. They become an integral part of his moral character and mental constitution as well as determine his physical and social condition. This I have elsewhere termed the "karmic potential" of the self. It is that hidden self which may spring into life under the proper circumstances, so that a man suddenly rises to unexpected heights of accomplishment and virtue—as when a robber suddenly becomes a saint. Now these possibilities are hidden from empirical examination or even from one's own introspection. Yet they are there, an integral part of him. And their real, though hidden, presence in every man (presumably) should prevent us from contemptuously dismissing men, any man, as of no worth because of present appearances. Who knows the degree of that man's karmic potential? He may be a future Buddha!

We pause to observe here that the difference between Christian and Buddhist at this point is mostly one of vocabulary. When the Christian sees unpredictable conversions of evil persons to goodness, or the rising of nobility and strength out of the unpromising soil of degradation and weakness, he speaks of the "grace of God." When the Buddhist sees the same event he calls it "stored-up merit and latent faculties." Just now and then he recognizes the similarity of his stored-up merit to Christian grace. Thus:

What others call Grace we name right effort and faculties latent in us only waiting to be discovered, developed, and used. Only by the application of such hidden forces do we become genuine Buddhists, the followers of the Perfect One.[8]

But obviously a caveat must be entered here. For this hidden self of karmic potential which may shower help and strength (as well as good fortune) upon us unexpectedly may also drop devastating and destructive gifts of unexpected evil into our laps. In some contexts, indeed, Buddhist writers tend to emphasize the extreme likelihood of this being the case rather than the other. This hidden karmic self may be depraved rather than angelic and represent a kind of Buddhist "carnal nature" in man. Now this does indeed somewhat qualify the nature of karma as a purely grace-structure, for it seems to dispense a negative destructive "grace" as well as positive healing grace. Nor can the Buddhist take comfort at this point in the Christian confidence that no matter how evil his present circumstances and how mysteriously hard the will of God for him, that will is in the end a good will, working even through calamities for his true welfare. For the Buddhist has only impersonal karma that as surely results in evil as it does in good.

Yet here too there are positive qualifying factors. Karmic manifestations from a man's past are still in great degree under his own control. Just as lightning in the clouds is attracted by the concentration of earthly electrical force, so is the blessing or curse of past karma attracted to a present deed of like quality. The man who does evil deeds in the present or nourishes evil dispositions is most likely to attract his past bad karma in devastating force. And the reverse, of course, is also true: to cherish purity and righteousness attracts the helpful forces of purity out of our own karmic past or from our own latent karmic potential. Here again it is free will and not mechanical determinism that governs the future.

Besides, there seems to be an implicit assurance that on the whole the structure of the universe favors the good influence rather than the evil. To be sure, a Buddhist will seldom be willing to say as much, but it is there between the lines. It is held, for example, that a man who has achieved the supramundane or supernormal psychic powers that enable him to do "miraculous" deeds will soon lose those powers if he attempts to use them for self-glorification or the injury of others. Great emphasis is also put upon the power of the good man to irradiate his environment—and, if a Buddha, this means thousands of universes—with the power of his good will. Of the miracles of the mental-moral taming of ferocious animals, of changing ill will into love, and of blessing other beings by emanated loving-kindness we have spoken earlier. And it seems to be assumed in the currently strong emphasis upon the possibility of creating good karma, that the universe, even the impartial karmic universe, is *slightly* more on the side of the good man than of the evil man—though this may be only the Buddhist *preacher's* helpful if unrealistic approach to reality.

To sum up: The Buddhist is unwilling to say that governing the conditions of sentient existence there is a God of grace and glory. He speaks, rather, of inexorable law that apportions results to each according to his own deserts, and his own alone. But this inexorable law is a loose-jointed law that allows for the escape or burning up of past evil deeds (the Christian calls it forgiveness) and the freedom of voluntary action (both Christian and Buddhist call it free will). Indeed, this karmic law is ethical throughout, preserving only those freely chosen deeds of each man for the future. And somewhere about, beyond, or within each of us is a hidden self with immense karmic potential from which may spring totally unexpected strength in time of need, or sainthood suddenly flash forth. So also it is a structure that makes possible the efficacious radiation of healing good will throughout all the universes by the man of purity and righteousness—more effectively than by the man of impurity and unrighteousness. Even the earth witnessed to the Buddha's good deeds during his temptations. So in the end, whatever the Buddhist may call it and whatever limits he may put upon its operation, the Christian will be inclined to sense even in the human situation the presence of active Grace, not of man's own creation.

4. *Grace as Transcendence*

We shall now finally consider grace under the aspect of transcendence. Accordingly, our terms must be defined. What is grace considered as transcendence? Grace as transcendence need not necessarily be thought of as active miraculous intervention by a supratemporal being in the lawful space-time order. It is rather the encompassing, permeative presence of a structure or quality that bridges over the separateness of the individual moments of existence (thus transcending their separate individuality by continuity) and offers the possibility of final escape from the relativity and fragmentary nature of space-time existence. If there is such a quality or reality in the universe, available to those beings caught in or composed of the space-time fluxing elements, then it has the quality of grace. Even though this grace may not seek one out as in the Christian scheme, it is available and it represents what grace always and everywhere represents—the possibility of transcending the iron-linked determinism of circumstances and the fragmentary unmeaningfulness of our space-time lives. We ourselves do not create this possibility of significance and of escape; it is there, given to us by a power not of ourselves.

We may begin, therefore, by asking whether there *is* a transcendent element in Buddhism. Certainly, the transcendent element is almost completely hidden under the negative terminology that is so characteristic of Southern Buddhism. One must definitely read between the lines to find it. Since this negativity has been sufficiently described in previous chapters, here we may sum it up in a few sentences: Buddhism denies that there is any God, any allover moral purpose in the universe, any self or soul, and any life after death in the usual sense of that word. There is only law-governed process and the cyclic rise and fall of one meaningless, goalless world after another. The course of the individual sentient being through these worlds is a meaningless meandering through a series of point-moments of present pseudoreality strung along the line of force determined by karmic law. The only transcendence of this order is itself completely negative—the going out of existence in Nirvana.

Wherein, then, is there any "positive" transcendent factor that penetrates this meaningless law-ridden flux with meaning and hope, i.e., any grace from above or beyond? We have already noted some law-transcendent elements in karma itself. We may here speak of them again under a different aspect. Let us take the self, for example. The only self recognized by orthodox Buddhism is the not-self, or anatta, the self considered empirically as a series of psychophysical events causally related to each other in time and space but harboring no real identity within. Yet there is also the *karmic* self that goes on age after age cumulatively carrying the total results and quality of all past lives and deeds into each succeeding existence. While many of these results are canceled out by a kind of repetitious seesaw fluctuation of the ordinary life, there *are* those—the saints and Buddhas—who progress in an always-upward direction, so that goodness is accumulated up to that peak of infinite perfection which they embody. Thus, whatever we call this process of cumulative perfection, there is here a transmomentary, transindividual continuity that is transcendent of the discontinuities of the anatta-self, or momentary no-self.

But, of course, this is only a *relative* transcendence. By the progressive accumulation of good character one does transcend the momentary meaninglessness of the separate hours of his life, and to some extent of his separate existences. And something of time and space transcendence—in very considerable degree indeed—is gained in seeking the goal of a better rebirth. Yet be it repeated, this is only a relative transcendence, and hence in our terms only partial grace. For the better rebirth, on no matter how exalted and immaterial a level it may occur, is still within the realm of karma; and sooner or later even the most exalted and immaterial beings will be brought back again to human or even subhuman status. Thus there must be somewhere a linkage with an *absolutely* transcendent element if we are to speak of genuine full-bodied Grace even in a Buddhist context.

This points us directly to that one fully transcendent factor in all Buddhist teaching and experience: Nirvana. And it must be emphasized that the nirvanic quality of "grace" is far more fundamental to Buddhism than even the "grace" of the Buddha that we have earlier described. Here and here alone is full grace to be found in the Buddhist structure. Were Nirvana not there (wherever "there" is), not even a Buddha could offer men salvation. We may repeat the words of the Buddha as reported in the *Udāna Sutta:*

There is a not-born, a not-become, a not-created, a not-formed. If there were not this not-born, this not-become, this not-created, this not-formed, then here an escape from the born, the become, the created, the formed, could not be known.[9]

Now the whole process of Buddhist salvation points toward this not-born, not-become, not-created, not-formed transcendence by Nirvana. This grace-possibility is recognized throughout the whole length and breadth of the discipline of salvation. But we must be sure to understand the quality of its transcendence, and this is perhaps best done in relating Nirvana to karma in terms of the spiritual progress possible in each realm. First we may notice that the presence of Nirvana somehow enables one both to use and transcend karma at the same time and by the same actions. That is, two plus two, in karmic terms, may add up to five on the nirvanic scale. Karmic good deed added to karmic good deed will by itself yield only karmic result in a better rebirth. But if the deeds are done under the aspect of Nirvana, they do in the end add up to *more* than a merely better rebirth. They add up to progress on the absolute scale of measurement, i.e., toward the achievement of Nirvana itself. "Good" karma, though not ultimately good in the light of Nirvana, because even its cherished goodness represents a form of bondage to existence in the realm of birth and death, must still be cultivated in order to make progress toward Nirvana. Only by accumulating good karma in sufficient quantity can one achieve that saintly detachment which enables him at last to spurn the ladder of karmic deeds by which he has risen to sainthood, and take off, ladderless, on the wings of supramundane purity, into the realm of unconditioned Nirvana itself. The ladder—or the raft, in Buddhist terms—is necessary only in order that it may finally be discarded.

Secondly, we may note again that technique by which mere karma is transcended and a measure of ultimate and absolute "goodness" is achieved. This is, of course, the technique of meditation. It is by meditation alone, says orthodox Southern Buddhism, that man can free himself from the karmic ladder of good deeds, and from bondage to birth and death. Here it is that he finally realizes the emptiness of the self, of the space-time order, and the uselessness of karmic virtues so far as final liberation is concerned. Here it is that he is enabled to burn up past bad karma by the fires of meditational purging rather than suffer its unfortunate consequences in some future existence. Thus, by a negative discipline embodied in the Vipassana type of meditation—by which he realizes *in himself,* even in his own body-mind, the impermanence, unsatisfyingness, and unreal quality of *all* space-time existence—he is able to transcend the karma realm entirely.

Thirdly, we may observe that at some point along the line the *positive* essence of Nirvana itself appears. *How* it enters into human experience and precisely at what point it is difficult to ascertain. For Nirvana, as we have seen, represents absolute transcendence in all its dimensions. It is above time and space; it is beyond existence and non-existence; it is beyond consciousness and nonconsciousness; it is beyond *every* characterizing description. Hence, it must be approached only in negative terms. Yet when the negative terms have worn themselves out, destroyed the pseudo-realities, and dissipated the reality-hallucinations that hide Nirvana from perception, it is at last *experienced*. In its final form, to be sure, in its absoluteness, it is only realized by those who have passed into it. Yet the arahat sometimes experiences it directly in this life. And sometimes, in the language of contemporary Buddhists, *Nibbāna-dhātu,* or essence of Nirvana, may "descend" into a man's life. But even below such high levels a man may know that he is approaching this transcendent realm of "grace" by the experience of increasing peace and happiness that is his. Thus we find a layman writing about the experience of his fellows in Nirvana-realization, and perhaps impliedly of his own also:

In this connection I should like to mention that our [friend] has explained the Mahasatipatthana Sutta very clearly in his learned article. . . . So I take it for granted that he must have experienced a kind of happiness as the result of the complete cessation of all sorts of worldly feelings, thoughts, and emotions. . . . In the same way the other members present here must be Anagamins or must have gained the personal experience of transcendental happiness at least for a short duration whether they would admit it or not.[10]

Yet we may ask: Is there here a full transcendence, one of the quality of that Wholly Other in which some Christian theologians have been anxious to dress all the forms of Divine Grace? or is it in essence the highest possible reach of *self*-development? The Southern Buddhist would, of course, not agree to this latter term, even though Nirvana-realization be achieved within the depths of a self-awareness that is almost totally cut off from external stimuli, and is the product of intensive cultivation of interior states of mind. Hence, we must go to a Mahayanist statement for an *explicit* description of Nirvana-realization as the fullness of a perfected, self-transcendent self, if we may use the phrase:

> Our I, our true Atta, is essentially different from all the elements of personality. . . .
> This true I is therefore not to be discovered as an *object* of cognition; it does not enter into our consciousness in any way; it is transcendent.

This writer goes on to compare the awareness of this true self to the position of the driver of an automobile at night who can see everything that enters the span of his lights and recognize it in its relation to himself. "But he himself does *not* enter the light. . . . Since he sits behind it, hence he cannot see *himself*." And, most importantly for our context here, he goes on to identify this transcendent self with Nirvana. For the empirical self indeed passes away with all the objects of its cognition, which are anatta or not-I; and "nothing" becomes the object of the transcendent self:

> But though there . . . is no "anything," nevertheless . . . after having overcome the world I will be just as real as I really am now. . . . That "nothing" with which I find myself confronted . . . is nothing cognizable. *This* reality, i.e., this *conceptual* nothingness, is what the Buddha referred to in these solemn words: There is a not-born, a not-become, a not-created, a not-formed.[11]

In other words, Nirvana is one in essence with pure consciousness; it is the transcendent consciousness purely aware, but without objects. Whether we conceive of Nirvana as the fullness of a self-realization that is transcendent of all ordinary selfhood, yet of the essence of the *real* self, as with Grimm; or whether we consider it as transcendent of all selfhood whatever, as with Southern Buddhism, it is indeed transcendent of all that we know or can express. But by the same token of its utter inexpressibility it is also utterly real according to all varieties of Buddhism. *And because it is utterly real it is supremely full of grace.* Who produced it? For what purpose? Both foolish questions. It simply exists; it is. And just because it thus is, with an "existence" utterly beyond all changing individualized existence, independent of any human or other effort to create or destroy it, it can "save" man. In fact, it saves men by thus existing. It is a "gift of grace," for there *might* have been a world without Nirvana, hence a world without the hope of salvation. *But there it is, absolute transcendence, complete reality, unutterable Grace.*

Notes

I. Concerning the Christian Understanding of Buddhism

1. "The Buddha Dhamma Alone Can Save the World," *International Buddhist News Forum*, Vol. I, No. 2 (February, 1961), pp. 1–2. Published by World Buddhist Fellowship, Rangoon, Burma.

2. Hendrik Kraemer, *The Christian Message in a Non-Christian World* (Harper & Brothers, 1938), pp. 210, 211.

3. Hendrik Kraemer, *The Communication of the Christian Faith* (The Westminster Press, 1956), pp. 124–125. Italics added.

4. According to Southern Buddhism, "gods" are simply sentient beings (usually ex-men) who by virtue of good deeds are temporarily (some millions of human years) elevated to the heavenly worlds.

5. That there is a tension between the "self" that is to be denied and the "self" that denies it, the "self" that does not exist and the "self" that overcomes self-delusion, is obvious. I have treated this tension or contradiction in detail in a forthcoming volume, *In the Hope of Nibbana*, Chapters I–III. See also Chapter VI, in this book, on Buddhist and Christian selflessness.

6. *Udāna*, VII, 1–2. Quoted in J. Evola, *The Doctrine of Awakening* (Luzac, 1951), pp. 76–77.

7. Rudolf Otto, *The Idea of the Holy* (Oxford University Press, 1924), p. 39. Italics added.

8. It should be noted that many Buddhists dislike to have the term "mysticism" applied to Buddhism, because for them it

is equated with the occult, with possession by spirits contrary to the will of the possessed, or with emotional, audio-visual experiences. Buddhism emphatically rejects the equation of its higher experiences with these other experiences. Nevertheless, taken in the sense of direct experience or knowledge of ultimate realities, mysticism seems to be the best and only possible description of the higher Buddhist states and nirvanic experience in this life.

9. After completing some ten days in a meditation center in Burma, the author and his wife were somewhat embarrassed by a visit from some neighboring household servants bringing gifts and "shikoing" us (kneeling-bowing in front of us)—presumably because we were supposedly pilgrims on the higher way, even though foreigners and non-Buddhists.

II. God in Four Parts

1. The so-called Tri-Kaya doctrine. There is the *Dharma-kaya* "which is the ultimate cause of the universe and in which all existences find their essential origin and significance. . . . The Dharmakaya, however, does not remain in its absoluteness; it reveals itself in the realm of cause and effect. It then takes a particular form . . . adapting itself to the intellectual development of the people. . . . This is called *Nirmānkaya*, that is, the body of transformation. The Buddha who manifested himself in the person of Gautama . . . is a form of Nirmankaya. . . . The third one is called *Sambhogakaya*, or body of bliss. This is the spiritual body of a Buddha, invested with all possible grandeur in form and in possession of all imaginable psychic powers." D. T. Suzuki, *Outlines of Mahayana Buddhism* (Luzac, 1907), pp. 73–74.

Whether this is some form of personalistic theism, or more in the pantheistic order of Hinduism, is a question we cannot deal with in full here. It may be remarked that even in Mahayana Buddhism, and still more notably in Southern Buddhism, the category of the personal always tends to fade away into something else upon close examination—at least in the sense of personality as unitary, distinctive self-conscious awareness and being.

2. U Pu, "Foreign Questions and Their Answers," *The Light of Buddha*, Vol. VI, No. 4 (April, 1961), pp. 73–74.

Published monthly by the Burma Buddhist Society, Mandalay, Burma.

3. One elderly gentleman complained once to the author, almost with a sense of deep aggrievement, that it was "very, very hard to do anything with you Christians who believe so strongly in God and soul. It takes a long time to get rid of those beliefs."

4. Nārada Thera, ed. and tr., *Dhammapada*, Wisdom of the East Series (John Murray, Publishers, Ltd., London, 1954), p. 15.

5. Venerable U Thittila, "The Fundamental Principles of Theravāda Buddhism," *The Path of the Buddha*, Kenneth W. Morgan, ed. (The Ronald Press Company, 1956), p. 67.

6. *Ibid.*, p. 83.

7. *Dialogues of the Buddha*, Sacred Books of the Buddhists, Vol. IV (Luzac, 1957), p. 76.

8. Venerable U Thittila, *loc. cit.*, pp. 85, 87.

9. *Ibid.*, pp. 86–87.

10. *Ibid.*, p. 91. One Buddhist friend of mine, when asked whether the act of free will was a part of the causally determined series (and therefore not free), or outside that series (and therefore breaching the rigid causal order of dharma-karma), replied that every act of seeming free will was the result of some "past action in some past life"—and therefore incapable of direct investigation, of course. Thus was the essential element in free will admitted, while yet the face of strict karmic causality was saved.

11. A devout Buddhist acquaintance immediately after he had suggested that Nirvana was "the graveyard of consciousness," with nothing to know or to be known, further suggested that perhaps it was also a condition in which *everything* was known.

III. Love: Christian and Buddhist

1. This is of course rejected by Anders Nygren, in his *Agape and Eros* (The Westminster Press, 1953), as a valid interpretation. In his view the two are mutually exclusive.

2. In Southern Buddhism, where belief in rebirth in animal form is prevalent, there would seem to be greater opportunity for human-animal sympathy. But curiously this doctrine, which

makes it wrong to kill animals, seems to produce a certain callousness to animal suffering and no conspicuous love for animals as such. Is this because animals, as beings suffering grievously for past sins, are viewed with a certain subconscious horror? Or because each being is presumed able to bear its own burden of suffering? In Northern Buddhism, Zen in particular, there is some mystic sense of cosmic consciousness in which the meditator seeks to feel his "oneness with nature" and tries to absorb the nature, or "viewpoint," of the rock or tree or flower into himself. He seeks to experience its state of being from the "inside." This, of course, is not love in the Christian sense because of its mystic impersonality.

3. Sister Vajira, tr., *Sutta Nipata* (Maha Bodhi Society, Sarnath, India, n.d.); p. 6.

4. Venerable U Thittila, "Buddhist *Mettā*," *The Light of the Dhamma*, Vol. V, No. 1 (January, 1958), p. 51. Published quarterly by Union of Burma Buddha Sāsana Council of Rangoon.

5. Bhandatācariya Buddhaghosa, *The Path of Purification*, Nyāṇamoli translation (R. Semage, Colombo, 1956), pp. 347, 353.

6. *Ibid.*, p. 323.

7. *Ibid.*, pp. 347, 353.

8. *Ibid.*, p. 344.

9. *Ibid.*, p. 327.

10. *Ibid.*, p. 341.

11. *Ibid.*, pp. 344, 346, 352.

12. *Ibid.*, p. 352.

13. *Ibid.*, p. 344.

14. *Ibid.*, pp. 351, 352.

15. The acceptance of the theory of the biological evolution of man from lower creatures raises this same problem in another form for Christianity.

16. Each civilization has its rationale here. In the *West*, superior enterprise and material progress are often credited to racial and religious superiority (or even the superiority of Protestantism over Catholicism), and failings of Western civilization are attributed to historical accidents and nonreligious elements. In *Burma* it is put thus: The superior peaceableness of the East is due to the influence of Buddhism, but its static unprogressiveness in material and social areas is due to climate.

And conversely it is climate, not Christianity, that makes the Westerner more vigorous—lest he freeze to death by inaction.

17. For a fuller discussion of this whole area, see author's *In the Hope of Nibbana,* to be published in 1963 by Open Court Publishing Company.

IV. CHRISTIAN GUILT AND BUDDHIST DUKKHA

1. *Book of the Discipline,* tr. I. B. Horner, *Sacred Books of the Buddhists,* Vol. XIV (Luzac, 1951), Part IV (*Mahāvagga* I, Text 20, 2), p. 45.

2. William Temple, quoted in Carlyle Marney, *Structures of Prejudice* (Abingdon Press, 1961), p. 219.

3. James Leasor, *The Red Fort* (Reynal & Company, Inc., 1956), p. 348.

4. "Kamalanjali," quoted in *Sangīti,* Francis Story, ed. (Burma Buddhist World Mission, Rangoon, n.d.), p. 90.

5. Many forms of Northern, or Mahayana, Buddhism do not strongly emphasize the literal rebirth doctrine—though it is perhaps implicitly in the background. There it is rather the rapid continuity and stale repetitiousness of life from moment to moment that is stressed. In either case, the basic attitude and solution will be much the same.

6. Nirvana may, of course, be interpreted psychologically rather than metaphysically, i.e., as the psychological absence of greed, hatred, and stupidity. And some Mahayana philosophers put it in these terms: *Samsāra* (the realm of space-time, birth-death existence) *is* Nirvana—when one lives life in the proper spiritual attitude. But for the Southern Buddhist, Nirvana ends *Samsāra,* which latter is very real to him. And who can say, under the philosophically idealistic forms of much Hindu and Mahayana Buddhist thought, whether even a state of mind or being is not ultimately, i.e., metaphysically, real after all?

7. *Pali-English Dictionary,* Pali Text Society edition (Luzac, 1959), p. 324.

8. H. C. Warren, *Buddhism in Translations, Harvard Oriental Series* (Harvard University Press, 1909), p. 60.

9. H. Richard Niebuhr, "Protestant Movement and Democracy," in *The Shaping of American Religion,* Vol. I of *Religion in American Life,* J. W. Smith and A. L. Jamison, ed. (Princeton University Press, 1961), p. 32.

10. As always, exceptions must be made for Northern Buddhism. Several schools of Japanese Buddhism have depended upon the "grace" of the Buddhas to save them, in particular, Pure Land Buddhism. There are, of course, differences from Christian grace even here, but we have no space to enter into them.

11. This was dramatically pointed up to me by a Buddhist monk who exclaimed, when I suggested the suffering-with-and-for-others theme: "What! Do you save a drowning man by jumping into the water and drowning with him?"

12. Bhandatācariya Buddhaghosa, *The Path of Purification*, Nyāṇamoli translation (R. Semage, Colombo, 1956), p. 328, quoting stanza 125 of the Dhammapada.

V. Christian Prayer and Buddhist Meditation

1. Roger Hazelton, *The Root and Flower of Prayer* (The Macmillan Company, 1943), p. 49. Italics added.

2. J. Evola, *The Doctrine of Awakening* (Luzac, 1951), p. 266.

3. Friedrich Heiler, *Prayer* (Oxford University Press, 1937), p. 251.

4. *Ibid.*, p. 242.

5. *Ibid.*, p. 253.

6. *Ibid.*, pp. 239, 240.

7. Louis J. Puhl, S. J., tr., *The Spiritual Exercises of St. Ignatius* (The Newman Press, 1951), p. 1.

8. *Ibid.*, pp. 29–30.

9. *Ibid.*, pp. 49–51.

10. Evelyn Underhill, *Practical Mysticism* (E. P. Dutton & Co., Inc., 1915), p. 53.

11. Evelyn Underhill, *Mysticism* (Methuen & Co., Ltd., London, 1949), p. 313. Quotation from Jacob Boehme's *Dialogues on the Supersensual Life*.

12. Heiler, *op. cit.,* pp. 178, 177, respectively.

13. Underhill, *Mysticism*, p. 318.

14. *Idem.*

15. Tersteegen, quoted by Heiler, *op. cit.*, p. 178.

16. Underhill, *Mysticism,* pp. 442–443.

17. "Letters to the Editor," *The Guardian*, Rangoon, Burma (May 16, 1961).

18. Pe Maung Tin, *Buddhist Prayer* (Burma Christian Literature Society, Rangoon, Burma, 1960), p. 5.

19. *Ibid.,* pp. 1 and 11, respectively.

20. *Ibid.,* p. 7

21. *Ibid.,* p. 6.

22. In Pali-language (Southern) Buddhism, ordinary morality of the personal-social sort is called *Sīla.* The second stage, one of concentration, is named *Samādhi,* which is also the name used by Hinduism for the highest level of mystical realization. Buddhism, however, has a third term reserved for *its* highest level of knowledge, and that is *Paññā,* or insight wisdom.

23. Evola, *op. cit.,* pp. 262–263.

24. With regard to Zen Buddhism, at the opposite end of the Buddhist spectrum in many respects from Southern Buddhism, it *might* be true to say that a psychological, and not metaphysical, Nirvana is sought, since Zen appears to discard most of the rebirth schema.

25. This has led to the attribution of marvelous psychophysical powers as noted on page 40 f., but these are not of the essence of Buddhist spiritual attainment.

26. Nyanatiloka Thera, *Buddhist Dictionary* (Frewin and Co., Colombo, 1956), p. 101.

27. Since, for the Buddhist, my *present* self has a vast unconscious hinterland of karmic character, good or bad, accumulated through thousands of previous lives, the knowing of them gives a man full insight into all his own potentialities and tendencies. All his subconscious is brought to light, and by intelligently directed effort he may burn up the evil in himself, i.e., remake himself spiritually. Note again the likeness to Western psychological techniques, even though expressed in radically different language.

28. *Études sur le mysticisme,* p. 370, quoted in Evelyn Underhill, *Mysticism,* p. 330.

29. Harold K. Schilling, "Difficult Questions for 'Conversation,'" *Faculty Forum,* Nashville (October, 1961), No. 18.

30. *Reason in Religion, The Life of Reason* Series, Vol. III (Charles Scribner's Sons, 1905), p. 43.

VI. The Conquest of Self

1. J. Bernhart, ed., *Theologia Germanica* (Pantheon Books, Inc., 1949), p. 150.

2. *Ibid.,* p. 171.

3. *Ibid.,* p. 163.

4. *Ibid.,* p. 150.

5. *Ibid.,* p. 174.

6. *Ibid.,* p. 173.

7. *Ibid.,* p. 157.

8. *Ibid.,* p. 144.

9. *Ibid.,* p. 171.

10. *Ibid.,* p. 138.

11. *Ibid.,* p. 211. Italics added.

12. For a fuller statement, see author's *In the Hope of Nibbana,* to be published in 1963 by Open Court Publishing Company.

13. Venerable U Thittila, in *The Light of the Dhamma,* Vol. II, No. 1 (November, 1953), p. 5. Italics added.

14. *Ibid.,* p. 5.

15. The author once received a letter that read in part as follows: "Dear Professor King: Greetings! I hope you are happy and well! You are an Ever-Becoming, Cause-Effect, Fiery Comet shooting through Samsāra! . . . Wishing you all the best, with Blessings and Boundless loving-kindness to you." However, he did *not* go on to sign it "from Another Fiery Comet." And I appreciated being called a "Fiery Comet" rather than a mere "fiery comet."

16. In the Buddhist cosmology there are successive planes of existence progressively refined, in which the highest series is held to be "immaterial," entirely "mental" in essence and form.

17. Henri de Lubac, S.J., *Aspects of Buddhism* (Sheed & Ward, Inc., 1954), Ch. I.

18. Nyanaponika Thera Mahathera, "The Four Sublime States," *The Light of the Dhamma,* Vol. VI, No. 2 (April, 1959), p. 35. Italics added.

19. George Grimm, *The Doctrine of the Buddha* (George Allen & Unwin, Ltd., London, 1959), p. 201. This work is regarded in general as somewhat heretical in Southern Buddhist countries; but the above description of the arahat's con-

sciousness seems to be in keeping with the classical Pali tradition.

20. Fyodor Dostoevsky, *Brothers Karamazov* (Grosset & Dunlop, Inc., 1956). Italics added.

VII. GRACE AND FAITH IN BUDDHISM

1. "Dazzling Mansion," *Minor Anthologies of the Pali Canon,* Part IV (Luzac, 1942), p. 60.

2. *Ibid.,* p. 59. Italics added.

3. In Chinese Buddhism, probably borrowing from Nestorian Christianity, a massive apparatus for rescuing departed relatives from hells by good deeds, gifts to the monks, and chanted prayers for the dead, was constructed. See K. L. Reichelt, *Truth and Tradition in Chinese Buddhism* (Shanghai, 1927).

4. For a more detailed discussion of the whole concept of merit and merit-sharing, see Chapter II of the author's *In the Hope of Nibbana,* to be published in 1963 by Open Court Publishing Company.

5. From a leaflet published by the Burma Buddhist World Mission. No date. Italics added. Nibbana=Nirvana.

6. Nārada Thera, "Buddhist Doctrine of Kamma and Rebirth," *The Light of the Dhamma,* Vol. III, No. 1 (June, 1955), p. 45. Kamma=Karma.

7. Nyanatiloka Thera, *Buddhist Dictionary* (Frewin and Co., Colombo, 1956), pp. 125–126.

8. Nyanasatta Thera, "Practical Buddhism," *The Light of the Dhamma,* Vol. I, No. 3 (April, 1953), p. 38.

9. It may be remarked that logically it is as difficult to explain the existence of Nirvana—the non-created, the beginningless—as it is the existence of an Uncaused or First Cause.

10. U Khin Moung, *The Only Method for the Speedy Realization of Nibbana* (booklet) (Buddha Sāsana Samagama, Rangoon, Burma, 1959), p. 2.

11. George Grimm, *The Doctrine of the Buddha* (George Allen & Unwin, Ltd., London, 1959), pp. 497, 515–518.

Index